# THE ELECTIONS
# OF 2008

# THE ELECTIONS
# OF 2008

Edited by

## Michael Nelson
*Rhodes College*

CQ PRESS

A Division of SAGE
Washington, D.C.

CQ Press
2300 N Street, NW, Suite 800
Washington, DC 20037

Phone: 202-729-1900; toll-free, 1-866-4CQ-PRESS (1-866-427-7737)

Web: www.cqpress.com

Cover design: McGaughy Design
Cover photo: © Brooks Kraft/Corbis
Composition: C&M Digitals (P) Ltd.

☺ The paper used in this publication exceeds the requirements of the American National Standard for Information Sciences—Permanence of Paper for Printed Library Materials, ANSI Z39.48-1992.

Printed and bound in the United States of America

13  12  11  10  09        1  2  3  4  5

**Library of Congress Cataloging-in-Publication Data**

The elections of 2008 / edited by Michael Nelson.
   p. cm.
  Includes bibliographical references.
  ISBN 978-0-87289-569-0 (pbk. : alk. paper)
  1. Presidents—United States—Election—2008. 2. United States. Congress—Elections, 2008. 3. Elections—United States. I. Nelson, Michael II. Title.

JK19682008 .E54 2009
324.973'0931—dc22

                                            2009002824

# Contents

# Preface

Scholars knew several things about elections going into 2008. Of the list that follows, none turned out to be true.

First, we knew that Republicans win presidential elections. Of the ten elections from 1968 to 2004, the Republican nominee won seven, four times by landslides of more than four hundred electoral votes. In contrast, two of the Democrats' three victories in this period were secured with less than a majority of the national popular vote. The one exception was 1976, when the Democratic nominee won 50.1 percent. Additionally, all of the Democrats' victories were by southerners.

Second, we knew that governors win presidential elections and that senators lose them. Four of the five presidents elected from 1976 to 2004 were governors. The other was the incumbent vice president. Every senator nominated in this period lost.

Third, we knew that presidents are white males. Starting with George Washington, all forty-three of them had been. So had all the major party candidates nominated to oppose them.

Fourth, we knew that a political party never makes large gains in consecutive congressional elections. If it does well in one election, it almost certainly will do poorly two years later.

Finally, we knew that the South, which for most of its history had been solidly Democratic, had become solidly Republican. George W. Bush carried every southern state in 2000 and 2004.

On these five points, the elections of 2008 proved scholars wrong, wrong, wrong, wrong, and wrong. The presidential election was won by Barack Obama: a Democrat, a northerner, a senator, and an African American. He received a larger share of the national popular vote than any Democratic nominee since Lyndon B. Johnson in 1964, and he carried three of the largest southern states. Obama's party added to its considerable gains in the 2006 congressional elections with considerable gains in 2008 in both the House of Representatives and the Senate.

What a remarkable year 2008 was in the long history of American elections. And how fortunate that so excellent a team of political scientists has assembled to help make sense of what happened. Readers of this series of post-election studies, which began a quarter century ago with *The Elections of 1984*, will welcome the return of Gary Jacobson on the congressional elections, Paul Quirk on the presidency, Gerald Pomper on the general election,

Barry Burden on the nomination campaigns, Marian Currinder on campaign finance, and Nicole Mellow on voting behavior. Welcome additions to this talented group of scholars are Marjorie Hershey on the media, David Mayhew on the meaning of the elections, and Bruce Nesmith, who coauthored the chapter on the presidency with Quirk. I have claimed for myself the book's first chapter, which sets the stage for the elections.

In addition to reporting and interpreting the events of 2008, each of *The Elections of 2008*'s nine chapters looks back in time to place the year's events in their historical, institutional, and theoretical contexts. Each also looks forward, assessing the elections' consequences for politics and public policy. Carefully written and edited for clarity of meaning and felicity of expression, each can be read with profit and pleasure by research scholars, first-year students, and everyone in between.

On behalf of myself and the other contributors, much-deserved thanks are extended to the outstanding editorial, production, and marketing teams at CQ Press for the assurance, skill, warmth, enthusiasm, and helpfulness with which they worked on this book. We especially thank Charisse Kiino, chief acquisitions editor; Brenda Carter, executive director of college publishing; Lorna Notsch, project editor; Steve Pazdan, managing editor; Gwenda Larsen, senior production editor; Jason McMann, editorial assistant; Erin Snow, associate marketing manager; and Chris O'Brien, marketing manager.

Michael Nelson
January 2009

# Contributors

## About the Editor

**Michael Nelson** is Fulmer Professor of Political Science at Rhodes College and a nonresident senior fellow of the Miller Center of Public Affairs at the University of Virginia. A former editor of *Washington Monthly*, more than fifty of his articles have been anthologized in works of political science, history, and English composition, and he has won national writing awards for articles on music and baseball. In 2009 Nelson received the Southern Political Science Association's V. O. Key Award for the outstanding book on southern politics published in 2008: *How the South Joined the Gambling Nation: The Politics of State Policy Innovation*, with John Lyman Mason. His other recent books include *The Evolving Presidency: Landmark Documents, 1787–2008* (CQ Press, 2008) and *The American Presidency: Origins and Development, 1776–2007*, with Sidney M. Milkis (CQ Press, 2008). Nelson's articles have appeared in the *Journal of Politics, Political Science Quarterly, Leadership Quarterly, Presidential Studies Quarterly*, and numerous other journals. He is editor of the *American Presidential Elections* book series for the University Press of Kansas and is writing a book about the 1968 election.

## About the Contributors

**Barry C. Burden** is professor of political science at the University of Wisconsin–Madison. His research on U.S. politics emphasizes electoral politics and representation. He is author of *Personal Roots of Representation* (2008); editor of *Uncertainty in American Politics* (2003); and coauthor, with David C. Kimball, of *Why Americans Split Their Tickets: Campaigns, Competition, and Divided Government* (2002). Burden has also published articles in journals such as *American Political Science Review, American Journal of Political Science, Legislative Studies Quarterly*, and *Political Science Quarterly*. His current research focuses on election administration and the distribution of federal spending.

**Marian Currinder** is a senior fellow at the Government Affairs Institute at Georgetown University. She previously was an assistant professor of political science at the College of Charleston. Her research focuses on Congress, campaign finance, and congressional party organizations. She has published articles in *Legislative Studies Quarterly* and *State and Local Government Review* and is author of *Money in the House: Campaign Funds and Congressional*

*Party Politics* (2008). She was an American Political Science Association congressional fellow in 2003–2004.

**Marjorie Randon Hershey** is professor of political science at Indiana University. She specializes in the study of political parties, media coverage of American campaigns, and the construction of explanations for election results. She is author of *Party Politics in America* (now in its thirteenth edition) as well as other books, and her articles have appeared in the *American Journal of Political Science,* the *Journal of Politics, Public Opinion Quarterly, Political Communication, Polity,* and other professional journals and edited volumes. She directs the Leadership, Ethics, and Social Action program at Indiana University.

**Gary C. Jacobson** is professor of political science at the University of California, San Diego, where he has taught since 1979. He previously taught at Trinity College; the University of California, Riverside; Yale University; and Stanford University. Jacobson specializes in the study of U.S. elections, public opinion, parties, interest groups, and Congress. He is author of *The Politics of Congressional Elections* (7th ed., 2009); *A Divider, Not a Uniter: George W. Bush and the American People* (2007); *The Electoral Origins of Divided Government: Competition in U.S. House Elections, 1946–1988* (1990); and *Money in Congressional Elections* (1980). He is coauthor of *The Logic of American Politics* (4th ed., 2009) and *Strategy and Choice in Congressional Elections* (2nd ed., 1983). Jacobson is a fellow of the American Academy of Arts and Sciences.

**David R. Mayhew** has written books on American politics that include *Parties and Policies* (2008), *Divided We Govern* (2005), *Electoral Realignments* (2002), *America's Congress* (2000), and *Congress: The Electoral Connection* (1974). His recent articles include "Incumbency Advantage in Presidential Elections" (2008) and "Wars and American Politics" (2005). He is Sterling Professor of Political Science at Yale University, a fellow of the American Academy of Arts and Sciences, and a member of the American Philosophical Society.

**Nicole Mellow** is assistant professor of political science at Williams College, where she teaches classes on American political development, the presidency, political parties, and political geography. She has published articles on parties and partisanship, political leadership, education policy, and gender and politics, and is author of *The State of Disunion: Regional Sources of Modern American Partisanship* (2008).

**Bruce Nesmith** is Joan and Abbott Lipsky Professor of Political Science at Coe College in Cedar Rapids, Iowa. He teaches courses on American political institutions, religion and U.S. politics, and political philosophy. He is author of *The New Republican Coalition: The Reagan Campaigns and White Evangelicals* (1994). His current research is a collaboration with Paul Quirk examining policymaking by the president and Congress.

**Gerald M. Pomper** is Board of Governors Professor of Political Science (emeritus) at the Eagleton Institute of Politics at Rutgers University. He also held visiting professorships at Tel Aviv, Oxford, Northeastern, and Australian National Universities. He was editor and coauthor of a quadrennial series on national elections from 1976 to 2000. A new edition of his book *On Ordinary Heroes and American Democracy*, nominated for the Pulitzer Prize, was reissued in 2007.

**Paul J. Quirk** holds the Phil Lind Chair in U.S. Politics and Representation at the University of British Columbia. He earned his PhD at Harvard University and has held faculty appointments at several American universities. He has published widely on the presidency, Congress, public opinion, and public policymaking. Among other awards, he has received the Aaron Wildavsky Enduring Contribution Award of the Public Policy Section of the American Political Science Association and the Brownlow Book Award of the National Academy of Public Administration. He currently serves on the editorial boards of several scholarly journals, including the *American Political Science Review*. Among recent works, he is coeditor of *Institutions of American Democracy: The Legislative Branch* and coauthor of *Deliberative Choices: Debating Public Policy in Congress*. His chapter on presidential competence appears in the eighth edition of *The Presidency and the Political System*, edited by Michael Nelson (CQ Press, 2006). He is working with Bruce Nesmith on a book-length study of the presidency and Congress as policymaking institutions.

# 1

# The Setting:
# Diversifying the Presidential Talent Pool

## Michael Nelson

Every four years, candidates, consultants, commentators and, yes, political scientists all proclaim the historic nature of the current presidential election. America stands at a crossroads, we solemnly intone, and our nation is at a critical turning point. Usually we are wrong. Most elections are ordinary affairs. But not the election of 2008.

From the beginning, 2008 promised to be the first wide-open contest for president in all of American history. Not since George Washington was unanimously chosen as the first president in 1788 had there been an election in which it was clear from the outset that neither the incumbent president nor the incumbent vice president would be on the ballot. George W. Bush was barred from seeking a third term by the Twenty-second Amendment's two-term limit, which was added to the Constitution in 1951. Most recent vice presidents have made a run for the presidency, but Vice President Richard B. Cheney made known at the time he was selected that he had no ambitions of this kind.

The 2008 election was also wide open in a different, more significant way. The two leading candidates for the Democratic nomination were Sen. Hillary Clinton of New York and Sen. Barack Obama of Illinois. Never before had a major political party nominated a woman (not to mention a recent first lady) or an African American for president. The field of Republican contenders was equally unprecedented: it included a man older than seventy, Sen. John McCain of Arizona; a Mormon, former Massachusetts governor Mitt Romney; and a former mayor, Rudolph Giuliani of New York. By late summer, after the parties held their nominating conventions, the general election ballot guaranteed that the United States would elect either its first nonwhite president or a ticket consisting of its first woman vice president (Gov. Sarah Palin of Alaska, the Republican nominee) and the oldest person ever to assume the presidency.

To appreciate just how remarkable the 2008 election was in the diversity of its talent pool, I review the record of the previous 220 years to see what answers history long provided to the question of who can be president—that is, what kinds of people have any realistic chance of being elected to that office. I then describe and analyze how that record was transformed by the events of 2008, notably the Republican and Democratic nomination contests and the general election.

# Who Can Be President? The Constitutional Answer

The first answer to the question of who can be president is in the Constitution, which was written in 1787, ratified in 1788, and implemented in 1789. Article II, section 1, paragraph 5 states:

> No person except a natural born Citizen, or a Citizen of the United States, at the time of the Adoption of this Constitution, shall be eligible to the Office of President; neither shall any Person be eligible to that Office who shall not have attained to the Age of thirty five Years, and been fourteen Years a Resident within the United States.

Why the Framers chose to include this list of qualifications—thirty-five years or older, natural-born citizen, and fourteen years a resident—is hard to explain.[1] The recorded debates on presidential qualifications at the Constitutional Convention of 1787 are meager. The delegates labored through the first four months of the convention without any apparent interest in establishing qualifications for the presidency. Then, on August 20, Elbridge Gerry of Massachusetts moved that the convention's Committee of Detail recommend such qualifications. Two days later, it did: the president "shall be of the age of thirty five years, and a Citizen of the United States, and shall have been an Inhabitant thereof for Twenty one years."[2] On September 4, the newly formed Committee on Postponed Matters offered a revised recommendation, changing "Citizen of the United States" to "natural born Citizen" and "Twenty one years" to "fourteen years a resident." Although no debate or explanation accompanied Gerry's motion or either committee's recommendations, the convention unanimously approved the Committee on Postponed Matters version on September 7.

Why did the delegates decide, late in the game, to state qualifications for the presidency? Although they never said as much, their actions throughout the convention manifested a consistent principle: a constitution that states qualifications for those who fill an office need not state qualifications for the office itself, but a constitution that states no qualifications for the electors must do so for the elected. In the case of Congress, the need for a qualifications clause for members was agreed on from the beginning. Conversely, in the case of judges, ambassadors, consuls, ministers, heads of departments, "inferior officers," and other public officials mentioned in the Constitution, no qualifications ever were stated or even proposed. None were needed, the delegates seemed to assume, because these individuals would be selected by constitutional officials for whom qualifications had been established.

The presidency received more varied but no less principled treatment from the delegates. During most of the convention they remained wedded to the idea that the chief executive should be chosen by the legislature. Because requirements of age (twenty-five for representatives, thirty for senators), citizenship (at least seven years for a representative, and at least nine years for a senator), and residency (in their state, in either case) were included for members of Congress, the delegates saw no need to establish any for the president. They believed that constitutionally qualified legislators could be counted on not to select an unqualified president.

By midsummer, however, the tide of opinion in the convention clearly had turned against election of the president by Congress. Although it took until September for the Framers to agree that presidents would be chosen by the Electoral College, one thing was certain: however the president was chosen, it would not be by an electorate for which the Constitution stated qualifications. Hence, the logic behind Gerry's motion on August 20 to establish qualifications for the presidency, the two committees' prompt responses, and the convention's willingness to adopt a presidential qualifications clause without controversy.

Such qualifications would have to be high, in the delegates' minds, because of a second principle they deemed relevant: the greater the powers of an office, the higher the qualifications for holding that office must be. Just as senators had to satisfy stiffer eligibility requirements than House members, so would the president have to be more qualified than a senator: five years older and at least fourteen years a resident of the United States. As for the requirement that the president be a natural-born citizen, it was not only steeper than the unadorned citizenship requirement for legislators, but it also helped to solve a political problem that the delegates anticipated as they considered how to get the Constitution ratified.

The Framers realized that the presidency they were creating was the closest thing in the new constitution to a king. During the summer, rumors spread across the country that the delegates were plotting to import a foreign prince—perhaps even Frederick, Duke of York, the second son of King George III—to rule the United States. So vexatious did the situation become that the delegates momentarily lifted the convention's veil of secrecy with a leak to the *Pennsylvania Journal*:

> [August 22] We are informed that many letters have been written to the members of the Federal Convention from different quarters, respecting the reports idly circulating that it is intended to establish a monarchical government, to send for [Frederick] &c. &c.—to which it has been uniformly answered, "though we cannot, affirmatively, tell you what we are doing, we can, negatively, tell you what we are not doing—we never once thought of a king.[3]

However effective their squelching of this rumor may have been, the delegates knew that the mere presence of an independent executive in the Constitution would prompt further attacks on its latent monarchical tendencies. If nothing else, they could defuse the foreign-king issue by requiring that the president be a natural-born citizen.

The final reason for setting a special citizenship requirement for the president was the office's power as commander in chief. With troops at his disposal, it was feared that a foreign subversive serving as president could seize tyrannical power or lay down American arms before an invading army. John

Jay of New York sent a letter to this effect to George Washington, the president of the convention, on July 25:

> Permit me to hint, whether it would not be wise and reasonable to provide a strong check on the admission of foreigners into the administration of our National Government, and to declare expressly that the commander in chief of the American Army shall not be given to, nor devolve upon, any but a natural born citizen.[4]

One cannot be certain when Washington read Jay's letter or what effect it had. The record shows, however, that on September 2 Washington replied to Jay, "I thank you for the hints contained in your letter."[5] Two days later, the Committee on Postponed Matters recommended that the president be "a natural born citizen or a citizen of the US at the time of the adoption of this Constitution," a sharp departure from the Committee of Detail's recommendation, made on August 22, that the president merely be "a Citizen of the US."

How does the Constitution's presidential qualifications clause affect the choice of a president? One effect is to eliminate some highly accomplished people from the presidential talent pool. In 2000 Madeleine Albright was secretary of state, the second occupant of that office in recent history (Henry Kissinger was the first) to be fourth in the line of presidential succession yet constitutionally ineligible to become president because she was a naturalized rather than a natural-born citizen. The Czech-born Albright was in good company. In 2001, President George W. Bush appointed Elaine Chao, a native of Taiwan, as secretary of labor and Mel Martinez, who was born in Cuba, as secretary of housing and urban development.[6]

A second effect of the qualifications clause is to muddy the waters of presidential eligibility. "Natural-born citizen" is an especially murky term. At the time the Constitution was written, two meanings could be found in the English common law from which the term was borrowed: *jus sanguinis,* which held that anyone whose parents were citizens was a natural-born citizen, and *jus soli,* which held that one had to be born on a nation's soil to gain this status. American law is equally unhelpful. The Naturalization Act of 1790, for example, provided that "the children of the United States that may be born beyond the sea, or out of the limits of the United States, shall be considered as natural-born citizens." Yet in 1898, Supreme Court justice Horace Gray argued that natural-born citizenship was confined to those born "within the United States."[7]

Both effects of the qualifications clause were felt in 2008. Governors of large states ordinarily are regarded as presidential timber. But the Constitution ruled out Gov. Arnold Schwarzenegger of California, an Austrian by birth, and Gov. Jennifer Granholm of Michigan, a native Canadian, as unqualified because they were naturalized American citizens. The 2000 census revealed that nearly twenty-eight million individuals—around 10 percent of the American people—were either naturalized citizens or legal immigrants eligible for citizenship.

In addition, disputes arose about the constitutional eligibility of both major parties' nominees for president. Following the *jus soli* interpretation of the term, some argued that McCain was ineligible because he had been born in the Panama Canal Zone, where his father was stationed as a naval officer at the time. Others charged that Obama was actually born in Kenya, not Hawaii, or that having a Kenyan father disqualified him because he became a dual citizen at birth. Although lawsuits containing each of these allegations were thrown out of court, they served as a reminder of just how vexing the issues raised by the qualifications clause are.[8]

## Who Can Be President? Social Background, 1788–2004

The answer the Constitution provides to the question of who can be president is not very useful. The number of constitutionally qualified Americans in a modern presidential election is well over one hundred million. Yet the field of plausible contenders is comparatively tiny. As Thomas Cronin has noted, "There is an 'on-deck circle' of about fifty individuals in any given presidential year."[9] Historically, much of what has defined this small number involves the social background characteristics traditionally associated with presidents. Unlike the constitutional qualifications, these were never debated, much less codified in law. Instead, they have emerged from the habits and prejudices of the American people.

From the first presidential election in 1788 to the fifty-fifth presidential election in 2004, every president—indeed, every major party nominee for president—was white. In addition, all were men and Christians. All were older than forty and younger than seventy at the time of inauguration. Taken together, barriers of race, gender, religion, and age prevented more than half of the adult population from being seriously considered for the presidency.

Not every lesson from this long history is discouraging. During the latter half of the twentieth century, a host of other social barriers to the presidency fell. In a book published on the eve of the 1960 presidential campaign, Clinton Rossiter offered a catalog of "oughts" and "almost certainly musts" for would-be presidents that included: "northerner or westerner," "lawyer," "more than forty-five years old," "less than sixty-five years old," "Protestant," "a small-town boy," and "a self-made man."[10] None of these barriers remained standing for long. In 1960 forty-three (not forty-five) year-old John F. Kennedy, a rich (not self-made), urban (not small-town), Roman Catholic (not Protestant) candidate with no law degree, was elected president.

From 1960 to 2004, southerners Lyndon B. Johnson, Jimmy Carter, George Bush, Bill Clinton, and George W. Bush won seven of twelve presidential elections. Six of the nine presidents in this era—Kennedy, Johnson, Carter, Reagan, and both Bushes—were not lawyers. The class backgrounds of these presidents could not have been more varied. Kennedy and the Bushes were born into wealth; Johnson, Carter, and Gerald R. Ford grew up in middle-class families; and Nixon, Reagan, and Clinton were sons of the working class.

Barriers typically fell during the half-century prior to the 2008 election in one of four ways. *Facing the issue* was the strategy Kennedy employed to overcome widespread prejudice against Catholics in 1960. In an era when entering presidential primaries was generally regarded as a sign of political weakness, Kennedy had no choice but to do so in order to convince the leaders of his party (many of them Catholic) that a Catholic could win. In the midst of his crucial primary campaign in overwhelmingly Protestant West Virginia, Kennedy told a television audience: "When any man stands on the steps of the Capitol and takes the oath of office as President, he is swearing to support the separation of church and state."[11] In September, again with cameras rolling, he addressed the Greater Houston Ministerial Association, declaring: "I do not speak for my church on public matters; and the church does not speak for me."[12] In 1958, 24 percent of Americans had answered *no* to the Gallup Poll question: "If your party nominated a generally well-qualified candidate for president who happened to be Catholic, would you vote for that person?" Soon after Kennedy was elected that number fell to 13 percent and, by 1969, to 8 percent. By 2007 it was a negligible 4 percent.[13]

Kennedy's election also illustrates a second historical barrier-buster: *positive bias*. Although his religion cost him votes among anti-Catholics, it also won him support among Catholics proud to see one of their own contending for the presidency. Of those voters who participated in both the 1956 and 1960 presidential elections, about 6 percent switched from Democrat Adlai Stevenson in 1956 to Republican Richard Nixon in 1960. Nine out of ten of these voters were Protestants. But 17 percent of voters switched from Dwight Eisenhower, the Republican nominee in 1956, to Kennedy in 1960, and six of ten of them were Catholics. In general, anti-Catholic voting hurt Kennedy in the South, and pro-Catholic voting helped him in the much larger and more populous North.[14]

*Vice-presidential succession* has been a third means of toppling social barriers to the presidency. After Whig Party nominee Zachary Taylor of Louisiana was elected in 1848, no southerner was nominated for president by a major party for more than a century. Intense opposition among southern whites to the civil rights movement of the 1950s made it seem even less likely that either the Republicans or Democrats would nominate a southerner any time soon. The vice presidency, however, was a different matter. Kennedy of Massachusetts added Johnson of Texas to the ticket in 1960 to help carry the South. Three years later Johnson succeeded to the presidency when Kennedy was assassinated and, defying stereotype, the new president became an ardent champion of civil rights. By the time Johnson ran for a full term in 1964, anti-southern prejudice had nearly vanished from the electorate.

The fourth way barriers have fallen is through growing *social tolerance*. Like being a Catholic or a southerner, being divorced was long considered a disqualifier for the presidency. As recently as Stevenson in 1952 and Gov. Nelson A. Rockefeller of New York, who unsuccessfully sought the Republican nomination in 1964, divorce proved an insuperable obstacle to presidential candidates. In 1980, however, Reagan was elected president with scarcely a hint that his divorce from actress Jane Wyman should be held against him. Society's tolerance for divorce had grown so great during the 1960s and 1970s that it was no longer a barrier by the time Reagan ran.

## Who Can Be President? Career Background, 1788–2004

Although, historically, each of the major social background criteria for president eliminated tens of millions of people from realistic consideration, an additional unwritten requirement—a career that included recent, prominent experience in government—defined the pool of presidential possibilities most narrowly of all. Nearly everyone elected president from 1788 to 2004 was a current or former senator, governor, vice president, general, or cabinet member.[15]

The relative value of each of these credentials to would-be presidents varied over the years, not because of any changes in the Constitution but rather, as with the unwritten social background qualifications for the presidency, because of changing public expectations. In the early nineteenth century, secretary of state was the leading stepping-stone to the White House. Starting with Thomas Jefferson in 1801, four consecutive presidents held this office. Since then, no secretary of state has been elected president or even been nominated by a major party. Indeed, the only cabinet members of any kind to ascend to the presidency in the twentieth century did so more than eighty years ago: Secretary of War William Howard Taft in 1908 and Secretary of Commerce Herbert Hoover in 1928.

Military general was another much-valued credential for candidates seeking the presidency prior to the twentieth century. Washington, Andrew Jackson, William Henry Harrison, Zachary Taylor, and Ulysses S. Grant all became famous throughout the country as generals. After that, only Eisenhower successfully used his army service as a presidential springboard.

What cabinet members and generals have in common is that they are unelected officials, inexperienced and often uninterested in political campaigning. This was no barrier in the eighteenth and nineteenth centuries, when party leaders controlled the presidential nominating process and nominees did not campaign to get elected. Subsequently, the rise of primaries, joined to new public expectations that candidates run rather than stand for office, placed cabinet members and generals at a disadvantage. Former general Colin Powell was enormously popular in 1996, but chose not to undergo the ordeal of a modern presidential campaign. "I never woke up a single morning saying, 'Gee, I want to go to Iowa'," Powell told an interviewer.[16] Former general Wesley Clark sought the Democratic nomination in 2004, but was a poor campaigner.

Except for Taft, Hoover, and Eisenhower, every president elected since 1900 has been a senator, governor, or vice president. Each of these offices allows candidates to make a distinctive claim about their qualifications to be president. Governors, like presidents, have been chief executives. Senators, like presidents, have dealt with national and international issues. Vice presidents, although lacking independent responsibilities, have stood first in the line of presidential succession and, in most cases, were senators or governors before they became vice president.

During the past century, the persuasiveness of these competing claims by senators, governors, and vice presidents has waxed and waned. Governors dominated presidential elections in two periods: 1900–1932, when four of seven presidents were governors, and 1976–2004, when four of five presidents were. Compared to state governments, the government in Washington was unimportant during the first period, which preceded the federal government's rise to prominence after the New Deal, and was unpopular during the second, in the aftermath of the Vietnam War and Watergate crisis. Senators, in contrast, dominated the post–New Deal, post–World War II era. In the twelve-year stretch from 1960 to 1972, every major party nominee for president was either a senator or a vice president who had served as senator. The vice presidency became the leading stepping-stone to a presidential nomination when the Twenty-second Amendment was added to the Constitution. By imposing a two-term limit on presidents, the amendment freed second-term vice presidents to campaign actively for president themselves. Richard Nixon in 1960, George Bush in 1988, and Al Gore in 2000 each won his party's presidential nomination at the end of his second term as vice president.

## The 2008 Election

In 2008 the still-standing social background barriers of race, gender, religion, and age all came under assault, as did the career barrier that excluded everyone but senators, governors, and vice presidents from serious consideration for the presidency. Some of these barriers were challenged in the Republican nomination contest, others in the Democratic contest. The general election campaign brought further challenges. In the end some barriers fell, others were weakened, and still others proved sturdy.

### The Republican Field

The field of contenders for the 2008 Republican nomination included two candidates who fit the historical mold of white, male Christians who had served as senator or governor: former Arkansas governor Mike Huckabee and former senator Fred Thompson of Tennessee. Thompson's candidacy was lackluster from the start and went nowhere. Huckabee's campaign was woefully underfinanced, but he rode an argument that had worked well for governors in most recent elections—"I've actually managed a government for ten-and-a-half years"[17]—to a second-place finish in the battle for the nomination. Huckabee also benefited from being a Southern Baptist minister and a former president of the Arkansas Baptist Convention. These were especially appealing credentials among the GOP's many Christian conservatives.

Other Republican contenders, however, offered the voters less conventional profiles: Romney was a lifelong Mormon, Giuliani's highest office was mayor of New York, and McCain was older than seventy.

***Religion.*** Although adherence to Christianity was a requirement for office in several states at the time of the nation's founding, the Constitutional Convention voted unanimously that "no religious Test shall ever be required as a Qualification to any Office or public Trust under the United States." In practice, however, every president has been a Christian, at least in name. In 2000 Democratic presidential candidate Al Gore chose Sen. Joseph Lieberman of Connecticut as the first Jewish nominee for vice president. In election day exit polls, 72 percent of voters said they thought Lieberman's religion would make him neither a better nor a worse vice president, and of the remaining 28 percent, twice as many thought it would make him a better one.[18] In February 2007, only 7 percent of respondents to a Gallup poll said that they would not vote for "a generally well-qualified person for president who happened to be Jewish." But more than half—53 percent—said they would not vote for an atheist.[19]

The candidate who faced the most difficult religious challenge in 2008 was Romney. In the same Gallup poll, 24 percent said they would not vote for a Mormon. Other polls were even more discouraging. A January 2008 NBC News/*Wall Street Journal* survey, for example, found that 50 percent of voters either had "some reservations" or were "very uncomfortable" about electing a Mormon as president.[20] Christian leaders such as Richard Land of the Southern Baptist Convention said that they did not regard Mormons as Christians, and Huckabee wondered aloud, "Don't Mormons believe that Jesus and the devil are brothers?" At an "Ask Mitt Anything" forum in California, an audience member asked, "If you were elected president, how many first ladies could we expect?"[21]

Kennedy's challenge as a Catholic in 1960, during an era when candidates seldom discussed their religious beliefs in public, had been to convince voters that his religion did not matter. Romney's challenge was different: to persuade evangelical Christians, who expect candidates to speak freely about their faith, that he was one of them. In a much-publicized speech in December 2007, Romney declared, "I believe that Jesus Christ is the Son of God and the Savior of mankind." He then added: "My church's beliefs about Christ may not be the same as those of other faiths." The speech was heralded for its thoughtfulness, but it did little to unmuddy the waters for conservative Christian voters.

Romney ran a strong campaign for the Republican nomination, winning eleven primaries and caucuses and finishing second in several others before withdrawing in favor of McCain on February 7, two days after Super Tuesday. His candidacy benefited in some ways from his Mormonism: he won strong support from the 2 percent of Republican voters who are Mormon, as well as raising substantial contributions from Mormon donors, especially in Utah. Although rejected by many voters because of his religion, Romney's defeat had additional, more politically significant causes. The liberal stances on abortion and gay rights that he had taken while running for senator from

Massachusetts in 1994 were politically damaging in their own right, and his renunciation of those views as a presidential candidate compounded the problem by making him appear unprincipled.

*Career Background.* Only two presidents, Grover Cleveland of Buffalo, New York, and Calvin Coolidge of Northampton, Massachusetts, have ever served as mayor, and both of them were elected governor before becoming president. The credentials of candidates like Giuliani, whose highest office involved leading a city, are generally regarded by voters as too limited and too urban to qualify them for national office. The candidacy of John Lindsay, an attractive, articulate mayor of New York City who sought the Democratic nomination in 1972, foundered on these shoals.

Yet Giuliani transcended the limits of his office on September 11, 2001. Nearly every American saw him take firm command when the World Trade Center was destroyed by al-Qaida terrorists. Talk-show host Oprah Winfrey quickly crowned him "America's Mayor," broadening his appeal beyond New York with the hint that by defiantly condemning al-Qaida, Giuliani had qualified himself to lead the United States in a dangerous world.

Giuliani was a strong candidate. Throughout 2007, he consistently led the polls among Republican voters. Although his bid for the Republican nomination ended after he lost the January 29 Florida primary to McCain, it wasn't because of his résumé. What hurt Giuliani the most was that, as the campaign unfolded, more and more Republican voters discovered that he was pro-choice on the abortion issue, was a champion of gay rights, and supported gun control. That said, it is hard to imagine that many other mayors will ever have the opportunity to demonstrate the sort of strong national leadership credentials that enabled Giuliani to overcome the political limits of his office.

In terms of career background, the 2008 presidential election also was notable for the absence from the field of the incumbent vice president. Unlike nearly all of his recent predecessors, Cheney made clear from the time of his selection as Bush's running mate in 2000 that he had no presidential ambitions. In 1996 Cheney had explored the possibility of running for president and found that he "was uncomfortable with the pressure to reveal his feelings and talk about his family."[22] Between 1978 and 1988 he suffered three heart attacks. (He had another one two weeks after the 2000 election.) By temperament, Cheney was most comfortable outside the spotlight. His Secret Service codename while serving in the Ford administration was almost comically apt: "Backseat." Of all the leading figures in the first Gulf War, Cheney was the only one not to write a self-glorifying memoir.

Bush found Cheney's reticence enormously appealing. He knew he would never have to worry about the vice president's personal ambition interfering with his commitment to the president's interests. "When you're getting advice from somebody . . . ," Bush said, "if you think deep down part of the advice is to advance a personal agenda, . . . you discount that advice."[23] Following the Bush-Cheney model, Obama tapped Sen. Joseph Biden of Delaware as his running mate in 2008 in full awareness that in 2016, Biden will be seventy-four, too old to mount a credible presidential campaign. Thus, after serving as the leading stepping-stone to a presidential nomination ever since Vice President Nixon ran for president in 1960, the vice presidency may become a career-culminating office, its occupants chosen by presidents seeking vice presidents whose loyalty is uncomplicated by ambition.

*Age.* The Constitution includes a minimum age requirement for the presidency but places no limit on how old a president can be. The voters are different. An August 2007 Gallup poll offered a national sample of Americans a long and varied list of social and career characteristics of presidential candidates and asked if each "would be a desirable characteristic for the next president to have, an undesirable characteristic, or if it wouldn't matter much to you either way?" Of the twenty characteristics on the list, a majority of voters identified only two as undesirable. One was being a "government lobbyist." The other was being "70 years of age or older." Although an identical 52 percent of voters found both characteristics to be undesirable, 19 percent said lobbying experience was desirable, compared with only 5 percent who said this about age.[24]

Unlike religion, race, gender, and other distinctive characteristics of the 2008 candidates, commentators felt comfortable raising questions about McCain's age. "McCain's Age Is a Legitimate Issue" was the headline of one typical article; another was titled "Is McCain Too Old to Be President?"[25] Isolated pundits rose to McCain's defense, pointing out that several successful world leaders, including Nelson Mandela of South Africa and Konrad Adenauer of West Germany, had been older than McCain when they became their nation's chief executives.[26] But most trotted out actuarial tables attempting to prove that men of McCain's age and medical history were likely to deteriorate or die during the four to eight years that he would serve as president.[27] Comedians added to McCain's woes. David Letterman, for example, compared McCain to "a mall walker" and said, "He's the kind of guy who picks up his TV remote when the phone rings."[28]

McCain worked hard during the Republican nomination campaign to overcome, through words and actions, the political stigma of age. When actor Chuck Norris, a prominent Huckabee supporter, said he did not think McCain would have "the stamina to run the country for four years," McCain responded, "I'm afraid that I may have to send my 95-year-old mother to wash Chuck's mouth out with soap."[29] McCain's campaign days were long and vigorous, and he often introduced his energetic mother to audiences. He also asked voters to regard age as a proxy for experience. "My friends, I'm not the youngest candidate," he told a Wisconsin primary crowd, "but I am the most experienced."[30]

When McCain's first candidacy for president ended in 2000, he indicated that he probably would never run again. "If I were 43 or 53, it might be different," McCain said at the time. "But I'm 63, a pretty old geezer."[31] In 2008, he decided to hang a lantern on his problem with humor, joking that he was "older than dirt," leaving "the old soldiers' home for one last charge" and, referring to his two operations for skin cancer, had "more scars than Frankenstein."[32] McCain also appeared on *The Daily Show with Jon Stewart*, which reaches a young audience, more than any other candidate.

McCain overcame enough of the concerns about his age to win the Republican nomination. He was fortunate in his choice of party. Only 38 percent of Republicans in the August 2007 Gallup survey regarded being seventy or older as undesirable in a president, compared with 65 percent of Democrats and 55 percent of independents. The GOP also has a history of nominating established party leaders for president, which generally translates into greater openness to older candidates. When Eisenhower left the White House in 1961, he was, at age seventy, the oldest president in history. In 1980 the sixty-nine-year-old Reagan became the oldest president ever to be elected and in 1984, then seventy-three years, he became the oldest ever to be reelected. The 1996 GOP nominee, Robert Dole, was seventy-three, a year older than McCain was when he turned seventy-two on August 29, 2008. Indeed, in all but two elections between 1960 and 2008 the Republican presidential nominee was older than his Democratic opponent.[33]

## The Democratic Field

The roster of serious contenders for the Democratic nomination was rich in white, male Christian senators: Biden, Christopher Dodd of Connecticut, and John Edwards, a former senator from North Carolina who finished second in the 2004 presidential nominating contest and, as a consolation prize, earned the vice presidential nomination. Edwards started strong, finishing second in the January 3 Iowa caucuses, but faded fast. Neither Biden nor Dodd received more than 1 percent of the vote in any caucus or primary. All three quickly dropped out of the race, along with Gov. Bill Richardson of New Mexico. Richardson was the first Latino to seek the presidency, but he ran an uninspired campaign and failed to make much progress even in heavily Latino New Mexico, which held one of the four earliest contests. Indeed, Richardson dropped out of the race on January 10, nine days before Nevada voted.[34]

On January 29, when Edwards withdrew, the Democratic field narrowed to Clinton and Obama. Both fit the traditional social and career profile of presidential candidates in every way but one: Clinton was bidding to become the first woman president, and Obama to become the first African American president.

*Gender.* Clinton's candidacy was distinctive both because of her gender and because she was the spouse of a former president. Being a Clinton furthered her quest for the nomination in some ways: Bill Clinton had been a vastly popular president in Democratic circles, and both Clintons enjoyed ready access to large donors and talented campaign operatives. But it hurt her in others. Some voters were uncomfortable with the "dynastic" implications of Clinton's candidacy. If she were elected president and served two terms, it would mean that by 2017 the United States had been governed by a Clinton or a Bush for twenty-eight consecutive years. "I can't find any example of even the most rinky-dink 'democracy' confining power continuously for seven terms over 28 years to four people from two families," wrote liberal *New York Times* columnist Nicholas Kristof.[35] Others worried about the awkwardness of having a former president return to the White House as first spouse—what would he do? An anti-nepotism act passed by Congress in 1967 forbade former president Clinton from accepting a job, such as White House chief of staff or secretary of state, over which Hillary Clinton, as president, would have direct supervision.

More than anything else, however, Clinton's candidacy was distinctive because she is a woman. In surveys taken from 1937 to 2007, the Gallup poll found that Americans had become increasingly willing to vote for a "generally well-qualified" woman for president. In 1937 and 1945 only 33 percent said they would do so, but that number rose to 52 percent in 1955, 66 percent in 1971, 73 percent in 1975, 80 percent in 1983, and 88 percent in 2007. About 11 percent in 2007 still said they would not vote for a woman, but their numbers were offset by the many women and some men who were eager to elect the first woman president.[36] In addition, the ranks of women meeting the public's career background criteria for president had grown. As recently as 1976, no women served in the Senate and only one was a governor. By 2008 there were nine woman governors and sixteen woman senators, including Clinton, whom New Yorkers elected to the Senate in 2000 and reelected in 2006. In the 2004 election, about nine million more women voted than men, 67.3 million to 58.5 million.[37]

Feminists, however, argued that Clinton faced unfairly high hurdles because of her gender. Some novelty stores and airport kiosks started stocking the "Hillary Nutcracker," described by one reporter as "a device in which a pantsuit-clad Clinton doll opens her legs to reveal stainless steel thighs that, well, crack nuts." Facebook had a group with tens of thousands of members called "Hillary Clinton: Stop Running for President and Make Me a Sandwich."[38] "Gender is probably the most restricting force in American life, whether the question is who must be in the kitchen or who could be in the White House" argued Gloria Steinem in a much-quoted January 8, 2008, *New York Times* op-ed essay.[39] Former vice-presidential candidate Geraldine Ferraro complained that Obama, Clinton's main rival for the nomination, was "terribly sexist." In March, as Obama pulled ahead, Ferraro claimed that if Obama "was a woman of any color, he would not be in this position."[40] Two months later, Clinton herself protested against "the incredible vitriol that has been engendered" against her "by people who are nothing but misogynists."[41]

Clinton handled the gender dimensions of her campaign in two basic ways. One was to embrace her identity as the first woman with a serious chance to become president. Calling on voters to break "the highest and hardest glass ceiling in America" by electing her, Clinton often said in campaign speeches: "As I go by, shaking hands and meeting people, I often hear a dad or mom lean over to a little girl and say, 'See, honey, you can be anything you want to be.'"[42] In the early primary states she ran commercials featuring herself, her mother, and her daughter. In a May 2008 letter to the Democratic superdelegates, Clinton wrote, "I am in this race for all the women in their nineties who've told me they were born before women could vote and they want to live to see a woman in the White House. For all the women who are energized for the first time, and voting for the first time. For the little girls . . . ."[43]

Clinton's other gender-inspired strategy was to claim leadership qualities traditionally associated with men, especially strength. For fear of appearing weak, she refused to join other candidates who had voted to authorize the war in Iraq in 2002 by saying that she had made a mistake. "Apologizing would have been especially difficult for a female candidate," said one top Clinton campaign aide. "It would have made her look weak and vacillating."[44] Polls showed that Clinton far outdistanced her rivals as the "strongest leader" in the Democratic field.[45] Ironically, however, one of Clinton's most effective moments in the campaign came on the eve of the New Hampshire primary when she was asked, "as a woman," how she kept "upbeat and so wonderful" despite the ordeal of campaigning. Clinton's voice cracked and her eyes teared as she replied, "It's not easy, it's not easy, and I couldn't do it if I just didn't passionately believe it was the right thing to do." Although Clinton climbed from a double-digit deficit in the New Hampshire polls to victory on primary day, she initially feared that by showing vulnerability she had hurt her chances of being elected.[46]

In the end, Clinton was not elected president, but she came very close. In the nomination contest Clinton ran strongly among older white women. But younger women and African American women mostly supported Obama. Just as Clinton was not the candidate of all women, however, neither was she just a woman's candidate. White working-class men also supported her strongly for the nomination, and every group of Democratic primary voters preferred her to any of the white male candidates in the race.

*Race.* After two centuries of being closed to African Americans, the doors of the White House at last were ready to be opened when Obama announced his candidacy for president in February 2007. Americans had grown accustomed, at least notionally, to the idea of an African American president. "Colin Powell's flirtation with a presidential run was a critical turning point in this shift in white attitude," noted sociologist Orlando Patterson, "effectively priming the nation for the possibility of a black candidate."[47] In addition, viewers had seen several black presidents govern calmly and well in recent popular television series such as *24* and in movies like *Deep Impact.*[48] Steeply increasing numbers of constituencies with white majorities had elected African Americans to office, including Illinois, which sent Obama to the Senate with 70 percent of the vote in 2004.[49] In a February 2007 Gallup poll, 94 percent of voters said they were willing to support a "generally well-qualified" African American for president, a number that had risen sharply since 1937, when only 33 percent said they would.[50] And scholarly evidence emerged to demonstrate that this stated willingness to vote for an African American was real. In particular, Daniel Hopkins showed that since the mid-1990s the variously labeled "Wilder Effect" or "Bradley Effect," in which white voters overstate to pollsters their support for black candidates for governor and senator, had disappeared.[51]

Most political pundits assumed that Obama's main challenge would be to win votes from whites. Yet his candidacy initially was greeted with greatest skepticism in the African American community. In the first of a series of critical comments, Jesse Jackson lumped Obama in with the other presidential candidates whom, he said, "have virtually ignored the plight of African Americans in this country."[52] "You can't take black people for granted just 'cause you're black," warned Cornel West.[53] The forty-two-member Congressional Black Caucus initially split down the middle between Obama and Clinton, with older members from the civil rights era, most of them representing majority black districts, supporting Clinton. To them, Obama was a newcomer whom they did not know nearly as well as they knew the Clintons; nor did they want to support a candidate whom they expected to lose.[54] Some black ministers opposed Obama because he, unlike Clinton, disdained the custom of passing out "walking-around money" in the guise of primary day get-out-the-vote expenses.[55]

African American voters initially favored Clinton as well, by 46 to 37 percent in a November 2007 *Wall Street Journal*/NBC News poll and by more than 60 percent in the Clinton campaign's own polls.[56] Like the older black leaders, they thought highly of the Clintons and doubted that Obama could receive enough white votes to be elected.[57] Many also were concerned that Obama would be killed by a racist assassin. Indeed, a flood of racially hateful e-mails to Obama's Senate office convinced the Secret Service to grant him full protection eight months before the first primary, the earliest any candidate has received such protection.[58]

"The biggest race problem we had to start was not with white voters," said David Axelrod, Obama's campaign manager, "but with African-American voters, [who felt] a deep skepticism."[59] Consequently, Obama approached the January 3 Iowa caucuses knowing that he needed to win the overwhelmingly white state to erase the doubts of black voters and leaders that whites would vote for a black man for president. He succeeded, finishing first by a healthy margin. Right after Iowa both candidates' internal polls showed Obama garnering support from 75 percent to 80 percent of African American voters.[60] In the crucial January 26 South Carolina primary, in which Bill Clinton campaigned strenuously for his wife, Obama won nearly 80 percent of the black vote.

If Obama rallied black voters largely by winning the votes of whites, he won these white votes with a three-pronged strategy that was part substantive, part rhetorical, and part symbolic. Substantively, Obama based his campaign on issues that transcended race, such as tax cuts for the middle class, expanded health care, and his early opposition to the war in Iraq. He downplayed issues that white voters tend to associate with black political leaders, such as poverty, urban blight, and affirmative action. Rhetorically, Obama spoke constantly about the value of national unity. In his keynote address to the 2004 Democratic National Convention, which introduced him to the American people, his theme had been: "There's not a black America and white America and Latino America and Asian America; there's a United States of America." Declaring victory in the Iowa caucuses, he echoed that theme: "We are one people. And our time for change has come!"[61] Symbolically, Obama surrounded himself with white supporters at his campaign speeches, featured images of the white mother and grandparents who had raised him in his commercials, and never spoke, as Clinton often did when referring to her gender, about the historic importance of electing the nation's first black president.

Obama also benefited from his opponents' awkwardness in campaigning against a black candidate. Biden clumsily praised Obama as "the first mainstream African-American candidate who is articulate and bright and clean and a nice-looking guy"—the implication being that these are unusual qualities in a black person.[62] Bill Clinton testily dismissed Obama's primary victory in South Carolina by pointing out that "Jesse Jackson won South Carolina in '84 and '88," giving the impression that any African American could win the state because of his race.[63] And Hillary Clinton's charge that "Obama's support among working, hard-working Americans, white Americans, is weakening" seemed to imply that Obama's base consisted mostly of nonwhites who don't work hard.[64] Biden and the Clintons are hardly racists. The controversy that greeted their remarks simply bespoke the political perils that attended any white candidate's mention of Obama and race in the same sentence.

Obama's efforts to transcend race in his own campaign met their sternest challenge on March 13, 2008, when video recordings of some of his Chicago pastor's incendiary sermons were aired. Rev. Jeremiah Wright's declaration on the Sunday after September 11, 2001, that "America's chickens are coming home to roost. . . . God damn America" was shown endlessly on broadcast and cable news programs and on the Internet.[65] Overriding his campaign advisers' judgment, Obama chose the path Kennedy had taken in 1960 to address voters' concerns about his religion: he faced the issue directly in a speech. On March 18 Obama declared that Wright had "expressed a profoundly distorted view of this country—a view that sees white racism as endemic, and that elevates what is wrong with America above all that we know is right with America." In contrast, Obama said, "we may have different stories, but we hold common hopes; we may not look the same and we may not have come from the same place, but we all want to move in the same direction—towards a better future for our children and our grandchildren."[66] Obama's appeal to white working-class voters suffered as a result of the Wright controversy, but not as badly as it would have if he had not addressed the issue. Meanwhile, his support among young and college-educated whites soared.

## The General Election

The fall campaign between Obama and McCain began on a jittery note when it came to the race and age of the candidates. Rick Davis, a McCain operative, charged that Obama had "played the race card . . . from the bottom of the deck" when he told an audience, "What they're going to try to do is make you scared of me. You know, he's not patriotic enough. He's got a funny name. You know, he doesn't look like all those presidents on those dollar bills."[67] Democratic governor David Paterson of New York, an African American, claimed to hear "overtones of potential racial coding" in Palin's mockery of Obama's early work as a community organizer.[68] Alluding to McCain's age, Obama backhandedly praised him in early speeches "for his half-century of service to his country."[69] Liberal groups put subtlety aside in an attack ad that began, "John McCain is 72 and had cancer four times."[70]

Both candidates, however, moved swiftly to tamp down age and race as issues. Obama stopped making the "half-century" reference. McCain consistently rejected his supporters' advice to run ads linking Obama to Reverend Wright and publicly corrected a voter at a town hall meeting who said she "can't trust Obama . . . he's an Arab." "No, ma'am," McCain repeated four times. "He's a decent family man, a citizen, that I just happen to have disagreements with on fundamental issues."[71] The Obama campaign had prepared itself for a range of race-related attacks: Obama as "a dashiki-wearing black nationalist," a "secret Muslim," and "a black man from crime-ridden Chicago."[72] McCain always refused to allow any such insinuations, although he was unable to prevent the circulation of scurrilous, grassroots-generated e-mails charging that Obama had sworn his Senate oath of office on the Koran or might even be the Antichrist.[73]

In the end, race proved no obstacle to Obama's election. From 1968 to 2004, an average 39 percent of white voters had supported Democratic candidates for president.[74] In 2008 Obama won 44 percent of the white vote.[75] He did especially well among whites younger than thirty, earning 54 percent of their support. Among minority voters, Obama secured 95 percent of the black vote, up from Kerry's 88 percent share in 2004. This prize turned out to be all the more valuable because black turnout surged from 11 percent of the electorate in 2004 to 13 percent in 2008. Obama also won 66 percent of Latino votes, a thirteen-point improvement over Kerry's 53 percent showing.

In contrast, McCain's age was a political burden. In exit polls, 39 percent of voters said that age was a factor in their decision, and 66 percent of them voted for Obama. McCain's age problem was compounded by voters' lack of confidence in Palin, who was judged unqualified to "be president if necessary" by a 60 percent to 38 percent margin. Like Democratic presidential nominee Walter F. Mondale's choice of three-term representative Geraldine Ferraro as his running mate in 1984, McCain's selection of Palin, the second-year governor of a sparsely populated state, earned his candidacy a short-term boost in the polls. In principle, voters liked the idea of voting for a woman. But in both cases, growing awareness of the vice-presidential candidates' weak credentials eventually undermined their appeal.

## Conclusion

Election night inspired gracious oratory by both candidates. "If there is anyone out there who still doubts that America is a place where all things are possible," Obama told a cheering crowd, "who still wonders if the dream of our founders is alive in our time, who still questions the power of our democracy, tonight is your answer." Conceding defeat, McCain said, "This is a historic election, and I recognize the significance it has for African Americans and the special pride that must be theirs tonight. We both realize that we have come a long way from the injustices that once stained our nation's reputation."[76]

The elections of 2008 offered inconclusive answers to some parts of the question: Who can be president? It still is not clear whether Americans are ready to accept a candidate who is not a Christian, although strong evidence indicates that a Jewish nominee could be elected.[77] McCain's age probably impaired his candidacy, but it is hard to imagine any Republican running much better than he did in such a politically difficult year for the GOP. And Giuliani's candidacy was a poor test of whether someone who is not a senator, governor, or vice president can be elected because his liberal views on social issues were so out of step with his party's conservative majority.

Clearly, however, Clinton's closely fought campaign demonstrates that the gender barrier to the presidency has fallen. She lost the nomination not because she is a woman, but because she was offering Democratic voters experience in a year when they were looking for change. In the general election, the exit poll indicated that Clinton actually would have won by a larger majority over McCain than Obama did: eleven percentage points rather than seven points. And, in dramatic fashion, Obama's victory brought down the historic racial barrier. As Juan Williams exulted, "There is no other nation in the world where a 75 percent majority electorate has elected as their supreme leader a man who identifies as one of that nation's historically oppressed minorities."[78]

## Notes

1. A fuller account of the argument that follows may be found in Michael Nelson, "Constitutional Qualifications for President," in *Inventing the Presidency*, ed. Thomas E. Cronin (Lawrence: University Press of Kansas, 1989), 1–32.
2. Nearly all of the quotations from the Constitutional Convention in this section are from James Madison's notes of the debates, which are included (along with the other quoted material in this essay) in *The Records of the Constitutional Convention*, 4 vols., edited by Max Farrand (New Haven, Conn.: Yale University Press, 1911).
3. Quoted in Cyril C. Means Jr., "Is Presidency Barred to Americans Born Abroad?" *U.S. News & World Report*, December 23, 1955, 26–30.
4. Quoted in Charles C. Thach Jr., *The Creation of the Presidency* (Baltimore: Johns Hopkins University Press, 1969), 137.
5. Quoted in Means, "Is Presidency Barred to Americans Born Abroad?"
6. Michael Nelson, "Constitutional Qualifications for President," in *Understanding the Presidency*, 4th ed. (New York: Pearson Longman, 2007), 14–22.

7. Michael Nelson, "Who Vies for President?" in *Presidential Selection*, eds. Alexander Heard and Michael Nelson (Durham: Duke University Press, 1987), 120–154.
8. Carl Hulse, "McCain's Canal Zone Birth Prompts Queries about Whether that Rules Him Out," *New York Times*, February 28, 2008; Christopher Beam, "Must Obama Prove He's a Natural-Born Citizen?" Slate.com, October 29, 2008, www.slate.com/id/2203346; and Kate Phillips, "Justices Turn Back a Challenge on Obama," *New York Times*, December 9, 2008.
9. Thomas E. Cronin, *The State of the Presidency*, 2nd ed. (Boston: Little, Brown, 1980), 28.
10. Clinton Rossiter, *The American Presidency*, rev. ed. (New York: New American Library, 1960), 193–194.
11. Quoted in Theodore H. White, *The Making of the President 1960* (New York: Pocket Books, 1961), 128–129.
12. John F. Kennedy, "Address to the Greater Houston Ministerial Association," www.americanrhetoric.com/speeches/jfkhoustonministers.html.
13. George H. Gallup, *The Gallup Poll: Public Opinion, 1935–1971*, vol. 3 (New York: Random House, 1971), 1605, 1735, and 2190; and Jeffrey M. Jones, "Some Americans Reluctant to Vote for Mormon, 72-Year-Old Presidential Candidates," February 20, 2007, www.gallup.com/poll/26611/Some-Americans-Reluctant-Vote-Mormon-72YearOld-Presidential-Candidates.aspx.
14. Philip E. Converse et al., "Stability and Change in 1960: A Reinstating Election," in *Elections and the Political Order*, eds. Angus Campbell et al. (New York: John Wiley and Sons, 1966).
15. The exception was Abraham Lincoln, whose previous political experience consisted of several terms in the Illinois legislature and one term in Congress.
16. Quoted in David Remnick, "The Joshua Generation," *New Yorker*, November 17, 2008.
17. Pamela M. Prah, "Will Govs Lose Edge in Presidential Races?" Stateline.org, February 8, 2008, www.stateline.org/live/details/story?contentId=278622.
18. Michael Nelson, "The Election: Ordinary Politics, Extraordinary Outcome," in *The Elections of 2000*, ed. Michael Nelson (Washington, D.C.: CQ Press, 2001), 75.
19. Jones, "Some Americans Reluctant to Vote for Mormon, 72-Year-Old Presidential Candidates."
20. Suzanne Sataline, "Mormons Dismayed by Harsh Spotlight," *Wall Street Journal*, February 8, 2008.
21. Maureen Dowd, "Mitt's No JFK," *New York Times*, December 9, 2007; Libby Quaid, "Huckabee Asks If Mormons Believe Jesus, Devil Are Brothers," *Time*, December 11, 2008; and Ryan Lizza, "The Mission," *New Yorker*, October 29, 2007, 42.
22. Jacob Weisberg, *The Bush Tragedy* (New York: Random House, 2008), 170.
23. Stephen F. Hayes, *Cheney: The Untold Story of America's Most Powerful and Controversial Vice President* (New York: HarperCollins, 2007), 307.
24. Joseph Carroll, "Which Characteristics Are Most Desirable in the Next President?" September 17, 2007, www.gallup.com/poll/28693/Which-Characteristics-Most-Desirable-Next-President.aspx.
25. Bud Jackson, "McCain's Age Is a Legitimate Issue," *Politico*, May 22, 2008; and Steve Chapman, "Is McCain Too Old to Be President?" *RealClearPolitics*, September 9, 2007, www.realclearpolitics.com/articles/2007/09/is_mccain_too_old_to_be_presid.html.
26. Ryan Cole, "Is McCain Too Old?" *Wall Street Journal*, February 27, 2008.
27. Alexander Burns, "McCain and the Politics of Mortality," *Politico*, September 4, 2008.
28. Julie Bosman, "So a Senior Citizen Walks into a Bar . . . ," *New York Times*, March 9, 2008; and Dick Polman, "The Age Factor," *Philadelphia Inquirer*, May 25, 2008.

29. Michael Cooper, "McCain's Age May Figure in Choice of a Running Mate," *New York Times*, February 24, 2008.
30. Ibid.
31. Polman, "The Age Factor."
32. Holly Bailey, "An Answer for Every 'Little Jerk,'" *Newsweek*, June 2, 2008, 27.
33. The two exceptions were in 1968 and 2004.
34. A February 2007 Gallup Poll found that 87 percent of Americans said they were willing to vote for a Hispanic nominee for president, and 12 percent said they were not. Jones, "Some Americans Reluctant to Vote for Mormon, 72-Year-Old Presidential Candidates."
35. Nicholas D. Kristof, "The Dynastic Question," *New York Times*, January 31, 2008.
36. Jones, "Some Americans Reluctant to Vote for Mormon, 72-Year-Old Presidential Candidates."
37. Kate Zernike, "Both Sides Seeking to Be What Women Want," *New York Times*, September 15, 2008.
38. Marie Cocco, "Clinton Campaign Brought Sexism Out of Hiding," *RealClearPolitics*, May 13, 2008, www.realclearpolitics.com/articles/2008/05/clinton_campaign_brought_sexis.html; and Amanda Fortini, "The Feminist Reawakening," *New York Magazine*, April 13, 2008.
39. Gloria Steinem, "Women Are Never Front-Runners," *New York Times*, January 8, 2008.
40. Jodi Kantor, "Gender Issue Lives on as Clinton's Hopes Dim," *New York Times*, May 19, 2008; and Katharine Q. Seelye and Julie Bosman, "Ferraro's Obama Remarks Become Talk of Campaign," *New York Times*, March 12, 2008.
41. Lois Romano, "Clinton Puts Up a New Fight," *Washington Post*, May 20, 2008.
42. Anne E. Kornblut, "Encouraged by Women's Response, Clinton Stresses Female Side," *Washington Post*, October 14, 2007.
43. Michelle Goldberg, "Three a.m. for Feminism," *New Republic*, June 25, 2008, 29–31.
44. Roger Simon, "Lost in Hillaryland," *Politico*, August 25, 2008.
45. Karlyn Bowman, "Democrats' Intraparty Gender Gap," *Washington Post*, March 6, 2008.
46. Evan Thomas, "How He Did It," *Newsweek*, November 17, 2008, 49.
47. Orlando Patterson, "An Eternal Revolution," *New York Times*, November 7, 2008.
48. Recent seasons of *24* featured two admirable black presidents and one despicable white president. Joshua Alston, "Diversity Training," *Newsweek*, February 11, 2008, 55–56.
49. Rachel L. Swarns, "Quiet Political Shifts as More Blacks Are Elected," *New York Times*, October 14, 2008.
50. Jones, "Some Americans Reluctant to Vote for Mormon, 72-Year-Old Presidential Candidates"; and Linda Feldman, "In 2008, Many Presidential 'Firsts' Are Possible," *Christian Science Monitor*, February 16, 2007.
51. Daniel J. Hopkins, "No More Wilder Effect, Never a Whitman Effect: When and Why Polls Mislead about Black and Female Candidates," August 4, 2008, http://people.iq.harvard.edu/~dhopkins/wilder13.pdf. The effect took its name from two black candidates for governor, Tom Bradley in California in 1982, and Douglas Wilder in Virginia in 1989, who received many fewer votes on Election Day than pre-election polls predicted.
52. Jesse Jackson, "Most Democratic Candidates Are Ignoring African Americans," *Chicago Sun-Times*, November 27, 2007. Jackson also criticized Obama for "acting like he's white" when the candidate did not go to Jena, Louisiana, to protest a racial incident. After Obama gave a Father's Day speech urging black fathers to take more responsibility for their children, Jackson let slip a remark over a live

Fox News microphone that Obama had been "talking down to black people." Making a slicing gesture, he added: "I want to cut his nuts off." Remnick, "The Joshua Generation."

53. Richard Wolffe and Daren Briscoe, "Across the Divide," *Newsweek*, July 16, 2007, 24.
54. Matt Bai, "Is Obama the End of Black Politics?" *New York Times Magazine*, August 10, 2008.
55. Thomas, "How He Did It," 63; and Marc Ambinder, "Race Over?" *The Atlantic* (January/February 2009), 62–65.
56. Jonathan Kaufman, "Whites' Great Hope?" *Wall Street Journal*, November 10, 2007.
57. See, for example, Perry Bacon Jr., "Can Obama Count on the Black Vote?" *Time*, January 23, 2007; and Ambinder, "Race Over?"
58. Wolffe and Briscoe, "Across the Divide," 25. Since leaving the White House, Hillary Clinton had received Secret Service protection as a former first lady.
59. Bai, "Is Obama the End of Black Politics?"
60. Ibid.
61. Robin Toner, "In the South, Echoes of Jackson's Run," *New York Times*, January 24, 2008.
62. Xuan Thai and Ted Barrett, "Biden's Description of Obama Draws Scrutiny," CNN.com, February 9, 2007, www.cnn.com/2007/POLITICS/01/31/biden.obama.
63. Maria L. LaGanga and Mark Z. Barabak, "Race a Wild-Card Factor," *Los Angeles Times*, February 28, 2008.
64. Kate Phillips, "Clinton Touts White Support," *New York Times*, May 8, 2008.
65. Thomas, "How He Did It," 67.
66. "Barack Obama's Speech on Race," *New York Times*, March 18, 2008.
67. Michael Cooper and Michael Powell, "McCain Camp Says Obama Is Playing 'Race Card,'" *New York Times*, August 1, 2008.
68. Nicholas Confessore, "Code Words Hint of Race in Campaign, Paterson Says," *New York Times*, September 10, 2008.
69. Cooper, "McCain's Age May Figure in Choice of a Running Mate."
70. Jim Rutenberg, "Liberal PACs Ready Attack Ad on McCain," *New York Times*, September 25, 2008.
71. Monica Langley, "As Economic Crisis Peaked, Tide Turned Against McCain," *Wall Street Journal*, November 5, 2008; and Thomas, "How He Did It," 108.
72. Adam Nagourney, Jim Rutenberg, and Jeff Zeleny, "Near-Flawless Run Is Credited in Win," *New York Times*, November 5, 2008.
73. Nicholas D. Kristof, "The Push to 'Otherize' Obama," *New York Times*, September 21, 2008.
74. John Harwood, "Level of White Support for Obama a Surprise," *New York Times*, November 3, 2008.
75. All exit poll results are from "President: National Exit Poll," CNN.com, www.cnn.com/ELECTION/2008/results/polls/#USP00p1.
76. Adam Nagourney, "Obama Is Elected President as Racial Barrier Falls," *New York Times*, November 6, 2008.
77. In a July 2003 Pew Research Center survey, 38 percent said they would not be willing to vote for a "generally-well-qualified" Muslim for president, and 56 percent said they would. Pew Forum on Religion and Public Life, "Religion and Politics: Contention and Consensus," July 24, 2003, http://pewforum.org/docs/?DocID=26.
78. Juan Williams, "What Obama's Victory Means for Racial Politics," *Wall Street Journal*, November 10, 2008.

# 2

# The Nominations:
# Rules, Strategies, and Uncertainty

Barry C. Burden

*What a long strange trip it's been.*
—The Grateful Dead, "Truckin'"[1]

In 2008 the presidential nominating campaigns were especially long and strange. For the first time in decades both the Democratic and Republican nominations were hotly contested. The competition between the two leading Democrats was especially lengthy and intense. The eventual nominees—Republican John McCain and Democrat Barack Obama—were not traditional standard-bearers. Nor were they the frontrunners at the outset of the campaign. Although the 2008 nominations reinforced some of our understandings of the process from earlier elections, they also challenged popular assumptions about how the process works.

An immediate and unsurprising conclusion to draw from the 2008 contests is that "rules matter." But the precise ways in which the rules governing such things as the dates of primaries and delegate allocation formulas end up shaping the nominations are complex. Moreover, they are often in flux as the campaign proceeds and the field of candidates evolves. This makes it difficult for candidates to plot their strategies in advance. Until a party's nomination has been settled no one can be sure which rules will matter and how. Because the game cannot be won in advance, it is not clear that candidates' strategies have much effect at all. McCain and Obama won their parties' nominations despite their strategies as much as because of them.

## Unique Features of the 2008 Election

Every election is unique, but the 2008 presidential nominations were historic in several respects. Their anomalies limit the ability of traditional understandings of presidential selection to apply as neatly as in the past. Even at the outset there were three ways in which 2008 would clearly differ from earlier elections.

First, it was an open seat election. For the first time since 1928, there was neither a sitting president seeking reelection nor a sitting vice president seeking to become president. This all but guaranteed vigorous campaigns for both the

Democratic and Republican nominations. Both major parties had large fields of qualified candidates. But the Democrats were more enthusiastic about their choices than were the Republicans.[2] The "enthusiasm gap," as it came to be known during the campaign, allowed Democrats to enter the general election in a strong position despite a longer and more contentious nomination.

Second, the presidential contenders in 2008 represented an unusually diverse array of backgrounds. As is common in many presidential elections, both parties attracted the standard field of U.S. senators and governors. But the pool also included some less likely candidates, including a big city mayor and several members of the House of Representatives, positions that had never launched candidates to the White House. Aside from a few candidates with clear ties to particular states, this also was a particularly "rootless" pool, largely unconnected to specific parts of the country.[3] Moreover, some of the strongest candidates had personal characteristics not typically seen in presidential contenders. Mitt Romney was a devout Mormon. Hillary Clinton was not only a woman but also a former first lady. Barack Obama was African American, the son of a white mother and a Kenyan father. For the first time both presidential nominees turned out to be sitting senators, making 2008 only the third election to elevate a senator directly to the White House.[4]

Third, the United States was a nation at war, with about 150,000 combat troops committed to military operations in Iraq and Afghanistan. Since George W. Bush's reelection in 2004, public support for the war in Iraq had fallen significantly. By the time the presidential nomination season began in early 2007, a majority of Americans believed that the invasion had done more harm than good. But because neither President Bush nor Vice President Richard Cheney was on the ballot, it was unclear at the outset who would pay the price for this discontent. In the end, the effect of the war differed by party. Obama's steadfast criticism paved the way for his candidacy, whereas McCain's military expertise and support for Bush's infusion of additional troops in Iraq—the "surge"—were critical to his success.

## The Rules

Central to any presidential nomination is the calendar of events that marks the process. Candidates win delegates in events that typically begin with the Iowa caucuses and New Hampshire primary. The period after candidates declare their candidacies but before any votes are cast is known as the "invisible primary."[5] Debates, endorsements, fund-raising reports, and polls define both this invisible primary and the gauntlet of state primaries and caucuses that follows. In addition to the dates on which events occur, the rules also govern procedural matters such as campaign fund raising and delegate allocation. No single entity is responsible for writing the rules, which are the result of decisions made by the national parties, state parties, the candidates, the media, and state lawmakers. Moreover, every four years these rules are revised, if not entirely rewritten. And as 2008 demonstrated, the rules are not always solidified by the time the campaigns get underway, making a successful path to the nomination something of a moving target.

Although the Democrats have been more apt to reform their rules than have the Republicans, both major parties invariably tinker with the process between presidential elections. Often these changes are instituted to correct the imperfections of the last nomination contest. "Fighting the last war," as it were, produces unintended consequences; reforms designed to rectify peculiarities of the previous election cannot anticipate what new concerns will emerge in the next. How the rules operate depends on the candidates, and that field changes every four years. Three sets of reforms turned out to be especially important in 2008. The first expanded the use of primaries and proportional allocation of delegates, the second created the position of superdelegate, and the third altered the calendar of delegate selection.

The first and most notable wave of reforms took place following the controversial nomination of Vice President Hubert Humphrey at the 1968 Democratic National Convention in Chicago. After the election the Democrats created a commission led by Sen. George McGovern to make the process of selecting convention delegates more democratic. The McGovern-Fraser Commission recommended more open delegate selection processes as well as quotas to guarantee proportional representation of women and minorities among the delegates.[6] In response to the commission's mandate, many state parties adopted primary elections and proportional representation as their means for selecting delegates. Republicans soon followed with similar reforms. In 1968 only fifteen states held presidential primaries; by 1980 the number was thirty-five and rising. Only in 2000 and 2004 did some states, concerned about the cost of running statewide elections that often were of little consequence, begin moving away from primaries toward caucuses.[7] Although states often adopted one or the other for idiosyncratic reasons, the distinction between caucuses and primaries would become critical in the 2008 Democratic nomination.

The second significant reform of the nomination process occurred between the 1980 and 1984 elections. After Sen. Ted Kennedy's bitter challenge to incumbent president Jimmy Carter's renomination in 1980, party officials decided to de-democratize the process. They created a commission led by North Carolina governor Jim Hunt to recommend reforms that would allow for more party control.[8] The Hunt Commission's recommendations led to the creation of additional convention delegates, called Party Leaders and Elected Officials (PLEOS). Popularly known as "superdelegates," these individuals were not pledged to any candidate and their identities were known before any primaries or caucuses took place. In 1984 they comprised roughly 15 percent of all delegates; by 2008 they numbered close to one in five votes at the Democratic National Convention. (Republicans adopted a version of this system with a smaller number of automatic delegates.) Superdelegates helped insider Walter Mondale secure the Democratic nomination in 1984, but were not again pivotal until 2008.[9]

The third, most recent wave of reforms affected the calendar of primaries and caucuses. The 2008 nomination intensified the process of "front-loading" primaries and caucuses that had marked the previous thirty years.[10] In 1976 only 10 percent of convention delegates were selected by March 2. By 2004 the figure had risen to 58 percent. In 2008 more than 70 percent of delegates were selected by that date, a full eight months before the general election. Based on recent history, most observers believed that the 2008 nominating contests would be settled early, leaving later states to hold expensive primary elections that would be inconsequential.

As states moved their primaries and caucuses forward on the calendar, Iowa and New Hampshire jockeyed to maintain their privileged positions. The New Hampshire secretary of state, Bill Gardner, was granted unilateral power to move his state's contest to any date that would ensure its historical place as the first primary. The date of the Iowa caucuses was ultimately set at January 3, 2008, but that was not known until October 2007, when both national parties selected the date. Likewise, New Hampshire did not announce until late November that its primary would be on January 8.

To address the concern that Iowa and New Hampshire were unrepresentative of the demographics of the nation and possessed too much influence, in 2004 the Democrats created the Commission on Presidential Nomination Timing and Scheduling. The commission quickly recommended that Iowa and New Hampshire maintain their privileged positions but that one or two other states be permitted to host early events as well. Specifically, two additional states would be authorized to hold their events after Iowa and New Hampshire but before the opening of a "window" on February 5. Then starting on February 5 any remaining state could schedule its primary or caucus on whichever date it preferred.[11] In selecting the two new early states, preference would be given to those with racially and economically diverse populations and high concentrations of union members. In the end the party selected Nevada and South Carolina. Other states would receive bonus delegates for holding events later in the season or would be penalized by losing their delegates if they held events before the opening of the window.

Not all state party leaders were satisfied with this solution. Michigan was among the states whose bids to hold early events were rejected by the Democratic National Committee (DNC). The state's Democratic leaders nonetheless scheduled their primary for January 15. In Florida Democratic state legislators signed on to a bill scheduling their state's primary on the prohibited date of January 29, even though Florida had not submitted a bid to hold an early event.

Following the rules outlined by the commission, the DNC threatened that it would not seat the delegates from Florida and Michigan, despite the obvious importance of the two states in the general election. In September 2007 all of the leading Democratic candidates signed a "four-state pledge," promising not to campaign in Florida or Michigan. All except Hillary Clinton removed their names from the Michigan ballot. The battle of wills between the DNC and Democrats in Florida and Michigan remained unresolved throughout the nomination process. Party leaders in both states demanded that their delegates be seated, either by acknowledging the primary votes that were cast (Clinton's preference) or by holding a re-vote (the option acceptable to Obama and DNC leaders). As the campaign wore on, however, it became evident that neither the time nor the money was available to rerun the elections.

The stalemate was a dramatic example of nomination rules that could not have been anticipated by the candidates because they were in flux during most of the nomination season. Until a compromise emerged in late May, no one knew what role, if any, Florida and Michigan delegates would play at the convention. Clinton needed them fully seated to have a chance at being nominated.

As a result of the commission's window policy, many other states moved their events to the first date available to them: February 5. This created the biggest "Super Tuesday" in presidential nomination history.[12] Nearly half of the states held their events on that date, when 45 percent of Republican delegates and 52 percent of Democratic delegates were chosen. Most observers assumed that both parties' nominations would be settled on Super Tuesday and that the candidates with the most money and best organizations would emerge victorious. These assumptions turned out to be wrong.

## The Republican Nomination

The Republican nomination contest began early and ended early. In the 2006 midterm election, the Republicans had lost control of both chambers of Congress. Perhaps because of this defeat, the presidential contenders drawing the most interest in early 2007 were not typical Republicans.

Atop the field at the beginning of the invisible primary was former New York City mayor Rudolph Giuliani. Giuliani had risen to fame for his handling of the aftermath of the September 11 attacks on the city's World Trade Center and had been dubbed "America's Mayor." His appeal in the national security realm, however, was offset among Republicans by his liberal moderate positions on social issues and by the fact that a mayor had never been elected president.

Just behind Giuliani in early polls was Sen. John McCain, a self-described "maverick" who eight years earlier had challenged George W. Bush for the presidential nomination. At seventy-two years of age, McCain would have been the oldest person ever elected president. He boasted foreign policy credentials and a compelling personal story as a courageous prisoner of war in Vietnam. He worked to establish ties to the Republican Party base during Bush's second term and was known for his strong support of the U.S. invasion of Iraq and of the surge. But as public opinion toward both Bush and the war soured, so did McCain's campaign, allowing other candidates to outpace him in the early going.

Other candidates looked to fill the void left by discontent with Giuliani and McCain, neither of whom excited the most conservative Republicans. Former Massachusetts governor Mitt Romney used his personal wealth, large and attractive family, and successes in business and in organizing the 2002 Salt Lake City Winter Olympic Games to build his support in several early primary and caucus states. Unlike Giuliani and McCain, who focused on foreign policy, Romney emphasized economic and social issues. His victory in the March 2007 straw poll at the Conservative Political Action Committee (CPAC) convention helped thrust him into the top tier of candidates, despite some concerns about his Mormon faith and the inconsistency of his support for conservative positions on social issues.

The imperfections of the Republican field also opened the door for Fred Thompson to enter the fray. A television and film actor and a former senator from Tennessee, Thompson's name began to be circulated as a potential candidate just after Romney's victory at the CPAC meeting. Many conservative activists in the party had not yet endorsed a candidate, and they eagerly anticipated his arrival on the scene. Thompson eventually joined the race during the summer, but he disappointed many of his supporters with his lackluster campaigning. He had not fully prepared for the campaign, making him a more attractive candidate out of the race than in it.

Meanwhile, the Republican field grew to ten candidates. In addition to Giuliani, McCain, Romney, and Thompson, several other Republicans also sought the nomination. Former Arkansas governor Mike Huckabee entered the race without much national recognition or many resources. But as an ordained Southern Baptist minister from the South he laid claim to the "moral" issues that had motivated the Republican base during the Bush years. Former Wisconsin governor and Bush administration cabinet secretary Tommy Thompson ran as a mainstream Republican, while Sen. Sam Brownback of Kansas emphasized a return to conservative positions on such social issues as abortion, stem cell research, and the teaching of evolution in schools. Also in the mix were three members of the House of Representatives: Ron Paul, an antiwar candidate from Texas, had once run for president as the nominee of the Libertarian Party; Duncan Hunter, a foreign policy hawk from California, chaired the House Armed Services Committee; and Tom Tancredo of Colorado focused his campaign almost entirely on the eradication of illegal immigration. Others, such as former Speaker of the House Newt Gingrich, were also mentioned but chose not to run.

Despite the depth of the Republican field, none of the candidates looked like a traditional Republican presidential nominee. Each was grounded in one of the three prominent wings of the Republican Party: national security conservatives (Giuliani, Hunter, and McCain), fiscal conservatives (Romney, Thompson, and Paul), or social issues conservatives (Brownback, Huckabee, and Tancredo). Unlike Bush and Reagan, who had managed to bridge these intraparty cleavages, each of the Republican candidates in 2008 lacked credibility with at least some elements within the party. This led them to try to broaden their credentials. For example, Giuliani and McCain stressed that they would oppose the appointment of "activist judges," whereas Romney traveled abroad to establish a foreign policy profile and eventually began to emphasize illegal immigration. But as Adam Nagourney of the *New York Times* put it, "It is hard to think of another campaign when Republicans have seemed less excited about their choices," since each was "hobbled by some failing of character, ideology, or record."[13]

The Republican invisible primary was not won by any of the candidates; no one emerged as the frontrunner. In 2007 an unprecedented number of televised candidate forums and debates were held that provided each of the contenders with some exposure. The first debate was in May, a full seven months before the Iowa caucuses, and even without Fred Thompson it included ten candidates. In these early days the challenge for each candidate was to stand out from the crowd at a time when many Republican activists and donors were sitting on the sidelines waiting for a leader to emerge from the pack. Figure 2-1 shows the standings of the leading Republican candidates starting in August 2007, using political stock market data from the Iowa Electronic Market.[14] The data show that while Giuliani led throughout most of fall and early winter, no candidate yet dominated the field.

The lack of an early leader was surprising. Having made amends with President Bush, McCain initially appeared to be the Republican heir apparent. In August 2006 the *Washington Post* observed that McCain had "vaulted to the front of the GOP field." He was identified as "the early leader for the Republican nomination in 2008" by *U.S. News and World Report* just after the 2006 midterms. But by early 2007 McCain had faltered along with the Bush administration. He tried to jumpstart his campaign by reinstating his "Straight Talk Express" bus tour from 2000, but it had little effect. His fundraising totals were disappointing and suffered from a high "burn rate" of heavy expenditures relative to contributions. In the second quarter of 2007 he raised $11 million, whereas Romney pulled in $20 million (including $6 million of his own funds) and Giuliani raised $17 million. Even fringe candidate Ron Paul had more cash on hand than McCain, much of it raised from fellow libertarians over the Internet. In July two of McCain's top aides resigned, and the campaign appeared to be in freefall. He all but skipped the traditional Iowa straw poll in August, which provided a lift for the victor, Mitt Romney, as well as for Huckabee, who finished a surprisingly strong second. Subsequent debates were dominated by tough exchanges among Giuliani, Romney, and Thompson, leaving McCain a bystander without much chance of victory. Yet despite McCain's slump, none of his opponents was able to take control of the race.

As the January 2008 delegate contests in Iowa and New Hampshire approached, the logjam of the fall gave way to fluidity. Brownback's withdrawal from the race and Thompson's inability to motivate social conservatives provided Mike Huckabee with an opening, and he seized it by making his first serious ad buys of the campaign in Iowa. Tancredo's withdrawal gave Romney, who had begun to emphasize cracking down on illegal immigration, something of a lift. And McCain returned to the strategies that had worked for him in New Hampshire in 2000: open access to reporters, bus tours of the state, and dozens of town meetings. McCain also secured the endorsement of

**Figure 2-1**    Republican Candidate Standings, August 2007–May 2008

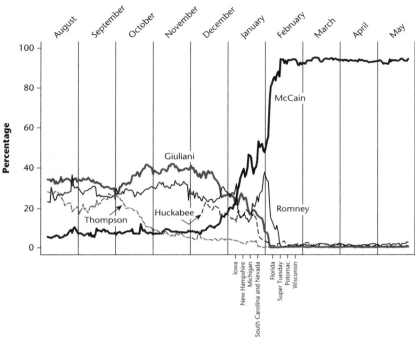

*Source:* Figure prepared using data from the Iowa Electronic Market. Data available online at www.biz.uiowa.edu/iem.

Sen. Joseph Lieberman, the Democratic nominee for vice president in 2000 who had run as an independent in 2006.

In late 2007 Giuliani found himself in a strange situation: leading in the national polls but not in any of the key early states.[15] Spooked by Giuliani's inability to penetrate in New Hampshire, Iowa, and South Carolina, his campaign took the unprecedented step of skipping the first six primaries and caucuses to focus on Florida. Giuliani assumed that the other candidates would split the vote in the early states, leaving the nomination wide open by the time of the January 29 Florida primary. His decision further reduced the field in Iowa and New Hampshire, providing McCain an even greater opportunity to rebound. As one report put it, by camping out in Florida, Giuliani made a decision to "zag while the rest of the candidates zig," assuming that a win there would render the mixed results of the first six states irrelevant.[16] As the immediate drop in Giuliani's mid-December standings in Figure 2-1 indicates, this view turned out to be incorrect.

What few anticipated was that the January 3 Iowa caucuses would give the first victory of 2008 to Mike Huckabee. Despite lagging well behind the other leading candidates in fund raising, Huckabee took 34 percent of the vote to Romney's 25 percent. He did especially well among rural evangelicals, with organizational help from networks of Christian volunteers such as the mothers of home-school children.[17] Huckabee won 40 percent of the female vote and 46 percent of born-again evangelicals, an important group that comprised a majority of Republican caucusgoers. He also drew support from those who endorsed the theme of "change" while still supporting traditional social values. Although Romney finished a clear second, it was a disappointing outcome considering how much time and money he had devoted to Iowa.

Meanwhile McCain was surging in New Hampshire. Huckabee had failed to gain traction in the Granite State, which has relatively few evangelical Christians, and Romney was working to make up lost ground. McCain was helped on primary day by independent voters, who were permitted to vote in the state's open primary. In the end, McCain edged out Romney in New Hampshire by 37 percent to 32 percent. Romney's second-place finish again failed to meet expectations. As governor of neighboring Massachusetts with a vacation home in New Hampshire, anything less than an outright victory was a severe setback. McCain grabbed the momentum mantle, with supporters chanting at his primary night victory speech that "Mac is back!" After the primary McCain and Romney turned their attention to Michigan, while Huckabee mined conservative votes in South Carolina.

On January 15 Romney finally won a primary in Michigan, the state where he was born and his father once was governor. He beat McCain by nine points by emphasizing his personal ties to Michigan and promising economic assistance to a state with one of the highest unemployment rates in the country. But four days later McCain's narrow victory over Huckabee in South Carolina, the state that had ended McCain's 2000 campaign, overshadowed Romney's in Michigan. By defeating the leading social conservative in the race, McCain laid claim to being the best candidate to unite the party's social and foreign policy conservatives. Fred Thompson's withdrawal three days after finishing a disappointing fourth in South Carolina only helped strengthen McCain's case for the nomination. Romney won the uneventful Nevada caucuses the same day that Thompson withdrew, but this was an empty victory because the other candidates had ceded the state to him due to its large Mormon population. That McCain beat Huckabee, Romney, and Thompson in South Carolina defined him as the candidate to beat in the head-to-head battle with Giuliani, who awaited him in Florida.

The dramatic increase in McCain's prospects shown in Figure 2-1 documents how his fortunes continued to rise during the week before the Florida primary. He earned several influential newspaper endorsements in the Sunshine State as well as critical backing from Florida's popular governor, Charlie Crist. Despite Giuliani's heavy investment of time and money in the state, McCain's accumulation of victories and media attention allowed him to win the Florida primary by five points over Romney. Giuliani's meager 15 percent of the vote was a stinging defeat for a candidate who had once seemed strong. He failed to win a single demographic group measured in the state's exit polls. Giuliani had bet that a victory in Florida would provide a launch pad for wrapping up the nomination a week later on Super Tuesday, but instead he dropped out of the race the day after the primary and endorsed McCain.

The Republican debate on January 30, the day after the Florida primary, featured only four candidates, a far cry from the ten who had debated six months earlier. Romney's many silver and bronze "medals" in the January primaries and caucuses forced him to attack McCain more directly in the hopes of defeating him in a two-man race. This became increasingly difficult as the party establishment coalesced around McCain. At the end of the month the governors of California and Texas both endorsed McCain.

McCain did well on Super Tuesday, winning nine contests, most of them in populous states such as California and New York that are traditionally Democratic in general elections. Beyond his "home" states of Massachusetts and Utah, Romney only managed to win small primary and caucus states, none of which provided many delegates or even symbolic victories. Despite a shoestring budget, Huckabee remained viable with surprising victories in five southern and border states.

McCain was helped in two ways on Super Tuesday, one related to the field of candidates and the other to the rules. First, because Huckabee and Romney split the social conservative vote in many states, McCain was able to beat both of them with support from moderates in the party. Second, because Republicans relied heavily on winner-take-all rules for allocating delegates, McCain began building an impressive lead in the delegate count. For example, although he beat Romney by just eight points in California, he earned 158 delegates to Romney's 12.

McCain's remaining challenge was to reassure the most conservative elements in his party that he was one of them. Romney's departure two days after Super Tuesday and his endorsement of McCain a week after that left Huckabee as the only remaining obstacle to the nomination. For a candidacy that in late 2007 had been declared all but dead, McCain's turnaround was dramatic. The remainder of the nomination campaign was merely a question of when McCain would accumulate a majority of the pledged delegates and nudge Huckabee from the race. In mid-February he defeated Huckabee in head-to-head competition in Washington and Wisconsin, but by now he was focusing his critiques more on the Democrats than on Huckabee, whose support he wanted. After besting Huckabee in a diverse set of four states on March 4, it became clear that McCain had clinched the nomination, and Huckabee ended his campaign. Bush endorsed McCain at the White House the next day.

In just two months of voting, the Republicans winnowed a large field of candidates to one nominee. This was not a typical nomination contest for the GOP. McCain may have been viewed as the presumptive nominee in 2006 because of his greater name recognition, but during the crucial invisible primary Giuliani had emerged as the leading contender. Because of Giuliani's failed Florida strategy and the lack of a single candidate to represent social conservatives, McCain was able to use victories in New Hampshire and South Carolina to overcome his fund-raising disadvantages and the disorder in his campaign. Whether he succeeded because he had momentum or simply because he peaked at the right time remains unclear.

McCain's opponents failed in their efforts to take advantage of the system. Romney could not translate his heavy spending in the four early states into victories. Giuliani mistakenly believed that he could wait until the end of January to begin earning media attention and votes. Huckabee was unable to parlay a win in Iowa into additional victories elsewhere. As much as McCain's own efforts, the flaws and miscalculations of his competitors left him the only candidate to emerge successfully from the contests between New Hampshire and Super Tuesday. His victory was not manufactured by his careful manipulation of the rules; it was mostly due to weaknesses in the field of candidates in which he found himself.

## The Democratic Nomination

In some ways the battle for the Democratic Party's presidential nomination resembled that of the Republicans. The contest drew a large field of qualified contenders. As with the Republicans, observers assumed that the early frontrunner would wrap up the nomination on Super Tuesday because of fund-raising advantages and a strong network of loyalists within the party, only to see those assumptions proven wrong. But that is where the similarities end. Hillary Clinton's campaign did not suffer the same implosion and rebirth that the McCain campaign did in 2007. Nor was her major task uniting the economic, national security, and cultural wings of her party. While Republican voters sought to find a candidate who was merely acceptable, Democratic voters were enthusiastic about several candidates; they saw their task as selecting the one who best represented their view of the party and had the best chance of winning the general election. Finally, unlike McCain, Clinton lost the nomination to a relative newcomer in a difficult nomination struggle that lasted a full three months longer than the Republican contest.

It was common knowledge by the time of the 2006 midterm election that Hillary Clinton would seek her party's nomination for president. In her Senate reelection campaign that year Clinton raised more than $30 million despite facing weak opposition. This signaled that she was ready for the fund-raising challenges of a presidential bid, and provided a way for her to ingratiate herself with other Democratic officials to whom she transferred some of those campaign funds. Clinton also shifted $10 million in leftover Senate campaign funds to her own presidential campaign. Without John Kerry or Al Gore in the race, the former first lady was the closest thing to an establishment candidate in the Democratic Party. Some Democrats feared that she would be too polarizing a figure to win a general election, but many also felt indebted to the Clintons, who had dominated party politics since the early 1990s.

Former North Carolina senator John Edwards, Kerry's running mate in 2004, began developing his own presidential campaign right after the Democrats lost that election. Despite his wife's recurrent cancer diagnoses, Edwards pursued the nomination with a message of rectifying economic inequalities between the "two Americas."

A junior senator from Illinois named Barack Obama also decided to seek the party's nomination. Obama was a newcomer to national politics. He had delivered an impressive primetime keynote speech at the 2004 Democratic National Convention about what Americans in "blue" and "red" states have in common and had been elected to the Senate that year in an easy victory. His initial message as a candidate for president focused on his early opposition to the Iraq War and his desire to foster national unity.

Joining Senators Clinton, Edwards, and Obama were two senior senators, Joe Biden of Delaware and Chris Dodd of Connecticut. Both had considered running in the past and Biden had launched and then abandoned a serious presidential campaign in 1988. Neither was able to generate much interest in 2008. Also in the field were Rep. Dennis Kucinich of Ohio and former senator Mike Gravel of Alaska, the two most liberal candidates. Finally, there was New Mexico governor Bill Richardson. Richardson was the only Latino, the only governor and, aside from Gravel, the only candidate from the West in the field, all of which distinguished him from the other contenders. Richardson also sported the most impressive résumé, having been a member of Congress, an ambassador to the United Nations, and a cabinet secretary before becoming governor. But those credentials meant little to Democratic voters in 2008.

The Democratic Party establishment did not quickly rally behind Clinton the way Republican leaders had behind George W. Bush in 2000, indicating that her path to the nomination would be challenging. Neither 2000 nominee Al Gore nor 2004 nominee Kerry endorsed her. Yet Clinton initially campaigned as if she were the presumptive nominee, touting her experience and assembling a team of seasoned political operatives. Campaign contributors did not shower the Clinton campaign with funds. In the first quarter of 2007 Obama nearly matched her $20 million haul and did so with many more small donors. By the end of the second quarter he had raised about $10 million more than Clinton, with support from 250,000 donors.

The first Democratic debate in April 2007 featured a field of eight candidates. As the other Democrats highlighted the differences among them, Clinton's approach was to contrast the two parties, essentially a general election message. As several more debates and other invisible primary events took place in the second half of 2007, Obama's early criticism of the war—including his 2002 speech and Clinton's vote in favor of the Senate resolution in favor of action—elevated his standing in the polls. Obama also benefited when Oprah Winfrey joined him at December rallies in Iowa, New Hampshire, and South Carolina. Edwards and to a lesser extent Richardson also emerged as "first-tier" candidates, with the rest of the field getting much less attention. As Figure 2-2 shows, Clinton's strategy slowly unraveled as winter turned to spring and the first nominating events approached in January.

Although it was clear from polling that Obama was steadily gaining ground and Clinton was losing it, it took the Iowa caucuses to challenge Clinton's status

**Figure 2-2**   Democratic Candidate Standings, August 2007–May 2008

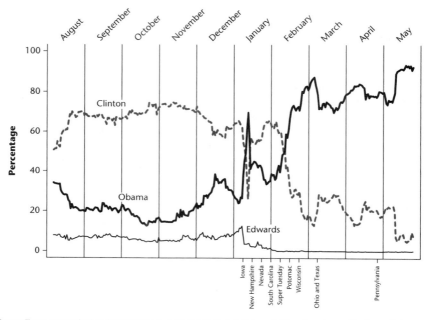

*Source:* Figure prepared using data from the Iowa Electronic Market. Data available online at www.biz.uiowa.edu/iem.

as the leading candidate for the nomination. She had won the endorsement of the *Des Moines Register,* which was viewed as critical to Edwards's strong showing in the 2004 caucuses, and had focused on mobilizing dependable female and elderly caucusgoers. But Obama won in Iowa with 35 percent of the vote, easily outdistancing the 25 percent for Clinton and 24 percent for Edwards. Obama won nearly every demographic group, including women. It was a stunning result, suggesting that Obama could defeat Clinton and do it mainly with the support of white voters. Although an African American, Barack Obama was no Jesse Jackson, dependent on black votes.

The Iowa results foreshadowed two trends that would unfold during the rest of the nomination contest. First, Democratic enthusiasm was high, with an astounding turnout of 239,000 Iowa caucusgoers. This was double the previous Democratic record and far higher than the turnout in the Republican caucuses the same day. The new surge of Democratic voters spelled trouble for Clinton and Edwards, both of whom relied on the party's traditional rank-and-file, but also demonstrated concretely the enthusiasm gap between the two parties. It became clear in Iowa that Obama's mantra of "change" was resonating strongly, drawing new participants into the electoral process.

Second, Iowa was a caucus state. As the process unfolded, Obama continued to dominate caucus results across the country, whereas Clinton performed better in primaries. Never before 2008 had the differences between caucus and primary voting been so strong or consequential. Clinton's campaign fell into a tailspin just before the critical New Hampshire primary in which an infusion of independent voters and momentum from the Iowa victory were expected to provide Obama with a second victory.

The tumult in the polls is evident in Figure 2-2, which shows the lead changing several times in early January. During the five days between Iowa and New Hampshire, Clinton tried to regroup, defending herself vigorously against Obama in a national debate. She also teared up at a forum in New Hampshire; video of the event was endlessly replayed on television and the Internet. Even though the last published polls had Obama up by double digits, Clinton pulled off a narrow victory in New Hampshire. She won a plurality of women and older voters, whereas Obama did better among men and much better among young people. Although Clinton beat Obama by just two points, the victory felt big because it came as such a surprise and quickly revived her campaign. As she told supporters that night, "I listened to you and in the process, I found my own voice."

Many in the political community, especially those within the Clinton campaign, believed that the Super Tuesday contests on February 5 would prove the end of the race, making the events before then critical. Richardson ended his campaign on January 10 without endorsing a candidate or even waiting for the heavily Latino Nevada caucuses. John Kerry endorsed Obama in South Carolina the same day. Several days later Clinton used the results of the anticlimactic Michigan primary to energize her campaign. Obama and the other leading Democrats had removed their names from the Michigan ballot several months earlier in response to the DNC's vow to punish the state for holding its primary prematurely. Clinton decided to remain on the ballot and won 55 percent of the votes cast. Four days later she won a rare caucus victory in Nevada with support from women, older voters, Latinos, and rural voters.

At about the same time, the campaign's discourse sharpened and for the first time focused on Obama's race. Bill Clinton took on the visible role of attack dog in his wife's campaign. Among other things, his statement that South Carolina was not important because Jesse Jackson had won the state's primary twice went over poorly, raising the possibility that the former president might be a drag on his wife's presidential aspirations. Obama went on to win South Carolina handily, helped in large part by overwhelming support from the state's black voters. South Carolina was the first contest in which clear racial voting patterns emerged. Edwards, a South Carolina native, finished a disappointing third despite winning the white vote. Two days later Obama picked up endorsements from Sen. Ted Kennedy and others in the Kennedy clan, who compared him favorably to President John Kennedy. Clinton again found her campaign in a difficult and unexpected position, in part because of her husband's actions.

Despite threats from the DNC identical to those leveled at Michigan, as well as the absence of real campaigning in the state, Florida's primary was held as scheduled on January 29. As she had done in Michigan, Clinton won with a 50 percent majority of the vote, hoping once again to use the victory to restore energy to her campaign. Edwards dropped out the next day without endorsing anyone, which turned the Democratic nomination into a two-way competition. A cordial debate between Clinton and Obama in Los Angeles two days later was the first of many, not all of them so friendly.

Super Tuesday arrived on February 5, the biggest single nominating day in history, with more than half of the Democratic delegates up for selection. Although Super Tuesday was expected to settle the nomination, its mixed outcome left the Democratic nomination unsettled. Obama won more states (thirteen to Clinton's nine) but Clinton won the large industrial states of California, Massachusetts, and New York. Obama's victories were concentrated in smaller, generally Republican states and in those with caucuses rather than primaries. This ambiguous result reinforced the patterns coming out of Iowa and New Hampshire that would persist until the nomination was settled. Clinton was applauded for holding off Obama in California and for winning a majority of Latino votes, which would be critical for Democrats competing in the Rocky Mountain West in the general election. At the same time, Obama argued that he was able to win in traditionally Republican states, which would be important for Democrats hoping to improve on their performance in 2004.

Starting on February 5, the delegate count became the most salient metric for judging who was ahead and who was behind. As Figure 2-3 shows, Obama's advantage in pledged delegates was established on Super Tuesday. The result of those events was that he led Clinton 931 to 876, a 55-delegate difference.

Midway through the campaign, it was clear that although Clinton sported high-priced talent, her team lacked the dexterity of the Obama campaign. One postmortem reported that Clinton's chief strategist, Mark Penn, mistakenly assumed that delegates were awarded on a winner-take-all basis, which would have given Clinton an insurmountable lead after she won the California primary.[18] The Clinton campaign also was wrong to undervalue caucus states and to assume the nomination would be settled on February 5. In truth, the rule of proportional representation used in Democratic contests made it difficult for any trailing candidate to catch up to the leader.[19]

As Figure 2-2 documents, the rest of February belonged to Obama. While Clinton struggled to put together a campaign in states where she had not expected to have to compete, Obama took advantage of strong fund raising and the extensive grassroots operations he built in many states. On February 9 he swept Louisiana, Nebraska, and Washington, three states with varying demographic profiles and delegate selection rules. The next day he won the Maine caucuses. Sensing a need to shake up her campaign in the face of these losses, Clinton replaced her campaign manager, Patti Solis Doyle, with Maggie Williams, a long-time associate who had worked for her when she was first lady. Yet Obama continued his winning streak with victories in the three "Potomac Primaries" of Virginia, Maryland, and the District of Columbia on February 12. For the first time he led in the total estimated delegate counts—that is, those that included both superdelegates and pledged delegates.

**Figure 2-3**    Pledged Delegate Counts for Clinton and Obama, January–May 2008

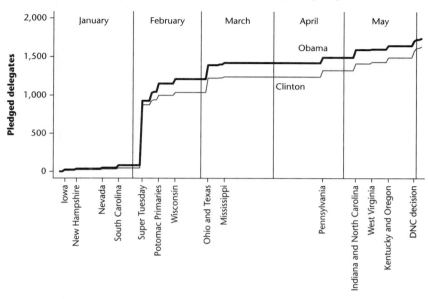

*Source:* Figure prepared using data from "Results: Democratic Delegate Count," the *New York Times.* Data available online at http://politics.nytimes.com/election-guide/2008/results/delegates/index.html.

Figure 2-3 documents Obama's widening lead in the pledged delegate count throughout February. But Clinton still appeared to be ahead in total delegates because of her support from superdelegates. (Clinton operatives referred to these as "automatic" delegates to remove their antidemocratic connotation.) While Clinton concentrated her resources on the upcoming contests in Ohio and Texas, dispatching her husband to stump in small communities across the two states, Obama reached the zenith of his success, winning the Wisconsin primary by a large margin even though the state's blue-collar demographics and primary laws were thought to favor Clinton. At this point Obama had won ten events in a row and led Clinton in pledged delegates 1212 to 1039, a difference of 173. If ever there was momentum in the Democratic nomination contest, it was in Obama's corner on February 20.

But in the next week Clinton and Obama participated in two more debates, raising the total number of Democratic debates to twenty. Clinton tailored her message to blue-collar white voters and began to criticize Obama more sharply. She suggested that he had plagiarized a campaign slogan, referring to mocking his message of "Change you can believe in" as "Change you Xerox." More effectively, her campaign aired a controversial television spot questioning whether Obama could be trusted to handle an emergency phone call in the White House in the middle of the night. The "3 a.m." ad and other attacks on Obama worked to some degree, and Clinton entered the early March contests with a new sense of optimism.

On March 4 Clinton and Obama split the small states of Rhode Island and Vermont, but she won the popular vote in both Ohio and Texas. Although this continued the pattern of Clinton victories in large states, the Texas result was complicated. The state used a two-stage process for selecting delegates: a primary during the day and a caucus in the evening—the so-called Texas two-step. Although both events were held on the same day with the same eligibility rules for participants, Clinton won the primary and Obama won the caucus. This further cemented the impression that Clinton had broader but less enthusiastic support than Obama. The Texas rules also prevented her from gaining much ground in the delegate count despite news coverage of a big victory in Texas.

The closeness of the total delegate count and national popular vote at this point refocused attention on the allegiances of the superdelegates and on how the delegate disputes in Florida and Michigan would be resolved. After Obama won quick victories in Wyoming and Mississippi, a six-week window in advance of the April 22 Pennsylvania primary opened, affording plenty of time to debate these procedural issues. The hiatus in primaries and caucuses facilitated several other developments as well. One was an intense focus on Obama's connections to his controversial minister, the Rev. Jeremiah Wright. Anti-American rhetorical sound bites from Wright's fiery sermons were heavily watched on television and on YouTube. To resolve the Wright issue, Obama delivered a major speech on race in Philadelphia, calling his minister "divisive." The speech marked an important turning point, temporarily quelling the controversy. At the same time, Obama snagged an endorsement from Bill Richardson, whom the Clintons had courted intensely. And Hillary Clinton was forced to admit that she misspoke about coming under sniper fire in Bosnia when videotapes of her visit revealed otherwise. She also completed the replacement of her top campaign staff by firing Mark Penn after it was revealed that he had lobbied for free trade agreements on behalf of Colombian officials.

Simultaneously, however, Obama was criticized as "elitist" for his connections to Wright, his failure to consistently wear an American flag lapel pin, and comments he made at a San Francisco fund-raiser, where he said that some working-class voters support Republicans because they "get bitter, they cling to guns or religion or antipathy to people who aren't like them or anti-immigrant sentiment or anti-trade sentiment as a way to explain their frustrations." These comments helped turn Clinton's campaign into a traditional appeal to lunch-pail Democrats in Pennsylvania and elsewhere. Rising economic concerns also worked to her advantage. Iraq and the economy were the two big issues throughout the campaign, but their relative importance changed. Initially, concern about Iraq drew Democrats into the process and attracted people to the Obama campaign. When Iraq began to recede as an issue, Obama lost some traction. In the wake of mortgage crises, rising gas prices, and a weak stock market, Clinton's traditional Democratic message began to resonate.

Clinton won the Pennsylvania primary by nine points, providing yet another lifeline for her campaign. She polled especially well among whites, Catholics, senior citizens, and longtime Democrats, all of whom were necessary for success in the general election. The victory helped her begin raising serious money again, but because of proportional representation it only shrank Obama's pledged delegate lead by twelve. Nonetheless, Obama was pressured to explain why he was unable to "close the deal" and wrap up the nomination despite leading in pledged delegates, polls, and fund raising.

After finally breaking with Wright when the reverend made additional controversial comments at the National Press Club, Obama entered May by winning the North Carolina primary and holding Clinton to a narrow victory in Indiana. Clinton continued to make promises aimed at working-class voters, such as a gas tax holiday, a move that Obama labeled a gimmick. It was also revealed that she had loaned her campaign millions of dollars to keep it afloat during fallow fund-raising spells. Obama finally passed her superdelegate total as party insiders, increasingly convinced that he was going to win, began to move decidedly in his direction. Indeed, it seemed that each of Clinton's small victories was offset by equally good news for Obama. For example, Clinton defeated Obama decisively in working-class West Virginia on May 13, but the next day Obama received the endorsement of John Edwards, thus diluting the impact of her win. A week later they split Kentucky (Clinton) and Oregon (Obama) in predictable fashion.

With only a few states left to vote, attention in late May returned to the national party's standoff with Florida and Michigan. The DNC's Rules and Bylaws Committee scheduled a meeting at the end of May to settle the matter. Clinton operatives lobbied to seat all of the two states' delegates based on the votes cast on January 15 and 29. This appeared to be the only way Clinton could win a majority of convention delegates. After a long day of testimony, the committee decided to grant each of the two states' delegates half a vote. The result was a net gain of just 24 delegates for Clinton, leaving Obama ahead by 178 with not much time left for her to catch him.

By almost any measure the contest between Clinton and Obama was nearly a tie. Which metric ought to be used to judge who was ahead changed during the campaign. Table 2-1 presents the results using several of the suggested standards that emerged. Clinton argued for fully including Michigan and Florida, although Obama had not been on the ballot in the former and neither candidate campaigned in either state. Including the popular votes from those states was the only way for Clinton to claim the advantage. Leaving out either state or relying on delegates rather than popular votes, Obama held a slight edge.

The final primary votes were cast on June 3, when Clinton won South Dakota and Obama won Montana. The results gave Obama enough delegates to secure the nomination. He delivered a preliminary acceptance speech in the St. Paul, Minnesota, arena where the Republicans would hold their nominating convention in September. Several days later Clinton endorsed

**Table 2-1**    Metrics for Assessing Who Won the 2008 Democratic Nomination

| Metric | Clinton | Obama | Obama % |
|---|---|---|---|
| Popular vote without Florida and Michigan | 16,846,712 | 17,293,328 | 50.7 |
| Popular vote with Florida | 17,717,698 | 17,869,542 | 50.2 |
| Popular vote with Florida and Michigan (apportioned)* | 18,046,007 | 18,043,404 | 49.996 |
| Popular vote with Florida and Michigan (actual) | 18,046,007 | 17,869,542 | 49.8 |
| Pledged delegates (as of June 3, 2008)** | 1,624 | 1,748 | 51.8 |
| Superdelegates (endorsements as of June 3, 2008)** | 286 | 394 | 57.9 |
| Total delegates and superdelegates | 1,910 | 2,142 | 52.9 |

*Source:* Real Clear Politics' 2008 Democratic Popular Vote, www.realclearpolitics.com/epolls/2008/president/democratic_vote_count.html.

*My apportionment of Michigan uses the exit poll to estimate the percentage of the "uncommitted" vote that would have gone to Obama had he been on the ballot. Approximately 75 percent of non-Clinton voters report that they would have voted for Obama, which translates to 126,775 votes.

**Estimated by CNN.

Obama. After almost two years of campaigning, the Democratic nomination was settled in an uneventful fashion and by the narrowest of margins.

## Lessons from 2008

Reviewing the events that defined the Republican and Democratic nominations in 2008, it becomes apparent how difficult it is for a candidate to game the system successfully in advance. No one can predict what strategies will work for candidates without knowing who the opponents are, and even then it is an uncertain business. And the field is constantly changing as candidates join the race (Fred Thompson in September 2007) and withdraw (Sam Brownback a month later). Voters, party activists, donors, and the media do not evaluate candidates individually; they compare them to the other contenders. A candidate cannot devise a foolproof strategy based on the rules alone, even if those are fixed in place well in advance of the campaign, which they were not in 2008. Rather, candidates develop their strategies in the context of competition against a large and dynamic field that will be winnowed over time. Had McCain not polled so well in New Hampshire in late 2007, Giuliani would not have shifted his focus to Florida. Had Al Gore been in the race, Hillary Clinton would not have been the initial frontrunner. Few anticipated that either party's nomination would continue to be contested after Super Tuesday on February 5. Almost no one predicted at the outset that the distinction between caucuses and primaries would be critical in determining the Democratic nominee. In short, just about every prediction about the 2008 nominations was wrong because nomination processes are inherently volatile and conditional. Candidates need sufficient resources and a sound strategy, but like McCain and Obama, they also need luck.

The 2008 nominations revise our understanding of "momentum." The term was popularized in 1988 when George H. W. Bush claimed the "Big Mo" for his campaign after winning the Iowa caucuses. Political scientists

John Aldrich and Larry Bartels had already treated the subject in thoughtful book-length analyses.[20] Since then the concept has been stretched and manipulated to the point where it lacks clear meaning.[21] Having momentum is surely more than simply rising in the polls. It entails a sudden and dramatic increase in standing that represents a rapid acceleration in political strength.

A long nomination season may or may not benefit a party in the general election, but it can be helpful to voters. Extended competition permits those in states with later events to shape the outcome, and they do so with more information than is available to early-state voters. Voters in New Hampshire were required to base their votes on debates, campaign advertisements, news coverage during the invisible primary, and the results from Iowa. Democratic voters in Montana and South Dakota had all of that background plus information derived from five months of caucuses and primaries. In addition, over time the field of candidates narrows. The field of eight Democrats who appeared in the early 2007 debates fell by March 2008 to two, each of them a well-defined contender whose record and positions had been in full public view for more than a year of campaigning. Moreover, a long campaign means that voters get to observe how candidates respond to changes in the political environment. As public concern shifted from the war in Iraq to mortgage failures and other economic woes, Clinton and Obama had to adjust their messages, just as a president needs to respond to changing developments. These reactions provided voters with a better sense of each candidate's judgment as a potential chief executive. The long Democratic nomination struggle also forced Obama to handle the Wright affair while seeking his party's endorsement, which helped take the controversy off the table in the general election.

Although a long campaign can make for better candidates, it also takes its toll. Clinton, McCain, and Obama missed most Senate roll-call votes because they were campaigning. And as Hillary Clinton stated in October 2007: "Can I tell you how amazing it was for me to realize that after I'd been doing this for nine months, October rolled around? My husband did not announce for president until October of 1991. I could have had a baby in the time that I've been campaigning."

The 2008 election might mark the end of the current public financing system for presidential campaigns. Obama's ability to raise unprecedented sums from small donors using the Internet was both a manifestation of his particular campaign and a continuation of earlier trends. In 2003 Howard Dean's campaign used the Web to introduce electronic networking, organizing, and fund raising. Dean was building on McCain's early attempt to use the Internet for fund raising in 2000 and even Jerry Brown's effort in 1992 to collect small donations on a toll-free telephone line. The "meet ups" of supporters finding each other on the Internet that were the hallmark of the Dean campaign all but disappeared in 2008, but Obama demonstrated the power of the Web to organize, mobilize, and raise funds. Both Clinton and Obama eschewed the public financing system during the nomination season, knowing that they could raise much more money on their own. After winning the Democratic nomination Obama became the first general election candidate to forgo public funds.

Finally, the 2008 nomination contests revealed the tension between states' desire to be influential and the national parties' ability to control the process. The disobedience of Democratic leaders in Florida and Michigan tested the DNC's authority as a party organization. The 2008 election was not the first in which states were stripped of delegates, but it was the first in which such a move affected the outcome. In 1996 Delaware was stripped of its Republican delegates because it held its primary too early, but in a small state in a year without a closely fought nomination battle this passed without notice. But as former DNC chair Donald Fowler put it, in 2008 "the closeness of the contest revealed all the weaknesses of the system."[22] Following old patterns, the Democrats are likely to make the most radical adjustments in their rules in advance of the 2012 nominations, with Republicans adopting milder versions of the same reforms.

## On to the General Election

Despite nearly identical calendars and similar rules, the Democratic and Republican nomination processes shared little in common. Republicans tend to wrap up their nominations earlier than Democrats, a difference that was especially apparent in 2008.[23] McCain became the clear frontrunner with his January 29 victory in Florida, and the party rallied behind him after his victories on Super Tuesday six days later. By mid-February the GOP was healing its wounds, providing McCain with ample time to soothe ruffled feelings within the party, engage in aggressive fund raising, and begin assembling a general election campaign team and strategy.

The Democrats, in contrast, became bogged down in a lengthy battle between two frontrunners, the closest and lengthiest nomination contest since Gary Hart and Walter Mondale battled in 1984.[24] The Clinton and Obama camps became increasingly contemptuous of one another as the primaries and caucuses dragged on. Obama did not emerge as the undisputed nominee until June, leaving just a couple of months for the party to unite and turn its attention to the general election. How to handle Clinton's pledged delegates complicated planning for the national convention. Generally, the party with the more divisive nomination is more likely to lose the general election.[25] Based on the distributions of votes cast in the 2008 primaries and caucuses, one would have expected the Republicans to be at a great advantage in the general election.

But that relationship did not hold in 2008. Fundamental political conditions heavily favored the Democrats no matter who they nominated. Public discontent with the Iraq War, the weak national economy, and President Bush's severe unpopularity put the Republicans at a decided disadvantage. Democrats were far more enthusiastic than Republicans about their chances and their party's presidential contenders. This enthusiasm gap plus the heated battle between Clinton and Obama produced tremendous increases in voter turnout in Democratic primaries and caucuses. This in turn increased the number of registered Democrats and strengthened Obama's organizations in many states. And the many debates and campaign speeches allowed Democrats not only to criticize each other, but also to remind voters of their displeasure with the Republican Party, Bush, and McCain. In some ways, then, the extended Democratic nomination season gave the party a platform for highlighting the GOP's flaws. Moreover, because most of Obama's campaign contributions were small, he was able to go back to his donors in the general election for additional contributions. It was a "long strange trip" for the Democrats, and although it was not one that many in the party envisioned or desired, it had an unexpected payoff for Barack Obama in the general election.

# Notes

I thank Matt Holleque for research assistance and David Canon for guidance in calculating pledged delegate totals in Table 2-1.

1. This quotation comes from the Grateful Dead song "Truckin'," and is the most famous phrase written by the band's lyricist, Robert Hunter. The line became a metaphor for the band's career.
2. In May 2007 a CBS/*New York Times* poll showed 63 percent of likely Democratic primary voters "satisfied" with their candidates, compared to just 38 percent of Republicans who felt the same way. In September 2007 a poll conducted by the Pew Center for the People and the Press showed that nearly two-thirds of Democrats had an "excellent" or "good" impression of their party's candidates, compared to 49 percent of Republicans.
3. Jonathan Martin, "2008 Field Sprouts Rootless Candidates," Politico.com, February 8, 2007, www.politico.com/news/stories/0207/2671.html.
4. Barry C. Burden, "United States Senators as Presidential Contenders," *Political Science Quarterly* 117 (2002): 81–102.
5. Arthur T. Hadley, *The Invisible Primary* (Englewood Cliffs, N.J.: Prentice-Hall, 1976).
6. Ironically, McGovern would win his party's nomination in 1972 in part because of these rules. See Nelson W. Polsby, *The Consequences of Party Reform* (New York: Oxford University Press, 1983). See also Byron Shafer, *Quiet Revolution: The Struggle for the Democratic Party and the Shaping of Post-Reform Politics* (New York: Russell Sage Foundation, 1983).
7. Barry C. Burden, "The Nominations: Technology, Money, and Transferable Momentum," in *The Elections of 2004,* ed. Michael Nelson (Washington, D.C.: CQ Press, 2005).
8. Gary R. Orren, "The Nomination Process: Vicissitudes of Candidate Selection," in *The Elections of 1984,* ed. Michael Nelson (Washington, D.C.: Congressional Quarterly Press, 1985).
9. In addition to official superdelegates, endorsements from prominent actors within each party surely play a role in selection of nominees. See Marty Cohen et al., *The Party Decides: Presidential Nominations before and after Reform* (Chicago: University of Chicago Press, 2008).
10. William G. Mayer and Andrew E. Busch, *Front-Loading in the Presidential Nomination Process* (Washington, D.C.: Brookings Institution, 2004).
11. Note that other ideas, such as a one-day national primary or rotation of several regional primaries, were rejected.

12. To distinguish it from lesser Super Tuesdays in earlier election years, reporters variously referred to February 5 as "Super Duper Tuesday," "Tsunami Tuesday," and other monikers. See Joanne Kaufman, "A Sweet Sundae? No, It's Primaries," *New York Times,* January 28, 2008.
13. Adam Nagourney, "For Republicans, Falling in Love Is Hard to Do," *New York Times,* December 16, 2007.
14. In markets such as the IEM investors may buy shares of candidate futures. As a result, their share prices reflect the collective expectations about each candidate's chances of winning the nomination. For example, a share price of 40 cents indicates a candidate with a 40 percent chance.
15. Michael Leahy and Michael D. Shear, "For Giuliani, the Trip South Started Early," *Washington Post,* January 30, 2008, A01.
16. Michael Cooper and Marjorie Connelly, "Giuliani Has Decided to Zag while the Other Candidates Zig," *New York Times,* December 20, 2007.
17. Thomas Beaumont and Lisa Rossi, "Home-Schoolers Help Propel Huckabee," *Des Moines Register,* December 11, 2007.
18. Karen Tumulty, "The Five Mistakes Clinton Made," *Time,* May 8, 2008.
19. Brian C. Mooney, "Two-Way Race Puts Rules to the Test," *Boston Globe,* February 6, 2008.
20. See John H. Aldrich, *Before the Convention: Strategies and Choices in Presidential Nomination Contests* (Chicago: University of Chicago Press, 1980); and Larry M. Bartels, *Presidential Primaries and the Dynamics of Public Choice* (Princeton, N.J.: Princeton University Press, 1988).
21. Drake Bennett, "The Momentum Equation," *Boston Globe,* March 25, 2007.
22. Adam Nagourney, "A Primary Calendar Democrats Will Never Forget," *New York Times,* June 2, 2008.
23. Marty Cohen et al., *The Party Decides: Presidential Nominations before and after Reform.* See also Wayne P. Steger, John Hickman, and Ken Yohn, "Candidate Competition and Attrition in Presidential Primaries, 1912 to 2000," *American Politics Research* 30 (2002): 528–554.
24. Barbara Norrander, "The End Game in Post-Reform Presidential Nominations," *Journal of Politics* 62 (2000): 999–1013; and Orren, "The Nomination Process: Vicissitudes of Candidate Selection."
25. Martin P. Wattenberg, *The Rise of Candidate-Centered Politics* (Cambridge, Mass.: Harvard University Press, 1991).

# 3

## The Presidential Election:
## Change Comes to America

### Gerald M. Pomper

*It is great*
*To do that thing that ends all other deeds;*
*Which shackles accidents and bolts up change*
— William Shakespeare, *Antony and Cleopatra*, V:2:4

The election of President Barack Obama was inevitable. Or maybe not.
In the contest between the Democrat Obama, senator from Illinois, and
the Republican John McCain, senator from Arizona, a Democratic victory
had been predicted as historically certain.[1] After two Republican terms in
the White House, the calendar called for a change of parties. Job ratings of
the incumbent Republican president, George W. Bush, had plunged to record
lows. Economic conditions were grim, the worst in twenty-five years:
unemployment reached ten million, stocks lost 40 percent of their value, and
the government scrambled to rescue a financial system nearing worldwide
collapse. Given this, most political scientists foretold Obama's certain success.[2]

But many others regarded that prediction as farfetched. It seemed
improbable that the United States would ever elect a black man as president,
given its sad historical inheritance of slavery and racial discrimination. Social
scientists "knew" that Americans still held racist views that would affect their
votes,[3] and commentators "knew" that respondents to opinion polls were
lying when they said they would mark their ballots for Obama. The evil
heritage of racism, analysts wrote, meant that Democrats could win neither
southern states[4] nor Latino votes in the West.[5] And, however bad economic
conditions might be, gullible voters would eventually fall prey to manipulators
of their social conservatism on issues such as abortion and gay marriage.[6]

These sentiments were reinforced by the apparent recent emergence of
a Republican majority in the nation, defined by issues of race, religion, and
national security.[7] This new dominant coalition would overwhelm the
Democratic candidate. Obama was black, surely a fatal political flaw in a
white and allegedly racist populace. He bore a Muslim name, but sought
votes from a nation that had been attacked by Islamic terrorists. He had
never served in the military and had limited experience in foreign affairs, in
contrast to his opponent, a Vietnam War hero who had pointed the way to

a possible, if limited, "success" in the U.S. war in Iraq. If there truly were a new Republican majority in the country, McCain ought to win.

The presidential election of 2008 was an exhilarating contest, a display of innovative campaign techniques, a contest of two unusually qualified and admired candidates. After half a century (or more, by some reckonings),[8] neither an incumbent president nor an incumbent vice president would be on the ballot, providing open contests for both parties' nominations. It would be the nation's first Internet election, featuring new networking Web sites such as YouTube, Facebook, and Twitter. Its historic results also tested competing theories of voter behavior.

So what happened?

## The Election Results

In the real political world, Obama won a decisive victory over McCain. The Democrat's margin in the popular ballot count was nearly ten million (53.7 percent of the two-party vote), and he secured more than two-thirds of the electoral votes (365 to 173). He became only the second Democrat since Franklin Delano Roosevelt (along with Lyndon Johnson) to win a decisive majority of the national popular vote. And his victory margin outshone those of all but three of his party's nominees throughout American history, including Woodrow Wilson, Harry Truman, John Kennedy, and Bill Clinton. In the post–New Deal period, Obama also outperformed every first-term Republican winner except Dwight Eisenhower.

The election results evinced a decided shift in voter sentiment from the two previous contests. In 2000, Democrat Al Gore won a thin plurality of the popular vote, but Republican George W. Bush gained a bare margin of four votes in the Electoral College, after a favorable ruling by the U.S. Supreme Court. In 2004, Bush achieved reelection by gaining a slight lead in the national popular vote and by carrying the critical state of Ohio.

Obama's mandate in 2008, in contrast to these close matches, was decisive.[9] He increased the Democratic vote by ten million, a 17 percent increase over John Kerry's losing tally in 2004. McCain not only lost the election; he also lost votes, garnering two million fewer than Bush's previous tally (a 3 percent decline). These results can be explained by three factors: turnout, geography, and demography.

### Turnout

The presidential election created great excitement, with nine-tenths of the electorate expressing marked interest. These feelings led more than 131 million Americans to cast ballots, a noticeable rise of some 9 million in the turnout numbers. Proportionate participation also increased from 2004, with 61.6 percent of eligible citizens casting votes in 2008, an increase of 1.5 percent from 2004.

Turnout varied considerably among the states. It increased by double digits in seven southern states, as well as Arizona, Colorado, Hawaii, Indiana, and Nevada, largely because of registration drives by the Obama campaign focused on African Americans and Latinos. In all of these states, the Democratic proportion of the vote also rose considerably, and seven of the twelve eventually fell into Obama's column. Turnout also dropped slightly in six noncompetitive states, where either Obama or McCain conceded the state in advance, reducing the stimulus to voter participation.

Expectations of high turnout had come from the large number of new registrants and the heavy participation in early and absentee voting before election day itself. More than thirty million ballots were cast before November 4, comprising at least a quarter of the total vote and representing an increase of at least five million early votes since 2004. In some states, the early voters comprised as much as three-fourths of the total vote in the previous election. By encouraging this heavy advance turnout, the Obama forces won significant victories in North Carolina, Colorado, and Nevada, all of which had voted for Bush in 2004.[10]

It is possible that some Republicans deliberately avoided the presidential balloting. Throughout the campaign, McCain supporters had shown less enthusiasm for their candidate, possibly keeping them at home. A leading student of turnout attributes their abstention largely to McCain's selection of Alaska governor Sarah Palin as the party's vice-presidential nominee. According to Curtis Gans, "By election time many culturally conservative Republicans still did not see him as one of their own and stayed home, while moderate Republicans saw the nomination of Palin as reckless and worried about McCain's steadiness."[11] Republican voters may also have been discouraged by the widespread pre-election predictions that Obama was certain to win.

Whatever the motivation, more self-identified Democrats participated in the balloting, outnumbering Republicans by 39 percent to 32 percent in exit polls. These partisan turnout rates marked considerable change from 2004, when the parties' ranks were essentially equal (36 percent Democrats, 37 percent Republicans). However, the turn toward the Democrats began as early as 2007, when a prominent academic study found that considerable erosion of Republican loyalties among both committed partisans and independents had given the Democrats an overall advantage in party identification of 50 percent to 36 percent.[12] The 2008 difference between Republican and Democratic turnout probably reflected longer-term changes in attitudes, rather than reactions to specific campaign events.

## Geography

In winning the electoral vote, Barack Obama forged new paths across the states of the Union. In the two most recent contests, Democrats had restricted their efforts to electoral fortresses in the Northeast, Florida, parts

**Figure 3-1**    The Electoral Map of 2008

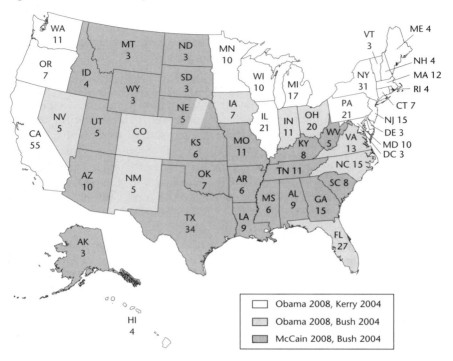

of the Midwest, and the Pacific Coast. In this minimalist strategy, winning the White House required victories in almost all of these states, neglecting wide swathes of the nation. Losing just one large targeted state—Florida in 2000 and Ohio in 2004—also meant losing in the national electoral count.

Obama changed the Democratic strategy, extending the contest to more states and to more areas, often Republican bailiwicks, within these states. A huge campaign treasury enabled him to implement what became a winning strategy on election day. The Illinois senator won a majority of the states, twenty-eight, and the District of Columbia. Holding all of the twenty constituencies won by John Kerry in 2004, Obama added nine states carried by Bush to his tally, as well as a single electoral vote from Nebraska.[13] Sweeping the Midwest (including three states won by Bush in 2004), carrying three of the former Confederate states in the South, and mobilizing new voters to win three of the eight Rocky Mountain domains, Obama won a national victory. The changing geographical results are clearly seen in Figures 3-1 and 3-2.

Even as Obama extended the Democrats' reach, the parties remained distinctive in their geographical bases of support. The Democrats did particularly well in the Northeast, the upper Midwest, and the Pacific Coast; the Republicans did best in the South Plains, and the smaller Mountain states. The geographical lines of party division remained substantially as they had

**Figure 3-2**    The Electoral Map of 2004

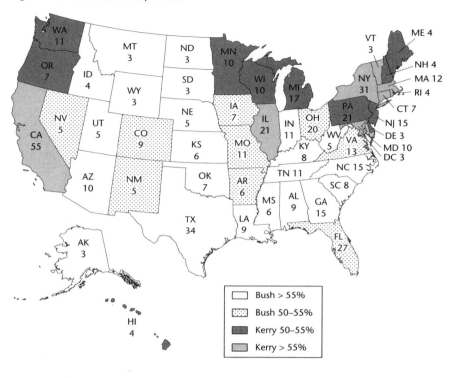

been in 2004,[14] but results varied more widely among the states, indicating increased polarization in the country.[15] Details of the presidential vote are shown in Table 3-1.

Obama shifted the lines of party cleavage to the Democrats' advantage.[16] Although he gained votes, compared to Kerry in 2004, he did not build his victory by simply focusing on the party's customary areas of strength. The party did gain popular vote share in its reliable states of the Northeast, upper Midwest, and Pacific Coast. But the largest gains, as seen in Table 3-1, came in areas in which Democrats previously had underperformed. They did especially well at the polls in such unfamiliar campaign sites as the Atlantic South, the Mountain states, and even North Dakota and Indiana. Obama did not win all of these states, but he set new benchmarks for future Democratic contenders.

The movement of the vote from Republican to Democrat could be seen in finer detail in maps of the results by counties rather than states.[17] While the Democratic trend was apparent in most of the nation, 22 percent of counties showed more support for McCain than they had for Bush in 2004. The pattern was consistent with the analysis of voter demography discussed below. The Democrats gained most in counties that had denser and growing populations and those with larger proportions of African American, Hispanic, Catholic, and college-educated residents. Republicans did better in counties

**Table 3-1** The Presidential Vote of 2008

| State | Popular vote (1,000s) Obama | Popular vote (1,000s) McCain | Two-party vote %, 2008 Obama | Two-party vote %, 2008 McCain | Two-party vote %, 2004 Kerry | Two-party vote %, 2004 Bush | Turnout % gain 2004–2008 | Democrat vote % gain 2004–2008 |
|---|---|---|---|---|---|---|---|---|
| Alabama | 813 | 1,267 | 39.1 | 60.9 | 37.1 | 62.9 | 11.2 | 2.0 |
| Alaska | 124 | 194 | 39.0 | 61.0 | 36.8 | 63.2 | 5.3 | 2.2 |
| Arizona | 1,035 | 1,230 | 45.7 | 54.3 | 44.7 | 55.3 | 13.4 | 1.0 |
| Arkansas | 422 | 638 | 39.8 | 60.2 | 45.1 | 54.9 | 1.6 | -5.3 |
| California | 8,274 | 5,012 | 62.3 | 37.7 | 55.0 | 45.0 | 8.4 | 7.3 |
| Colorado | 1,289 | 1,074 | 54.5 | 45.5 | 47.6 | 52.4 | 12.4 | 6.9 |
| Connecticut | 998 | 629 | 61.3 | 38.7 | 55.3 | 44.7 | 4.9 | 6.0 |
| Delaware | 255 | 152 | 62.7 | 37.3 | 53.8 | 46.2 | 9.4 | 8.9 |
| Dist. Columbia | 246 | 17 | 93.5 | 6.5 | 90.5 | 9.5 | 17.4 | 3.0 |
| Florida | 4,282 | 4,046 | 51.4 | 48.6 | 47.5 | 52.5 | 10.3 | 3.9 |
| Georgia | 1,844 | 2,049 | 47.4 | 52.6 | 41.6 | 58.4 | 18.7 | 5.8 |
| Hawaii | 326 | 121 | 72.9 | 27.1 | 54.4 | 45.6 | 4.9 | 18.5 |
| Idaho | 236 | 403 | 36.9 | 63.1 | 30.7 | 69.3 | 8.3 | 6.2 |
| Illinois | 3,420 | 2,032 | 62.7 | 37.3 | 55.2 | 44.8 | 4.1 | 7.5 |
| Indiana | 1,374 | 1,346 | 50.5 | 49.5 | 39.6 | 60.4 | 11.1 | 10.9 |
| Iowa | 829 | 682 | 54.9 | 45.1 | 49.7 | 50.3 | 1.1 | 5.2 |
| Kansas | 515 | 700 | 42.4 | 57.6 | 37.1 | 62.9 | 3.8 | 5.3 |
| Kentucky | 752 | 1,048 | 41.8 | 58.2 | 40.0 | 60.0 | 1.0 | 1.8 |
| Louisiana | 783 | 1,148 | 40.5 | 59.5 | 42.7 | 57.3 | 0.5 | -2.2 |
| Maine | 422 | 295 | 58.9 | 41.1 | 54.6 | 45.4 | -1.4 | 4.3 |
| Maryland | 1,629 | 960 | 62.9 | 37.1 | 56.6 | 43.4 | 9.7 | 6.3 |
| Massachusetts | 1,904 | 1,109 | 63.2 | 36.8 | 62.7 | 37.3 | 4.8 | 0.5 |
| Michigan | 2,873 | 2,049 | 58.4 | 41.6 | 51.7 | 48.3 | 2.7 | 6.7 |
| Minnesota | 1,573 | 1,275 | 55.2 | 44.8 | 51.8 | 48.2 | 2.0 | 3.4 |
| Mississippi | 555 | 725 | 43.4 | 56.6 | 40.5 | 59.5 | 13.2 | 2.9 |
| Missouri | 1,442 | 1,446 | 49.9 | 50.1 | 46.4 | 53.6 | 6.4 | 3.5 |
| Montana | 232 | 243 | 48.8 | 51.2 | 39.5 | 60.5 | 8.0 | 9.3 |
| Nebraska | 333 | 453 | 42.4 | 57.6 | 33.2 | 66.8 | 2.5 | 9.2 |

*(Continued)*

**Table 3-1** The Presidential Vote of 2008 (Continued)

| State | Popular vote (1,000s) | | Two-party vote %, 2008 | | Two-party vote %, 2004 | | Turnout | Democrat vote |
| | Obama | McCain | Obama | McCain | Kerry | Bush | % gain 2004–2008 | % gain 2004–2008 |
| --- | --- | --- | --- | --- | --- | --- | --- | --- |
| Nevada | 534 | 413 | 56.4 | 43.6 | 48.7 | 51.3 | 16.1 | 7.7 |
| New Hampshire | 385 | 317 | 54.8 | 45.2 | 50.7 | 49.3 | 4.5 | 4.1 |
| New Jersey | 2,215 | 1,613 | 57.9 | 42.1 | 53.4 | 46.6 | 6.9 | 4.5 |
| New Mexico | 472 | 347 | 57.6 | 42.4 | 49.6 | 50.4 | 9.5 | 8.0 |
| New York | 4,770 | 2,742 | 63.5 | 36.5 | 59.3 | 40.7 | 3.2 | 4.2 |
| North Carolina | 2,143 | 2,128 | 50.2 | 49.8 | 43.8 | 56.2 | 22.5 | 6.4 |
| North Dakota | 141 | 169 | 45.5 | 54.5 | 36.1 | 63.9 | 0.6 | 9.4 |
| Ohio | 2,933 | 2,674 | 52.3 | 47.7 | 48.9 | 51.1 | 0.1 | 3.4 |
| Oklahoma | 502 | 960 | 34.3 | 65.7 | 34.4 | 65.6 | -0.1 | -0.1 |
| Oregon | 1,037 | 738 | 58.4 | 41.6 | 52.1 | 47.9 | -1.9 | 6.3 |
| Pennsylvania | 3,276 | 2,656 | 55.2 | 44.8 | 51.3 | 48.7 | 3.5 | 3.9 |
| Rhode Island | 297 | 165 | 64.3 | 35.7 | 60.6 | 39.4 | 7.7 | 3.7 |
| South Carolina | 862 | 1,035 | 45.4 | 54.6 | 41.4 | 58.6 | 18.6 | 4.0 |
| South Dakota | 171 | 203 | 45.7 | 54.3 | 39.1 | 60.9 | -2.1 | 6.6 |
| Tennessee | 1,087 | 1,479 | 42.4 | 57.6 | 42.8 | 57.2 | 6.0 | -0.4 |
| Texas | 3,529 | 4,479 | 44.1 | 55.9 | 38.5 | 61.5 | 8.8 | 5.6 |
| Utah | 328 | 596 | 35.5 | 64.5 | 26.7 | 73.3 | 2.1 | 8.8 |
| Vermont | 219 | 99 | 68.9 | 31.1 | 60.3 | 39.7 | 4.3 | 8.6 |
| Virginia | 1,960 | 1,725 | 53.2 | 46.8 | 45.9 | 54.1 | 16.2 | 7.3 |
| Washington | 1,751 | 1,229 | 58.8 | 41.2 | 53.6 | 46.4 | 5.9 | 5.2 |
| West Virginia | 304 | 397 | 43.4 | 56.6 | 43.5 | 56.5 | -6.7 | -0.1 |
| Wisconsin | 1,677 | 1,262 | 57.1 | 42.9 | 50.2 | 49.8 | -1.0 | 6.9 |
| Wyoming | 83 | 165 | 33.5 | 66.5 | 29.7 | 70.3 | 3.8 | 3.8 |
| Totals | 69,457 | 59,935 | 53.7 | 46.3 | 48.8 | 51.2 | 6.9 | 4.9 |

*Sources:* Dave Leip's Atlas of U.S. Presidential Elections, uselectionatlas.org/RESULTS; elections.gmu.edu.

*Notes:* The total national vote was 131.4 million, 61.6 percent of those eligible. The total minor party vote was 1.98 million, 1.5 percent of the total vote, for 21 candidates, including Independent Ralph Nader, 0.56 percent, and Libertarian Bob Barr, 0.40 percent.

**Figure 3-3**    Increases in Democratic Vote, 2004–2008

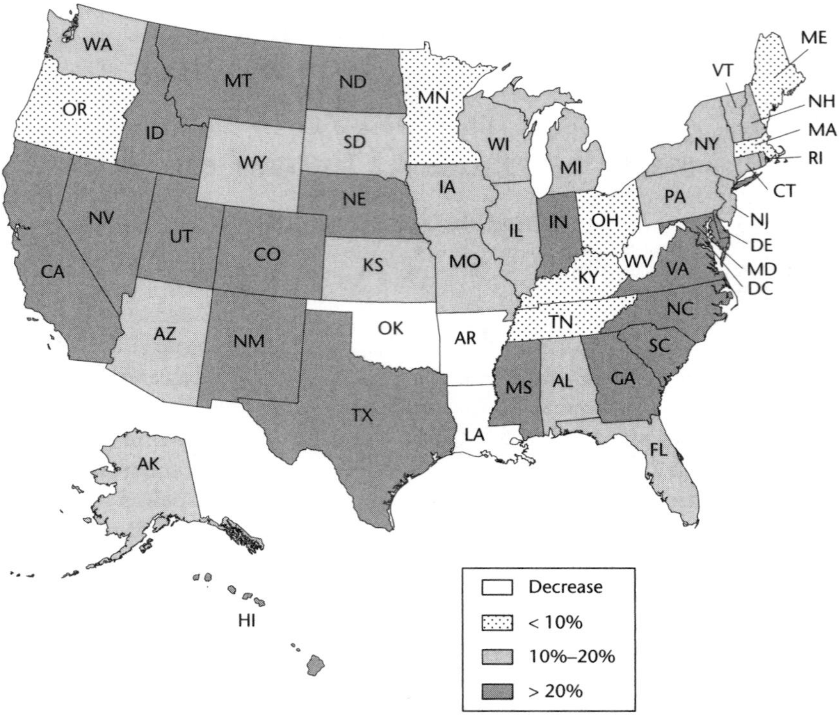

whose residents were poorer, less educated, Southern Baptist, and white. The combined effect of these characteristics was that Republican gains were concentrated in the poorer and less developed areas of the South and border states and along the southern Appalachians, as shown in Figure 3-3.

## Demography

Change was also evident in the behavior of individual voters, as seen in the patterns detailed in Table 3-2. Democrats and Republicans held to their partisan loyalties, with nine of ten Democrats supporting Obama and nine of ten Republicans supporting McCain. Hillary Clinton's backers followed her lead and returned to their party, joined by a majority of independents. The voters also divided as expected along ideological lines, particularly liberals who cohesively supported the Democratic candidate. McCain lost both the swing moderate voters and a sizable fraction of independent conservatives.

The demographic patterns in the vote were similar to those of the past. Obama did better among women (with a gender gap of 5 percent), the unmarried, the young, Catholics, Jews (contrary to pre-election murmurs),[18] urban residents, gays, persons with lower incomes, less religiously committed

**Table 3-2**  Demography of the Vote in 2008

| % of vote | | % Obama | % McCain | % shift 2004–2008* |
|---|---|---|---|---|
| | *Partisanship and ideology* | | | |
| 15 | Democratic liberals | 96 | 3 | 1 |
| 19 | Democratic moderates | 87 | 13 | 0 |
| 5 | Democratic conservatives | 77 | 20 | 1 |
| (14 | Clinton Democrats | 83 | 16 | - - ) |
| 5 | Independent liberals | 81 | 15 | 2 |
| 16 | Independent moderates | 56 | 41 | 3 |
| 8 | Independent conservatives | 26 | 70 | 7 |
| 1 | Republican liberals | 29 | 67 | 7 |
| 10 | Republican moderates | 17 | 82 | 6 |
| 21 | Republican conservatives | 4 | 95 | 1 |
| 22 | Liberal | 89 | 10 | 4 |
| 44 | Moderate | 60 | 39 | 6 |
| 34 | Conservative | 20 | 78 | 5 |
| 11 | First-time voters | 69 | 30 | 16 |
| 89 | Previous voters | 51 | 48 | 3 |
| | *Sex and race* | | | |
| 36 | White men | 41 | 57 | 4 |
| 39 | White women | 46 | 53 | 2 |
| 5 | Black men | 95 | 5 | 9 |
| 7 | Black women | 96 | 3 | 6 |
| 4 | Latino men | 64 | 33 | 8 |
| 5 | Latino women | 68 | 30 | 12 |
| 5 | Other men and women | 64 | 32 | 6 |
| | *Age* | | | |
| 18 | 18–29 | 66 | 32 | 12 |
| 29 | 30–44 | 52 | 46 | 6 |
| 30 | 45–59 | 49 | 49 | 2 |
| 23 | 60 and older | 47 | 51 | –2 |
| | *Yearly income* | | | |
| 38 | Less than $50,000 | 60 | 38 | 4 |
| 36 | $50,000–$100,000 | 49 | 49 | 5 |
| 26 | More than $100,000 | 49 | 49 | 6 |
| | *Education* | | | |
| 24 | No college | 54 | 44 | 7 |
| 31 | Some college | 51 | 47 | 5 |
| 28 | College graduate | 50 | 48 | 4 |
| 17 | Postgraduate | 58 | 40 | 3 |
| | *Religion* | | | |
| 54 | Protestant | 45 | 54 | 5 |
| 27 | Catholic | 54 | 45 | 7 |
| 2 | Jewish | 78 | 21 | 4 |
| 18 | Other/None | 74 | 23 | 8 |
| | *Church attendance* | | | |
| 40 | Weekly | 43 | 55 | 4 |
| 42 | Occasionally | 57 | 42 | 4 |
| 16 | Never | 67 | 30 | 5 |

*(Continued)*

**Table 3-2**    Demography of the Vote in 2008 (Continued)

| % of vote | | % Obama | % McCain | % shift 2004–2008* |
|---|---|---|---|---|
| | *Family status* | | | |
| 32 | Married women | 47 | 50 | 3 |
| 21 | Unmarried women | 71 | 29 | 9 |
| 33 | Married men | 47 | 53 | 8 |
| 14 | Unmarried men | 59 | 37 | 6 |
| | *Relationships* | | | |
| 40 | Parents of children < 18 | 52 | 41 | 7 |
| 21 | Union household | 59 | 39 | 0 |
| 42 | Gun owner | 37 | 62 | 1 |
| 15 | Veteran | 44 | 54 | 3 |
| 4 | Gay, lesbian, bisexual | 70 | 27 | −7 |
| | *Size of place and region* | | | |
| 11 | Large cities | 70 | 28 | 8 |
| 19 | Smaller cities (50,000–500,000) | 59 | 39 | 9 |
| 49 | Suburban | 50 | 48 | 2 |
| 7 | Small towns | 45 | 53 | −4 |
| 14 | Rural | 45 | 53 | 5 |
| 21 | Northeast | 59 | 40 | 3 |
| 24 | Midwest | 54 | 44 | 6 |
| 32 | South | 45 | 54 | 3 |
| 23 | West | 57 | 40 | 7 |
| | *Whites only* | | | |
| 74 | All | 43 | 57 | 2 |
| 11 | Age 18–29 | 54 | 44 | 10 |
| 13 | Age 65 and older | 40 | 58 | −4 |
| 25 | Income less than $50,000 | 47 | 51 | 0 |
| 49 | Income more than $50,000 | 43 | 56 | 5 |
| 39 | No college degree | 40 | 58 | 3 |
| 14 | Postgraduate education | 55 | 45 | 4 |
| 42 | Protestant | 34 | 65 | 2 |
| 26 | Evangelical | 24 | 74 | 3 |
| 19 | Catholic | 47 | 52 | 4 |
| 23 | Democrats | 85 | 14 | −2 |
| 23 | Independents | 47 | 49 | 1 |
| 29 | Republicans | 8 | 91 | 3 |

*Source:* National Exit Poll, as reported on cnn.com and election.cbsnews.com/election2008.

*Difference of percentage of two-party vote for Obama compared to Kerry.

voters, and both the least and the most educated. More important to the election outcome were shifts within these groups. Obama won new support for the Democratic ticket, compared to Kerry in 2004, in virtually every demographic and affinity group, as defined by sex, race, age, religion, education, income, family status, residence, and region.

Some shifts were larger than others. A group's effect on the overall vote depends on two measures: the size of the group and the division of its vote between the competing candidates. Some groups are so large—such as whites or women—that even a small advantage for one candidate may be decisive. Other groups have an impact because they give their support primarily to one candidate. One such group in 2008 was young voters. Although persons aged eighteen to twenty-nine hardly increased their share of the total vote (18 percent in 2008, up from 17 percent in 2004), they did change their preferences markedly. A small 54 percent to 46 percent margin for Kerry over Bush became an overwhelming 66 percent to 32 percent preference for Obama over McCain. That shift added two to three million votes to the Democrats.[19]

Minority voters had the greatest effect on the election result. African Americans and Latinos affected the outcome both by increased turnout, as they voted in larger numbers than in 2004, and by more marked support of the Democratic candidate. The strong support of Latinos for Obama holds a special portent for the future. Latinos are already the largest minority group in the nation, and their share of the electorate will grow considerably as the children of recent immigrants (citizens even if their parents are not) reach maturity. Republican hopes to build a national majority coalition depended on their support, but these hopes crumbled in 2008. Asian Americans, although small as a percentage of the overall population, also voted for Obama. The total effect of ethnic minorities, as detailed in Table 3-3, was to add more than seven million votes to Obama's tally, the lion's share (nearly three-fourths) of the Democrats' overall gain in votes.[20]

Although minority voters were critical to the Obama victory, it remains true that he won only because he also gained substantial support from whites, the largest ethnic group in the electorate. Rather than showing racial repugnance toward a black candidate, whites increased their support of the Democrats. The white shift was limited, and a majority of whites continued to vote Republican, as they had for forty years. But Obama actually did better among white voters than most recent Democratic candidates, all of whom were themselves white.

As seen in the bottom portion of Table 3-2, strong white opposition to Obama was limited to a few demographic groups; others increased their Democratic vote, and party loyalties largely overrode racial defections. There was considerable opposition to Obama in the white working class, as expected, but this opposition cannot be attributed simply to racism, since these "Reagan Democrats" have also been voting for years against the party's white candidates. In fact, Obama did considerably better among the white working class than Kerry did in 2004, adding five points to gain a 41 percent share of their votes.[21]

Regional residence had a considerable effect on white voters. In eight of the eleven southern states (as well as in five other states), Obama fell below 35 percent among whites—and plummeted below 20 percent in the Deep South. In these areas, the vote against Obama—who scored lower than Kerry—likely reflected racial prejudices. But in other states, most whites apparently overcame whatever racist feelings they may have held. In eighteen states, a majority of whites actually voted for Obama.[22]

Although race certainly had an effect on the outcome, that effect was direct and open. During the campaign, many observers had anguished that the influence of race would be both hidden and malevolent. Commentators showed particular concern over a "Bradley effect," the possible tendency of poll respondents

Table 3-3    Ethnic Shifts and Impact in the 2008 Presidential Vote

|  | 2008 | 2004 |
|---|---|---|
| Total two-party vote | 131,371 | 121,058 |
| Total Democratic vote | 69,457 | 59,029 |
| White % of vote | 0.74 | 0.77 |
| White % for Democrat | 0.43 | 0.41 |
| White vote for Democrat | 41,802 | 38,218 |
| White increase for Obama | 3,584 | |
| Black % of vote | 0.13 | 0.11 |
| Black % for Democrat | 0.95 | 0.88 |
| Black vote for Democrat | 16,224 | 11,718 |
| Black increase for Obama | 4,506 | |
| Latino % of vote | 0.09 | 0.08 |
| Latino % for Democrat | 0.67 | 0.56 |
| Latino vote for Democrat | 7,922 | 5,423 |
| Latino increase for Obama | 2,498 | |
| Asian/other % of vote | 0.04 | 0.04 |
| Asian/other % for Democrat | 0.63 | 0.57 |
| Asian/other vote for Democrat | 3,311 | 2,760 |
| Asian/other increase for Obama | 550 | |
| Total minority % of vote | 0.26 | 0.23 |
| Total minority % for Democrat | 0.80 | 0.71 |
| Total minority vote for Democrat | 27,457 | 19,902 |
| Total minority increase for Obama | 7,555 | |
| Minority % of Democratic vote | 39.5% | 33.7% |
| Minority % of Democratic increase | 72.4% | |

Source: Author's calculations, based on presidential vote (Table 3-1) and National Election Poll.
Note: Votes are in 1,000s.

to falsely declare their support for a black candidate to meet social expectations of tolerance, while intending to vote against the minority candidate in the privacy of the polling booth.[23] In reality, there had never been such an effect (even in the original reported instance), and it could not be located in opinion surveys, despite ingenious investigations by pollsters. Logically, the entire fear was senseless, because there was no reason for voters to lie to anonymous pollsters about their vote intention when they could easily disguise racist motivations. Still, the discussion provided grist for commentators' mills and added one more item to the list of urban legends about public opinion.

## The Campaign

The 2008 election year started with bad news for the Republicans and ended worse, with the victory of Barack Obama. The intervening months saw a series of astonishing events and turns in political fortunes.

As the year opened, Democrats had many reasons to be optimistic. In the congressional elections of 2006, they had wrested back control of both houses, giving them a platform to criticize and investigate the Republican administration. Public evaluations of the incumbent president, a consistent predictor of the November vote, were sharply negative: in January 2008 only 32 percent approved of George W. Bush's job performance (half of them only tepidly), whereas 66 percent disapproved (three-fourths fervently). Voters were also pessimistic about the country's course: three-fourths saw the nation on "the wrong track," whereas only a fifth saw it going in "the right direction." The economy was showing signs of decline, most obviously in the collapse of housing values and mortgage credit, which ultimately would threaten foreclosures on four million homes. These troubles made the economy the most important issue in the election, emphasizing a traditional source of Democratic strength.

The most important action of the Bush administration, the invasion of Iraq, had become the longest war in U.S. history since its independence, and there appeared to be no end in sight. On that issue, too, the public rejected the Bush administration, with two-thirds believing that the war was "not worth fighting." The conflict had brought both Obama and McCain prominence in their parties—Obama for his early opposition, McCain for his fervent support, even in times of military stalemate. Ironically, the issue faded even as the two won their parties' nominations, although it would still leave a mark on the election: long before the nominations were settled, voters had a more favorable impression of Obama than of McCain.

The presidential nominations (analyzed fully in chapter 2) did little to change the favorable outlook for Democrats. Although their contest concluded quickly, Republicans fought it in ways that limited their potential appeal to moderate voters in the general election. In televised debates, most of the party's aspirants competed in doubting the theory of evolution and in testifying to the literal truth of the Bible to prove their credentials to their most conservative activists. Pursuing similar tactics, McCain proudly asserted that 90 percent of his Senate votes had supported President Bush's initiatives—a boast he would later regret.

The Democratic nominating contest went on far longer, eventually reaching every state and territory by early June. By then Obama had won a narrow victory in popular votes[24] and a clear majority of delegates. Although often heated and sometimes personal, the close contest did no apparent harm to the party: Obama continued to lead McCain in national surveys (as illustrated in Figure 3-4). In the end, the nominating race may have actually benefited the Democrats by sharpening Obama's debating skills and by enlisting large numbers of voters into the party ranks. Ultimately, nearly forty million voters participated in the Democratic primaries, an astonishingly high proportion of the party's eventual vote in November.

The two nominees, McCain and Obama, could hardly have been more different. They were of two different generations, twenty-five years apart in age. Nor would any voter miss the difference between a white and a biracial candidate. Their lives also had been sharply distinct—the Republican a scion of a prominent military family and himself a distinguished veteran of the Vietnam War versus the Democrat abandoned by his Kenyan father and raised by an unconventional white mother and grandparents before achieving notable academic and professional success. McCain had been a

**Figure 3-4**    The 2008 Presidential Race in the Polls

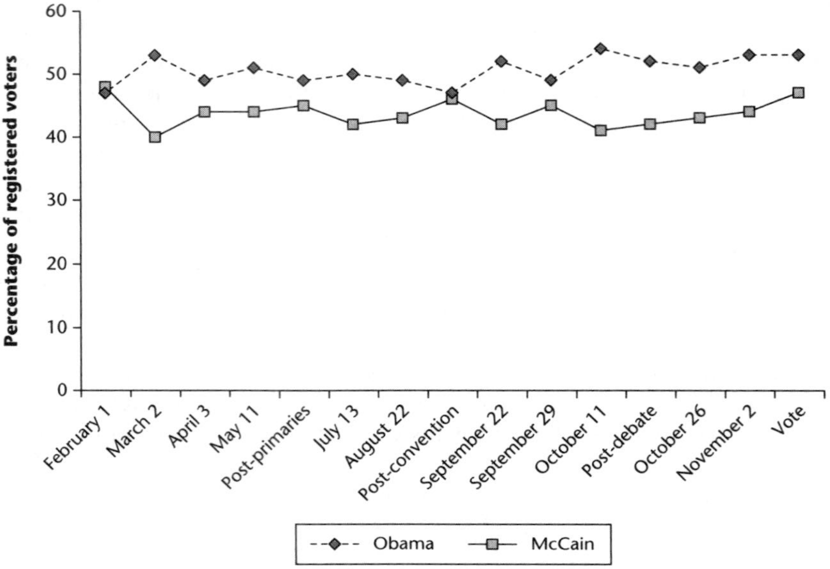

Source: Washington Post/ABC News

national legislator for more than twenty-five years, Obama for less than four. They disagreed on most issues, ranging from economic policy to the Iraq War, portending a vigorous combat in the presidential race.

The two candidates also embodied two mythic symbols, delineated by sociologist Todd Gitlin. McCain represented "the known quantity, the maverick turned lawman, fiery when called on to fight, an icon of the old known American story of standing tall, holding firm, protecting God's country against the stealthy foe." Obama represented a different archetype, "the new kid on the block, the immigrant's child, the recruit, fervent but still preternaturally calm, embodying some complicated future that we haven't yet mapped, let alone experienced."[25]

The candidates shifted into high gear after the parties' late-summer national conventions. In 2008, in contrast to most other years, the general election campaign did make a difference—it brought Obama rising support and ultimate victory. Four factors were important in determining the outcome: the nomination of Sarah Palin, the collapse of the economy, the candidates' performances in the televised debates, and the quality of the Obama and McCain organizations.

## The Nomination of Sarah Palin

As Democratic Party delegates left Denver the morning after their convention, still hearing Obama's stirring acceptance speech before a stadium crowd of eighty thousand, they were heady with the expectation of victory. McCain quickly deflated their joyful balloons by immediately announcing his surprising choice for the Republican vice-presidential nomination: Alaska governor Sarah Palin.

McCain, knowing all year that the circumstances of the election were unfavorable, and seeing that he trailed in the polls, looked to change the course of the race by making the daring choice of Palin to be his running mate. His personal favorite for vice president was Connecticut senator Joseph Lieberman, the Democratic vice-presidential candidate in 2000 who was both a personal friend and a fellow advocate of vigorous prosecution of the Iraq War. A cross-party ticket would change the arc of the campaign and reinforce McCain's vaunted image as an independent maverick. Lieberman, however, was unacceptable to Republican social conservatives because he supported abortion rights. Instead, McCain's staff convinced him to select Palin, the favorite of social conservative advisers.[26]

At first, choosing Palin appeared to be a brilliant stroke, the bold and unconventional choice of a woman who might appeal to former loyalists of Hillary Clinton, a conservative who would rally those on the right still skeptical of McCain's reputed moderation, and a state executive with some claims as a reformer of political ethics. Palin also cast an exotic personal figure .She lived in an atypical state; was a young, attractive mother of five children; and was so committed to the "right to life" that she knowingly gave birth to a child with Down Syndrome. She delivered a rousing acceptance speech at the Republican convention and drew ecstatic reactions from conservative commentators and large, energetic crowds. Suddenly, the race tightened, with McCain either tied or ahead of Obama in the polls.

Soon, however, the glamour faded. Televised interviews showed that Palin had little knowledge of most national issues, particularly those involving foreign policy. Admiration turned to ridicule in the news media and television comedies when, for example, she claimed expertise in international affairs because Russia is within sight of Alaska. Intensive investigations also raised questions about Palin's personal character, including her spending of $150,000 of party funds for campaign clothing, her use of Alaska state travel funds for days spent at home, and the possible abuse of her gubernatorial power in a dispute with her former brother-in-law.

Palin's ultimate effect on the election is uncertain, but it was probably harmful to McCain. Her nomination alienated some prominent Republican leaders, such as Colin Powell and Christopher Buckley. Three out of five voters considered her not qualified to step in as president, while only one of six rendered the same dour judgment of Obama's running mate, Joseph Biden. Palin's nomination probably also gave greater weight to McCain's age. The controversial governor, teamed with seventy-two-year-old McCain and, in the conventional phrase, "a heartbeat away from the presidency," led 39 percent of voters to say that age was an important criterion. McCain and Palin lost these voters overwhelmingly, carrying only 32 percent of that group.

## The Economic Collapse

More serious matters quickly came to dominate the election. The nation's financial system, already weak, appeared in mid-September to be on the verge of collapse. Losses from bad mortgages rippled through the web of financial institutions—banks, brokers, investors, lenders, and borrowers. A torrent of bad economic news changed the electoral frame. Inflation spiked in response to record high prices for oil, with gasoline selling for more than $4 a gallon. At the same time, unemployment grew to a five-year high. One financial catastrophe followed another: seizure of the largest mortgage lender in the United States; the largest bank failure in U.S. history; forced sales of major stock brokerage firms; federal takeover of the secondary lenders holding half of the country's mortgages; government stock acquisition and huge loans to the world's largest insurance company; and the government-encouraged failure of Lehman Brothers, the largest bankruptcy in U.S. history. The consequent economic crisis caused large losses in the values of U.S. and global stocks, which dropped more than 25 percent from the time of the nominating conventions to election day.

Voters were frightened by the severe threats to their job prospects, lifestyles, savings, and retirement pensions. The political stakes also rose as the Bush administration proposed that Congress provide $700 billion to rescue the financial system and give the secretary of the Treasury virtually unlimited power to spend this gushing federal money. The credit crisis and the proposed "bailout" legislation made the economy the predominant issue in the presidential election.

The focus on the economy inevitably aided the Democrats, always more trusted by voters on these issues, and harmed the Republicans, who bore the burden of the Bush record. The candidates' reactions magnified these effects. Obama, while indicating reserved acceptance of the financial rescue plan, also tried to turn the crisis to his advantage by blaming the "failed economic philosophy" shared by McCain and Bush. McCain fumbled the opportunity, however limited, to gain support from the crisis. Trying to present himself as calm in the storm, he first said, "The fundamentals of our economy are strong," which hardly seemed true to fearful voters. Then, in an attempt to demonstrate leadership, he announced that he was suspending his campaign to return to Washington and develop an appropriate plan in consultation with other Republicans, even if that meant delaying or canceling the first presidential debate.

As it turned out, McCain's congressional colleagues were not interested in his advice, and House Republicans united to oppose the Bush proposal. Although most Democrats and their party leaders did support an amended bailout plan, Republican opposition defeated it, which led in turn to another plunge of the stock market. Obama, remaining cool, in effect called McCain's bluff. He continued to prepare for the first debate, eagerly awaited by the national audience. Despite the turmoil, McCain then decided, only hours before the scheduled time, to participate in the September 26 event.

**Table 3-4**    The Economic Issue

| Poll response | % of population | % Obama | % McCain |
|---|---|---|---|
| Economy most important issue | 63 | 53 | 44 |
| Very worried about economic conditions | 50 | 60 | 38 |
| National economic conditions poor | 49 | 66 | 31 |
| Family situation is worse | 42 | 71 | 28 |
| Very worried crisis will hurt family | 46 | 62 | 36 |
| Support financial bailout | 39 | 59 | 40 |
| Very worried about health care costs | 33 | 66 | 32 |
| Tax rise no matter who wins | 49 | 55 | 42 |
| Country on the wrong track | 75 | 62 | 36 |

*Source:* National Election Poll.

The economic issue dominated both the debates (discussed below) and the eventual voting. In March 2008, it had already become the most important issue on voters' minds, but at that time it was stressed by only 29 percent of those surveyed.[27] By election day, the economy was the principal issue to 63 percent of the electorate, a greater focus on one issue than had ever been recorded in opinion surveys—even more than Vietnam in 1968 or Iraq in 2004. Voters were worried for themselves and their families, and about national conditions, health care, and the general direction of the country. Table 3-4 presents the public's most typical responses to a series of questions. All show deep concern about the economy and, consequently, large support for Obama. Those worries were the determining influences on the election.

## Television: Deliberation, Debates, and Decisions

The economic issue and intense public interest in the election carried over to the televised debates between the candidates. Three featured Obama and McCain and one the vice-presidential contenders. Each debate drew an audience of sixty to seventy-five million viewers; the most watched event, uncharacteristically, being the confrontation between Biden and Palin. Its popularity surely resulted from interest in the Republican candidate. Some voters wanted to judge this controversial nominee; others may have expected a disaster for her, a political version of highly rated reality programs like *American Idol* or *Survivor.*

The first debate between Obama and McCain came as Congress was considering the financial rescue plan and inevitably focused on the economic issue. Next was the vice-presidential clash, in which Palin's folksy manner and language made her more likeable to some, more bizarre to others. The presidential candidates then addressed the electorate in a town-hall format, including questions gathered from YouTube videos, returning to a focus on economic and other issues. The debates concluded three weeks before the election with a face-to-face, but barely civil, discussion between McCain and Obama. Attention strangely focused on "Joe the Plumber," a working-class

McCain supporter who had recently conducted a street colloquy with Obama about taxes. Both candidates used this ballyhooed "common man" to exemplify their sharp differences on tax policy:

MCCAIN:     Joe wants to buy the business that he has been in for all of these years, worked ten, twelve hours a day. And he wanted to buy the business, but he looked at your tax plan, and he saw that he was going to pay much higher taxes. . . . Now Senator Obama talks about the very, very rich. Joe, I want to tell you, I'll not only help you buy that business that you worked your whole life for, and I'll keep your taxes low.

OBAMA:      I think tax policy is a major difference between Senator McCain and myself. And we both want to cut taxes, the difference is who we want to cut taxes for. . . . Now, Senator McCain, the centerpiece of his economic proposal is to provide $200 billion in additional tax breaks to some of the wealthiest corporations in America. What I've said is I want to provide a tax cut for 95 percent of working Americans, 95 percent. If you make less than a quarter million dollars a year, then you will not see your income tax go up, your capital gains tax go up, your payroll tax.

MCCAIN:     You know, when Senator Obama ended up his conversation with Joe the Plumber—[he said] we need to spread the wealth around. In other words, we're going to take Joe's money, give it to Senator Obama, and let him spread the wealth around. I want Joe the Plumber to spread that wealth around. The whole premise behind Senator Obama's plans are class warfare, let's spread the wealth around. Who—why would you want to increase anybody's taxes right now?

OBAMA:      I want to cut taxes for 95 percent of Americans. Now, it is true that my friend and supporter, Warren Buffett, for example, could afford to pay a little more in taxes in order . . . to give additional tax cuts to Joe the Plumber before he was at the point where he could make $250,000. . . . So, look, nobody likes taxes. I would prefer that none of us had to pay taxes, including myself. But ultimately, we've got to pay for the core investments that make this economy strong, and somebody's got to do it.

MCCAIN:     Nobody likes taxes. Let's not raise anybody's taxes. OK?

OBAMA:      Well, I don't mind paying a little more.

MCCAIN:     We need to cut the business tax rate in America. We need to encourage business. Now, of all times in America, we need to cut people's taxes. We need to encourage business, create jobs, not spread the wealth around.[28]

Taken together, the debates displayed the clear differences that existed in 2008 between the candidates and their parties. Although policy issues supplied the content of the debates, the essential political point for both candidates was to win votes, not to define positions. On this criterion, Obama clearly dominated.

In a year of voter discontent, the televised confrontations favored the Democrat by reinforcing the basic narrative of the campaign: Obama's focus on change, McCain's on experience. In the debates themselves, Obama presented the calmer demeanor, one more appropriate to the "cool" medium of television. McCain was more agitated, more critical of his opponent, and more erratic in his personal appearance, even wandering around the stage at times during the town-hall debate.

For Obama, the greatest benefit of the debates—and of the lengthy campaign—was simple exposure. He began his presidential quest with limited public recognition, an exotic and unconventional background, a thin record in office, and the inescapable but politically charged identity of a black man. The debates and the months on the stump made him both familiar and comfortable to the electorate. They provided a "prolonged tryout," enabling Obama to quiet "an ambiguous and slightly suspicious response from much of the public."[29] Macomb County, Michigan, the archetypal locale of Reagan Democrats, evidenced this change. Before the Democratic convention, only 40 percent of its voters were "comfortable with the idea of Mr. Obama as president." By election day, that comfort level had risen to 60 percent.[30]

Polls showed the effects. After each of the debates, presidential and vice-presidential, the national audience deemed the Democrat the "winner."[31] That judgment was quite different from previous elections, when evaluations changed from one debate to another and were skewed by partisanship. Relying on these television appearances, public evaluations of both Democratic candidates became more favorable, while judgments of both Republican candidates declined. Obama's onscreen behavior also gave him a new advantage. Voters now saw him as the candidate more likely to "deal wisely with a crisis," reversing McCain's previous lead on that criterion that had been based on his military experience.[32] During the debates, Obama opened a clear lead and kept it through election day.

## Campaign Organizations

The final important difference in the election stemmed from the respective quality of the two candidates' organizations. By every standard, Obama's organization dominated. He did not run a perfect race—despite post-election mythology, all winners make mistakes, and all losers do some things right. But the Obama campaign was probably the most effective in any modern election, combining the techniques Obama learned as a local community organizer on Chicago's South Side with the older effective practices of the city's ward politics.

The Democratic candidate had another advantage, unusual for his party's nominees: money. Obama declined the $84 million in federal campaign funds for which each major party nominee was eligible, the first candidate to abstain from the funding system since it was established in 1976. He instead relied on his pathbreaking organization to raise extraordinary amounts of money from private sources, a total of close to $500 million in the fall contest alone. But McCain—coauthor of the most recent campaign finance law—did accept the $84 million in government money and, with it, the law's ban on additional fund raising, incurring a definite disadvantage in the contest (see chapter 8).

The candidates campaigned vigorously: Obama flew eighty thousand miles, McCain seventy thousand. As detailed in Table 3-5, they and their running mates made personal appearances throughout most of the country, in contrast to previous elections, when the contenders concentrated their attention on a very few "battleground" states. At least one candidate was in thirty states after the conventions, and they had visited many of the others earlier during the nominating contests.

The wide geographical scope of the campaigns owed much to Obama's strategy of challenging the Republicans in their previous redoubts, as well as to his immense treasury, which enabled him to implement that strategy. The states most visited by the candidates were primarily those won by Bush in 2004. Of the fourteen states that hosted nine or more candidate appearances, ten had voted Republican previously. These were the new battlegrounds of 2008, and all but Missouri fell to the Democrats.

Obama had a consistent theme in his geographically broad campaign. His constant emphasis was "change," with rhetorical variations: "Change we can believe in," "The change we need," "We are the change." This appeal was itself quite vague, although backed by extensive policy proposals on a wide range of issues. In the conditions facing the country, however, change had great thematic resonance, much as it did when Dwight Eisenhower won support with his own vague promise of "Time for a Change" in 1952 or John Kennedy did with his unspecific invocation of a "New Frontier" in 1960.[33]

McCain lacked not only a shimmering slogan, but even a clear direction to his campaign. Much of his early effort was based simply on his personal attributes: his experience, heroism, and integrity. But his exemplary record was less resonant as the election turned away from foreign policy.[34] Since the electorate seemed to value Obama's "change" message more than McCain's countering appeal to "experience," McCain shifted to a more conservative message, hoping to recreate the Bush winning coalition and selecting Palin to underline that direction. At the same time, however, he tried to distance himself from his party's conservative but unpopular president, presenting himself as the exponent of true change.

When that did not work, McCain and Palin shifted to criticism of Obama, first deriding his oratorical skills as mere celebrity power, then attempting to portray him as a leftist, one who "pals around with terrorists" (specifically, a neighbor of the Obamas in Chicago who had been a leader of the 1960s radical group Weather Underground). But neither the heroic

**Table 3-5**  Candidate Visits in the 2008 Campaign

| State | Obama | McCain | Biden | Palin | Total | Bush states, 2004 | | Kerry states, 2004 | |
|---|---|---|---|---|---|---|---|---|---|
| | | | | | | Republican | Democrat | Republican | Democrat |
| Alabama | | | | | 0 | | | | |
| Alaska | | | | 2 | 2 | 2 | | | |
| Arizona | | 1 | | | 1 | 1 | | | |
| Arkansas | | | | | 0 | | | | |
| California | 1 | | | 2 | 3 | | | 2 | 1 |
| Colorado | 5 | 5 | 2 | 5 | 17 | 10 | 7 | | |
| Connecticut | | | | | 0 | | | | |
| Delaware | | | 3 | | 3 | | | | 3 |
| Dist. Columbia | 1 | 1 | 1 | | 3 | | | 1 | 2 |
| Florida | 10 | 7 | 4 | 6 | 27 | 13 | 14 | | |
| Georgia | | | | | 0 | | | | |
| Hawaii | 1 | | | | 1 | | | | 1 |
| Idaho | | | | | 0 | | | | |
| Illinois | 1 | | 1 | | 2 | | | | 2 |
| Indiana | 5 | 1 | 3 | 3 | 12 | 4 | 8 | | |
| Iowa | 1 | 4 | 1 | 3 | 9 | 7 | 2 | | |
| Kansas | | | | | 0 | | | | |
| Kentucky | | | | | 0 | | | | |
| Louisiana | | | | | 0 | | | | |
| Maine | | | | 1 | 1 | | | 1 | |
| Maryland | | 2 | 1 | | 3 | | | 2 | 1 |
| Massachusetts | | | | | 0 | | | | |
| Michigan | 3 | 3 | 2 | 2 | 10 | | | 5 | 5 |
| Minnesota | | 2 | | 1 | 3 | | | 3 | 0 |
| Mississippi | | | | | 0 | | | | |
| Missouri | 3 | 3 | 5 | 4 | 15 | 7 | 8 | | |
| Montana | | 1 | | | 1 | | 1 | | |
| Nebraska | | | | 1 | 1 | 1 | | | |
| Nevada | 4 | 1 | 1 | 3 | 9 | 4 | 5 | | |
| New Hampshire | 3 | 4 | 3 | 1 | 11 | | | 5 | 6 |
| New Jersey | | | | | 0 | | | | |
| New Mexico | 2 | 5 | 1 | 1 | 9 | 6 | 3 | | |
| New York | 1 | 4 | | 2 | 7 | | | 6 | 1 |
| North Carolina | 6 | 3 | 4 | 4 | 17 | 7 | 10 | | |
| North Dakota | | | | | 0 | | | | |
| Ohio | 7 | 12 | 8 | 13 | 40 | 25 | 15 | | |
| Oklahoma | | | | | 0 | | | | |
| Oregon | | | | | 0 | | | | |
| Pennsylvania | 6 | 11 | 7 | 12 | 36 | | | 23 | 13 |
| Rhode Island | | | | | 0 | | | | |
| South Carolina | | | | | 0 | | | | |
| South Dakota | | | | | 0 | | | | |
| Tennessee | | 1 | | | 1 | 1 | | | |
| Texas | | | 1 | 1 | 2 | 1 | 1 | | |
| Utah | | | | | 0 | | | | |
| Vermont | | | | | 0 | | | | |
| Virginia | 9 | 5 | 5 | 5 | 24 | 10 | 14 | | |
| Washington | | | 1 | | 1 | | | | 1 |
| West Virginia | | | 1 | | 1 | | 1 | | |
| Wisconsin | 2 | 5 | 1 | 4 | 12 | | | 9 | 3 |
| Wyoming | | | | | 0 | | | | |
| Totals | 71 | 80 | 57 | 76 | 284 | 99 | 89 | 57 | 39 |

*Sources:* Daily reports in *New York Times* and at abcnews.com.

Note: Days in Washington and home visits excluded.

McCain biography nor the attacks on Obama resonated in an election forty years after the Vietnam War and the polarizing politics it had engendered. As a sardonic columnist wrote, "I sometimes wondered whether most Americans thought the Weather Underground was a reunion band."[35] The final Republican tactic, which McCain deployed in the last televised debate, was to attack Obama on tax policy. It gained the ticket some, but far too few, votes. In all, McCain tried many themes, but none worked. To his credit, he refused to employ the one campaign thrust that might have succeeded—an emphasis on race, by tying Obama to his vituperative former pastor, Jeremiah Wright.

Beyond the different emphases on themes and issues, the two campaign organizations were mismatched tactically, with the Obama campaigners vastly superior. They contacted more voters personally—possibly more than twice as many;[36] they ran far more television ads; they commanded the new techniques of Internet campaigning; and they mobilized millions of paid and volunteer staff members to identify supporters, register them as voters, and get them to mark their ballots early or at the polls.

The statistics of the Obama effort are staggeringly impressive. Primarily using the Internet rather than traditional events, the campaign raised $750 million from over three million contributors, with a median contribution of less than $200.[37] In this effort, the candidate's organization developed an e-mail list of thirteen million addresses and sent a billion messages to the list. It also sponsored 35,000 volunteer groups, 3.2 million Facebook enrollments, and 3 million phone calls to spur turnout in the last four days before the election.[38]

Just as plane travel and television transformed electioneering in the twentieth century, the Obama campaign created a new politics for the twenty-first. Compared to previous operations, a former adversary conceded, "They were Apollo 11, and we were the Wright Brothers." Obama's innovators understood, and led, the changes wrought by cable television, the 24/7 news cycle, text messaging, and the Internet and its innumerable new sites, from individual blogs to social networking sites such as YouTube and Facebook. The success of the Obama campaign will certainly affect future candidacies. The campaign's fund-raising prowess has probably doomed public financing for future presidential elections. In a different portent for the conduct of politics, Obama's ability to withstand negative campaigning—from Hillary Clinton in the primaries and from McCain and particularly Palin in the general election—may set a new and promising tone in future contests.[39]

## Outcomes

### Voters' Decisions

These elements of the Obama campaign came together in the balloting that culminated on November 4. Substantial change was evident, not only in the total result, but also in the movement of voters, shown in Figure 3-5. Although

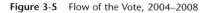

**Figure 3-5**    Flow of the Vote, 2004–2008

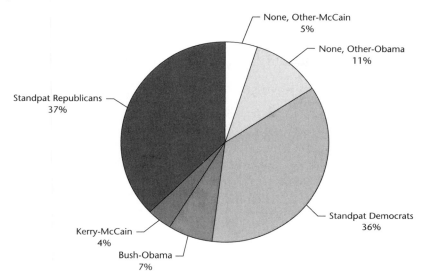

almost three-fourths ended up as standpat supporters of the same party in 2004 and 2008, many others changed their allegiance or became new participants. Obama won the election on the basis of those switchers and entrants.

Like the change in the vote between elections, Obama's strength grew during the course of the campaign as voters considered the positions and individual traits of the competitors. From September through the end of the campaign, Obama gained more positive evaluations from voters on most criteria (as detailed in Table 3-6). He became more trusted than McCain to deal with the economy, taxes, and an unexpected crisis, and was highly preferred on health care and Iraq. Obama resolved most voters' doubts about his readiness to be president and his personal values. McCain, on the other hand, lost ground on some criteria, even in his previous strengths, such as personal leadership, crisis management, and honesty.

As they came to their decisions, individual voters went through a silent, often unconscious, calculation. They emphasized either issues (as 60 percent claimed) or the candidates' personal traits (40 percent). Then they emphasized a particular issue or trait, and finally they voted for the man they preferred based on that criterion. Table 3-7 is an attempt to reconstruct their reasoning and estimate the contribution of each influence on the vote for Obama and McCain.

Obama's victory, not surprisingly, was based on the issue of the economy, with additional votes coming from the issues of Iraq and health care. He was overwhelmingly seen as the candidate of change and as empathetic to the needs of the electorate. McCain had some strengths too, on the issue of terrorism, his record of experience, and his values, but these were of lesser importance to the voters. Terrorism had faded as a concern in the seven years

**Table 3-6**    Changes in Candidate Evaluations

|  | % Obama | | % McCain | |
|---|---|---|---|---|
|  | Pre-election | September | Pre-election | September |
| Favorable ratings* | 51 | 48 | 41 | 39 |
| Trust more to deal with the economy** | 54 | 47 | 40 | 42 |
| Trust more to deal with unexpected major crisis** | 49 | 37 | 46 | 54 |
| Trust more to deal with taxes** | 52 | 45 | 43 | 44 |
| Shares Americans' values* | 65 | 66 | 64 | 61 |
| Understands your needs and problems* | 64 | 66 | 49 | 49 |
| Effective commander-in-chief* | 64 | 61 | 76 | 73 |
| Prepared to be president* | 56 | 48 | 64 | 71 |
| Spends time mostly attacking other candidate* | 22 | 35 | 64 | 53 |
| Would bring needed change in Washington** | 61 | 51 | 29 | 39 |
| Is the stronger leader** | 54 | 44 | 40 | 48 |
| Is more honest and trustworthy** | 44 | 38 | 40 | 44 |

*Sources:* *CBS News/*New York Times* polls October 23, 30; **Washington Post*/ABC News polls November 2, October 11.

**Table 3-7**    Influences on the Presidential Vote

| Influences on vote | % of total | Vote | | Contribution to the vote | |
|---|---|---|---|---|---|
|  |  | % Obama | % McCain | Obama | McCain |
| *Issues (60%)* | | | | | |
| Energy | 4.3 | 52 | 48 | 2.2 | 2.1 |
| Iraq | 6.1 | 60 | 40 | 3.7 | 2.4 |
| Economy | 38.6 | 55 | 45 | 21.2 | 17.4 |
| Terrorism | 5.5 | 13 | 87 | 0.7 | 4.8 |
| Health care | 5.5 | 74 | 26 | 4.1 | 1.4 |
| *Traits (40%)* | | | | | |
| Shares my values | 12.5 | 33 | 67 | 4.1 | 8.4 |
| Can bring change | 14.1 | 91 | 9 | 12.9 | 1.3 |
| Experience | 8.3 | 7 | 93 | 0.6 | 7.7 |
| Cares about people | 5.0 | 75 | 25 | 3.7 | 1.2 |
| Totals | 99.9 | | | 53.2 | 46.7 |

*Source:* Author's calculations from National Election Poll data. Contribution to the vote is calculated by multiplying the percentage emphasizing the issue or trait (column 2) by the percentage voting for the candidate (column 3 or 4).

since 9/11, and the cultural wars had come to a truce. In the new politics of 2008, McCain was out of date.

The election results were not inevitable, but they did fit with established models of political behavior. The fundamental causes were set months before the party conventions, the debates, and the campaign maneuvers. The voters' verdict in 2008 was a retrospective negative judgment of the Republican administration. It resembled similar past elections, grounded in the public's economic discontents (as in 1932), its wish for a change in political parties (as in 1952), and the unpopularity of the president (as in 1980).

Other predictive theories proved invalid. A majority of Americans proved they would vote for an African American, including a decisive majority of Latinos and a significant proportion of southern whites. The hyped culture wars, were muted, if not fully ended.[40] Conflicts over social issues such as abortion and gay marriage were hardly noticeable in voters' consciousness in 2008 and did not divert them from their focus on economic concerns. The vaunted new Republican majority disappeared. Based on politically constant, as well as immediate determining, features, the new politics of 2008, in the end, looked familiar.

## Future Implications

The 2008 election has been widely described as "historic." But its long-term import remains uncertain.

The election's most obvious significance was race. Obama's election culminated the long struggle of African Americans for political equality. Only forty-five years earlier, Martin Luther King Jr. had dreamed that someday the nation's children would be judged "not by the color of their skin but by the content of their character." In the figure of a child who was only two years old at the time, that dream became real on November 4. For whites it was also a time of personal liberation, a redeeming renunciation of the shame of racism. As Obama himself expressed the nation's pride: "If there is anyone out there who still doubts that America is a place where all things are possible; who still wonders if the dream of our founders is alive in our time; who still questions the power of our democracy, tonight is your answer."

Beyond the thrilling moment of equality and liberation, future consequences are less certain. By taking the presidential oath on January 20, 2009, Barack Obama released the nation from its self-inflicted bondage to a politics distorted by race. But what will happen during the next four years? Will there be enduring consequences beyond a day of stirring symbolism?

Obama's election does not demonstrate a clear ideological shift in the electorate. The proportion of liberals, moderates, and conservatives among voters in the 2008 election changed only marginally, and no large realignment was evident among social groups or regions. But the decisive results of the contest do present a warrant for change, providing the opportunity—although not the certainty—of a "reconstructive" presidency that will change the course of American politics.[41]

Mandates are usually created not by the voters but by the leaders they have chosen. Like Obama, FDR was elected to his first term on a vague platform. The content of his pledge of a New Deal came during his first administration and then was approved after the fact in the Democratic president's reelection. Another transformative leader, Ronald Reagan, barely achieved an initial popular vote majority for his conservative revolution, yet he also won sweeping retrospective approval in his second-term candidacy.[42]

Obama's initial mandate was a call from the voters for change from the Bush administration, which incurred a severe rebuke. In a general indicator of public attitudes, voters (by a 51 percent to 43 percent margin) endorsed the view that government should "do more to solve problems" rather than thinking that it is "doing too much." More specifically, voters do want government to take major actions to remedy the economic crisis, do favor extended health care coverage, and do insist on an end to the U.S. military involvement in Iraq. To advance that imposing agenda, Obama can legitimately invoke the power of the public will. To go further, he must rely on his party's majorities in Congress, his skills of persuasion,[43] and the mobilization of a new national will.

If successful in his agenda, Obama has the potential to create a new Democratic majority coalition, building on his impressive victory in 2008. The party has a wider geographical base now, reaching into the West and some of the South. The Democrats have broadened their reach, not only in presidential contests, but also in House districts. By 2008, they had won the congressional seats of a third of the districts carried by Bush four years earlier, and they controlled virtually all of those won by Kerry.[44]

The demographic foundation of a new party majority also has been laid. The groups that voted for Obama will likely grow in relative size in future years, including blacks, Latinos, the college-educated, secularists, and metropolitan residents.[45] Republican prospects are less bright, since McCain gained votes only in declining segments of the electorate—small-town residents, veterans, and those with less education. Inevitably, too, those who are now young and lean more Democratic will replace aging Republicans. Such generational change, when energized by political leaders, has often been the basis for fundamental partisan realignment.[46]

The Democratic majority, if it is built and built well, will rely on a different philosophy, "a new liberal order." Just as FDR brought order to undisciplined capitalism in the 1930s, and Nixon and Reagan sought social order out of the turbulent 1960s and their aftermath, Obama and the Democrats may be able to create a new stability. As Peter Beinart insightfully writes:

> The public mood on economics today is a lot like the public mood on culture 40 years ago: Americans want government to impose law and order—to keep their 401(k)s from going down, to keep their health-care premiums from going up, to keep their jobs from going overseas—and they don't much care whose heads Washington has to bash to do it.[47]

Attempting to accomplish that goal, President Obama is likely to employ pragmatic means toward progressive ends.

For now, American politics will seem familiar, as the new president copes with old and mounting problems. But one difference makes the 2008 election incomparable and brilliant. At last, the country has truly accepted its founding premise, the "self-evident truth" that "all men are created equal." That is cause enough for a celebration of American democracy.

# Notes

I gladly acknowledge the skillful editorial assistance of Marlene M. Pomper and of our sons, Miles, David, and Marc; the helpful comments of Robert Cohen, Milton Finegold, and Marc Weiner; and professional support from CBS News by Kathleen Frankovic, Fred Backus, and Craig Swagler.

1. Alan Abramowitz, using data from the end of June, predicted Obama would get 54.3 percent of the two-party vote, very close to the actual results. He relied on the three factors listed in this paragraph: the time in office, presidential approval ratings, and economic conditions. See "Forecasting the 2008 Presidential Election with the Time-for-Change Model," *PS: Political Science and Politics* 41 (October 2008): 691–696.

2. Of ten papers presented at the annual meetings of the American Political Science Association, only one predicted a Republican victory, and that prediction was later amended: "Symposium: Forecasting the 2008 National Elections," *PS: Political Science and Politics* 41 (October 2008): 679–728.

3. Finding that "one-third of white Democrats harbor negative views toward blacks" in a study conducted at Stanford University, reporters rushed to conclude that these "deep-seated racial misgivings could cost Barack Obama the White House if the election is close," Ron Fournier and Trevor Tompson, "Poll: Racial Views Steer Some White Dems Away from Obama," September 22, 2008, www.news.yahoo.com/page/election-2008. Although the AP-Yahoo! News Poll was conducted in nine waves throughout the election, these questions were not repeated. The surveys did, however, indicate that Obama was not in fact permanently damaged. The proportion of voters who eventually were "very favorable" in their evaluations (33 percent) and who intended to vote for him (51 percent) had tripled over the course of the campaign. See "The Associated Press/Yahoo Poll, Wave 9," October 28, 2008, www.knowledgenetworks.com.

4. Thomas Shaller, *Whistling Past Dixie: How Democrats Can Win without the South* (New York: Simon and Schuster, 2006).

5. Sergio Bendixen, a Hispanic adviser to Sen. Hillary Clinton, analyzing the coming vote in Democratic primaries in February, said, "The Hispanic voter—and I want to say this very carefully—has not shown a lot of willingness or affinity to support black candidates." Ryan Lizza, "Minority Report," *New Yorker,* January 21, 2008, www.newyorker.com.

6. Thomas Frank, *What's the Matter with Kansas?* (New York: Holt, 2004).

7. See chapters 1 and 4 in the previous volume in this series, *The Elections of 2004,* ed. Michael Nelson (Washington, D.C.: CQ Press, 2005).

8. In 1952, both parties had new nominees, Republican Dwight Eisenhower and Democrat Adlai Stevenson. However, incumbent vice president Alben Barkley had sought the Democratic presidential nomination. The previous election without any incumbent aspirant had been 1928.

9. For discussion of the absence of a mandate in 2004, see Marc D. Weiner and Gerald M. Pomper, "The 2.4% Solution: What Makes a Mandate?" *The Forum* 4 (2006): 2.

10. Michael McDonald of George Mason University provides the best source on early voting, as well as other aspects of American elections, through the United States Election Project, www.elections.gmu.edu.

11. Curtis Gans, "Much-hyped Turnout Record Fails to Materialize," American University, Center for the Study of the American Electorate, November 6, 2008.

12. "Trends in Political Values and Core Attitudes: 1987–2007" (Washington, D.C.: Pew Research Center for the People and the Press, 2007), 2.

13. All states other than Nebraska and Maine cast all of their electoral votes for the candidate who leads the popular vote in the entire state. These two states cast one vote for the winner in each congressional district, and two for the statewide leader. In 2008 Obama led in the Second Congressional District (Omaha), earning one of Nebraska's five electoral votes.

14. The correlation of the Democratic votes in 2004 and 2008 is very high, .92, excluding the outlying Democratic vote of the District of Columbia.

15. The standard deviation of the 2008 Democratic vote percentage was 9.58, a sharp rise from 8.50 in 2004.

16. The median shift was 5 percentage points toward the Democrats.
17. "For Much of the Country, A Sizeable Shift," *New York Times*, November 6, 2008, P11; November 11, 2008, A20.
18. Ethan Porter, "Rashid Who? Why the Jews Finally Came Home to Obama," *New Republic*, October 31, 2008.
19. In 2004, young voters were 17 percent of the total Kerry vote of 59 million, and gave him 54 percent, which resulted in a Democratic vote of 5.4 million from this group (.17 × 59 × .54). In 2008, young voters were 18 percent of the total Obama vote of 69 million, and gave him 66 percent, resulting in a Democratic vote of 8.2 million (.18 × 69 × .66).
20. A particularly significant impact came in the battleground state of Ohio. There, an early but incomplete analysis found that white turnout decreased by 538,000 (−11 percent). But black voting rose by 66,000 (+12.8 percent), and Latino voting by 39,000 (+22.7 percent). Turnout changes alone gave Obama an Ohio margin of 207,000: Greg Gordon, "More Minorities Voted this Year, but White Turnout Dropped," November 18, 2008, www.mcclatchydc.com.
21. Ruy Teixeira, "Digging into the 2008 Exit Polls," November 11, 2008, takingnote.tcf.org.
22. Chuck Todd et al., "First Thoughts," November 11, 2008, www.firstread.msnbc.msn.com.
23. The "effect" was named for Los Angeles mayor Tom Bradley, an African American, who lost a contest for governor of California in 1982, although some polls had shown him with a strong lead. See the conclusive refutation of the Republican pollster in this contest: V. Lance Tarrance, "The Bradley Effect—Selective Memory," October 13, 2008, www.realclearpolitics.com. After the elections, the spurious effect was consensually buried: Kate Zernike and Dalia Sussman, "For Pollsters, the Racial Effect that Wasn't," *New York Times*, November 6, 2008, A8.
24. Obama won 17,966,000 votes in all states and D.C., including caucus states and the "uncommitted" slate in Michigan, while Clinton won 17,770,000, an Obama majority of the two-candidate vote of 50.3 percent. Including territories not eligible to participate in the presidential election, Obama won 18,106,000 and Clinton 18,043,000, for a thin Obama edge with 50.1 percent. For full details, see the compilations on www.realclearpolitics.com.
25. Todd Gitlin, "Race for President Builds Characters," September 28, 2008, www.latimes.com.
26. Jane Mayer, "The Insiders," October 27, 2008, www.newyorker.com.
27. CBS News Poll, March 15–18, 2008.
28. Presidential debate transcript, www.latimesblogs.latimes.com/washington/2008/10/debate-transcri.html.
29. Adam Nagourney, "In Debating McCain, Obama's Real Opponent Was Voter Doubt," *New York Times*, October 5, 2008, A21.
30. Stanley Greenberg, the pollster who originated the category, in "Goodbye, Reagan Democrats," *New York Times*, November 11, 2008, A29.
31. Voters felt better (36 percent) rather than worse (12 percent) about Obama, while McCain drew fewer favorable (20 percent) than critical (26 percent) evaluations. See *Washington Post*-ABC News Poll, October 19, 2008, www.washingtonpost.com.
32. CBS News/*New York Times* poll, October 20, 2008. This poll re-interviewed respondents to its pre-debate survey. Obama went from a 5 percent lead on September 25 to a 13 percent margin on October 17–19. On the ability to handle a crisis, McCain previously had held a 53 percent to 44 percent advantage; after the debates, Obama held a 52 percent to 45 percent edge.
33. Illuminating accounts of the campaigns include Ryan Lizza, "Battle Plans" and David Grann, "The Fall," *New Yorker*, November 17, 2008, 46–66; and Adam Nagourney et al., "Near-Flawless Run From Start to Finish Is Credited in Victory," *New York Times*, November 5, 2008, A1.

34. John Judis, "Death Defying," *New Republic,* October 22, 2008.

35. Frank Rich, "It Still Felt Good the Morning After," *New York Times,* November 9, 2008, WK9.

36. In exit polls, 28 percent reported contact by the Obama campaign, 18 percent by the McCain campaign. The parties' own claims were 68 million contacts by the Democrats and 30 million (including ineffective robocalls) by the Republicans: Marc Ambinder, "Data that Helps Explain the Election," November 7, 2008, www.marcambinder.theatlantic.com.

37. However, many individuals made repeated small donations, so that the median contributor gave total contributions in the middle range, $201–$999. See "Reality Check," Campaign Finance Institute, November 24, 2008.

38. Jose Antonio Vargas, "Obama Raised Half a Billion Online," November 20, 2008, www.voices.washingtonpost.com/the-trail.

39. Adam Nagourney, "Change for Politics as We Know It," *New York Times,* November 4, 2008, A1.

40. Dick Meyer aptly undermines "5 Myths about Value Voters," *Washington Post,* October 26, 2008, B03.

41. Stephen Skowronek, *The Politics Presidents Make* (Cambridge, Mass.: Harvard University Press, 1997).

42. The meanings of an electoral mandate are skillfully presented in Stanley Kelley Jr., *Interpreting Elections* (Princeton, N.J.: Princeton University Press, 1983). The construction of Reagan's presumed mandate is analyzed well by Marjorie Hershey, "The Meaning of a Mandate," *Polity* 28 (Winter 1995): 225–254.

43. In his classic analysis, *Presidential Power* (New York: Wiley, 1960), chap. 3, Richard Neustadt emphasizes the central importance of the president's "power to persuade."

44. Ronald Brownstein, "The Bush GOP's Fatal Contraction," November 22, 2008, www.nationaljournal.com/njmagazine.

45. These trends were foreseen by John Judis and Ruy Teixeira, *The Emerging Democratic Majority* (New York: Scribner, 2002). Their analysis is updated in "Back to the Future," *American Prospect* 18 (July–August 2007): 12–18.

46. See Warren Miller and Merrill Shanks, *The New American Voter* (Cambridge, Mass.: Harvard University Press, 1996).

47. Peter Beinart, "The New Liberal Order," November 13, 2008, www.time.com/time.

# 4

## The Presidency:
## The Unexpected Competence
## of the Barack Obama Administration

### Paul J. Quirk and Bruce Nesmith

Among the astute judgments of his 2008 presidential campaign, Barack Obama was the first candidate in the election to conclude that one could run for president on a promise of "change," as if the word were self-explanatory. Apparently, many voters felt that almost any change in prevailing policies and national leadership would be an improvement. When he elaborated, however, Obama described changes on two levels. On one level, he outlined an ambitious agenda for policy change. He promised, among other things, to cut taxes "for 95% of all working families," to give every child "a world-class education," to provide affordable health care for all, to deal effectively with climate change, and to begin weaning the nation from its dependence on imported oil. On the international front, he said he would withdraw U.S. troops from Iraq and expand efforts to win the war in Afghanistan and defeat terrorism.[1] Later in the campaign, as economic troubles became the nation's major concern, he emphasized restoring the credit markets, creating jobs, and reforming financial institutions, although without abandoning his earlier promises. On another, deeper level, Obama promised to transcend the poisonous partisan conflict of American politics in recent years and bring the country closer together—as "not red states or blue states, but the United States"—changing the very practice of politics.

Two difficulties complicated Obama's notions of change. First, during the last two months of the campaign, the economic crisis threatened to undermine most of his plans for policy achievement. With $700 billion of federal funds already committed to reviving the credit markets by the outgoing George W. Bush administration, the crisis pointed to a presidency that would have to struggle to prevent or resolve the worst economic depression since the 1930s and to cope with the resulting hardship. Second, although the contradiction was rarely noted, Obama's two levels of change added up to an implausible overall conception: sweeping policy change, achieved by consensus. In American politics, dramatic policy change has occurred only when one political party or ideological faction has controlled both the presidency and a large congressional majority and proceeded to enact its policies over the opposition of the weakened minority.

Regardless of these difficulties with his plans, Obama's victory on November 4 produced an extraordinarily fervent, hopeful response—with huge, emotion-filled celebrations among his supporters not only in the United States, but around the world.[2] Much of the celebrating was inspired by the first election of an African American to the nation's highest office. Some of it expressed relief over the approaching end of the hugely unpopular Bush presidency.[3] But the enthusiasm undoubtedly also reflected expectations that Obama would deliver some attractive version of the change he promised. On the eve of his inauguration, the public remained optimistic despite consistently adverse economic developments. About three-quarters of respondents to a *New York Times* poll said Obama would create jobs and predicted the economy would be stronger in four years. Seventy percent expected him to "bring about real change in the way things are done in Washington," with seventy-nine percent saying they were "generally optimistic" about the next four years.[4]

This chapter considers the prospects for the Obama presidency: Can he succeed, substantively and politically? What can he accomplish for the country? And what effects will the election and the transition process have in shaping those prospects? In particular, we focus on three factors: the president's personal skills and dispositions for presidential leadership; his ability to control the government, especially Congress; and the possibilities and constraints of the policy agenda—including the monumental task of rescuing the U.S. economy.

As our account shows, Obama will have advantages both in his considerable abilities and in the large Democratic majorities in both houses of Congress. But he will encounter obstacles in promoting a centrist, "post-partisan" policy agenda in a Congress that is deeply partisan and ideologically polarized. And he will find even greater challenges devising policies that can deal effectively with the potentially intractable problems facing the country. We also show, more generally, that the deficiencies of campaign discourse in American elections have consequences for the performance of government.

## Competence and Leadership

A president's opportunity for success depends in part on the personal skills and dispositions he or she brings to bear.[5] By mid-December 2008, President-elect Obama's actions during the transition period quickly displayed, by most accounts, evidence of remarkable competence for the office.[6] Although some of his admirable traits had played a role in his election victory, some had become evident only late in the campaign, when he was already the likely victor, or even after the election. The election of a president of such ability was in that sense a stroke of good fortune for the country more than the result of any rigorous assessment in the electoral process.

### The Perils of Presidential Selection

The American political system promotes, indeed almost guarantees, a high rate of presidential failure. It creates a mismatch between the attributes that are required for presidents to perform effectively in office and those that are most likely to get them elected. On one hand, the functioning of the political system is exceptionally dependent on the president's performance. By comparison with the chief executives of most other developed democracies, American presidents have to deal with a far more independent legislature; a more decentralized and complex administrative system; less expertise and institutional memory in the executive branch, including the White House staff, which each president appoints and organizes himself; and a wider range of crisis-prone international involvements. In this context, presidents require a good deal of capability not only for them to get their way, but simply to avoid governmental chaos and incompetence. At the same time, presidents have greater authority to act unilaterally in some areas than other democratic chief executives, and they cannot be removed by something like a vote of no-confidence in the legislature. As President Bush famously pointed out, in such areas the president is "the decider." All these conditions put a premium on having presidents who can perform well when making decisions and promoting their policies.

There is no generally accepted list of attributes required for effective presidential performance. In our view, a reasonable list would include skills in policy deliberation (with some understanding of major areas of policy), political strategy (both for enacting legislation and maintaining popular support), organization and management, and communicating with the public— along with emotional stability.[7] Whatever the exact list of attributes, presidents benefit from relevant experience—that is, from holding one or more appropriate jobs for at least a few years. Such experience is the main means of developing necessary skills and understanding. The most useful jobs are those that provide opportunities to deal directly with the president or observe his activities at close range and that involve participation in national policymaking (for example, that of senator, White House staff member, or high-ranking executive branch official). Alternatively, a few other positions, primarily governorships, bear some similarity to that of the presidency. In addition to such learning, appropriate experience establishes a track record of performance from which observers can judge whether one has or lacks relevant attributes. If a candidate's abilities and dispositions have not been tested in a relevant setting, they are essentially unknowable by the voters.

To be sure, presidents can make up for their lack of particular kinds of experience by finding and relying on aides who have the right expertise.[8] But until they do so, one cannot count on that solution. Bill Clinton in 1993 had minimal experience in Washington and yet he appointed a chief of staff with none at all, contributing to numerous gaffes and scandals in the first two years of his presidency.[9]

In estimating a candidate's political, managerial, and other skills, it is crucial to distinguish three different arenas that they must deal with: campaign and electoral politics, the politics of policy adoption and implementation in Washington, and substantive policies and their consequences. A candidate who is highly expert in one of these arenas may be completely out of his or her depth in another. Indeed, few people are expert in more than one of them.

On the other hand, the structure of national institutions and the electoral process makes it impossible to have any confidence that a successful presidential candidate will assume office with adequate levels of the requisite skills. In the United States, there are normally few potential leaders, if any, who have the full range of relevant experience. To consider the two main sources of presidential candidates, senators usually have little or no experience managing a large organization, or in particular, any substantial part of the executive branch; mainly, they have vicarious experience of executive leadership gained by watching and discussing the president. Governors typically have only modest experience with national and international issues. But they are actively involved in some issues of particular interest to state governments, such as Medicaid, education, and highway funding. Those from large states with strong governors' offices (some governors have very limited powers) have somewhat comparable experience as executives; indeed, the single job most like that of the president may be the governorship of California. Parliamentary systems, by contrast, have a ready stock of leaders who have campaigned for office, served in the national legislature, and held positions in the cabinet or (for a member of a minority party) the shadow cabinet.[10]

Moreover, the presidential campaign—especially the nomination process, which narrows the field of candidates to two finalists, a Republican and a Democrat—does not select for the full range of relevant skills. Some have argued that the campaign itself is a good test of suitability for the office.[11] Certainly, some skills of a successful campaigner also serve a president well— for example, persuasiveness and likeability in public communications, sound strategic judgment, and effective management of a complex organization. But the differences between campaigning and governing make a great deal of difference with respect to these skills: running an organization that can choose effective campaign themes, produce persuasive campaign advertisements, calculate a strategy for the Electoral College, and coordinate local canvassing activities is very different from running one that can plan a military intervention, develop an economic program, or implement an effective response to a natural disaster. The differences explain why campaign consultants rarely moonlight as experts on governmental processes or public policy.[12]

In fact, it is easy to come up with examples of effective campaigns that led immediately to incompetent performances in the White House. Jimmy Carter, a dark horse candidate in 1976, threaded his way brilliantly through a new and complex nomination process, but once in office he was hindered by a habit of drowning himself in the details of policy, a staff inexperienced in Washington, and rigid adherence to policies that were dead-on-arrival in Congress. Bill Clinton's 1992 campaign was a model of focus in sticking to its centrist economic policy message, but in his first year in office Clinton lurched to the political left while failing to establish priorities among issues. Nor are campaigns always good predictors of presidential approaches. George W. Bush in 2000 advocated a humble approach to international relations that would avoid the perils of nation-building, but his presidency featured an aggressively unilateral approach to national security and involved the United States in massive projects of nation-building in Afghanistan and Iraq.

Televised debates—the feature of campaigns most celebrated as providing opportunity for voters to learn about the candidates—actually provide a confusing mixture of useful information and irrelevant noise. Above all, they test the candidates' poise and performance in a stressful situation before a television audience. Success in presidential debates turns largely on the candidates' ability to recall and integrate carefully rehearsed remarks; to strike appropriate balances on a variety of attitudinal and stylistic dimensions (firm, not angry; assertive, not domineering; informal, not crude; caring, not emotional; and so on); to repeat their campaigns' central claims and arguments multiple times; to "stay on message," despite the moderator's and opponent's efforts to divert them; to refrain from making embarrassing or harmful admissions, no matter the cost in candor; and above all to avoid any serious mistake— the dreaded "gaffe." Being knowledgeable about government and policy is of some value; but the voters' standards for assessing that knowledge are not demanding. Both Ronald Reagan in 1980 and George W. Bush in 2000 helped their respective causes by their performances in the debates despite offering very limited substantive information. In 1992 H. Ross Perot, a glib candidate with a simple message, easily outperformed George H. W. Bush, who had broad governmental experience.

Each debate is followed by exacting assessments of the candidates' performances, featuring opinion polls that seek to determine "who won." What is overlooked in all the commentary is that debate performances bear almost no resemblance to any significant presidential task. In particular, a president never has to make a decision and explain it publicly, without consulting anyone, in two minutes. If a candidate says something that is embarrassingly inaccurate or offends some constituency, he risks losing the election. If a president does so, the consequence is usually a round of jokes on late-night talk shows and a day or two of adverse commentary in the media.

Moreover, to the extent that debates do reveal significant qualifications, these may be overlooked by the news media and the public in favor of more gossipy, titillating, or amusing fare. Trivial elements dominate post-debate assessments—Richard M. Nixon's "five-o-clock shadow" in 1960, a mistaken remark about Poland by Gerald R. Ford in 1976, Michael S. Dukakis's failure in 1988 to display sufficient emotion on cue when asked how he would react if his wife were raped and murdered, and the distracting mannerisms of Al Gore in 2000 and John McCain in 2008. It is more important in a debate to avoid gaffes and "look presidential" than to demonstrate one's substantive qualifications for president.

The fundamental deficiency of the campaign as a test of relevant skills and experience for the presidency, however, is that the voters generally overlook some important attributes. They focus largely on a few qualities in each election, depending on the major issues of the day and the notable deficiencies of the incumbent president. The major qualities have included, for example, trustworthiness in 1976 (after Watergate), toughness in 1980 (after the Soviet invasion of Afghanistan), and compassion in 1992 (after a period of austere social programs). Voters pay less attention to the candidates' organizational capacity, cognitive or intellectual strengths, and, except for gross errors, substantive knowledge.

Most important, voters assign little value—and perhaps, indeed, negative value—to experience in Washington. Experience in national government is equated with being part of "the mess in Washington." Career politicians are derided for "never having met a payroll." The public may not actually penalize candidates for having experience in national government, but campaign rhetoric assumes they do. Carter, Reagan, and George W. Bush all proclaimed their lack of any Washington experience as a virtue, tarring their opponents as members of a vaguely unwholesome Washington establishment.

## Assessing Competence in 2008

The qualifications of candidates for the presidency were discussed at various times during the 2008 campaign, often with one candidate making a virtue of some credential he or she had that other candidates lacked. None of the leading candidates in either party had a notable lack of experience—as Republican Steve Forbes, a publishing executive who had never held public office, did in 1996 and 2000—or extremely limited knowledge of government and public policy—as George W. Bush did in 2000.[13] But the public discussion of qualifications in 2008 was burdened with omissions, distortions, and bizarre constructions.

*Democrats.* The field of contenders for the Democratic nomination presented an interesting dichotomy: a trio of well-funded, widely recognized candidates with comparatively thin records of public service, and another trio of experienced politicians who were less well-known to the general public.[14] Among the latter group, Delaware senator Joseph Biden, whom Obama ultimately selected to be his vice president, had served in the Senate for more than thirty years and was chair of the Foreign Affairs Committee after having previously chaired the Judiciary Committee. Connecticut senator Christopher Dodd had been in Congress since 1975, in the Senate since 1981, and had chaired the Committee on Banking, Housing and Urban Affairs. Bill Richardson was governor of New Mexico, with previous service as ambassador to the United Nations, secretary of energy, and member of Congress. All three touted records of policy achievement in addition to their long experience, but none ever gained much standing in public opinion polls, and all dropped out early in the contest for delegates.

The top-tier Democratic candidates were Obama, Hillary Clinton, and John Edwards. In order of governmental experience, Clinton had been elected in 2006 to her second term as senator from New York and before that had served eight years as first lady; Edwards had served one full term as senator from North Carolina, leaving the Senate as a result of his nomination for vice president in 2004; and Obama, the least experienced of any major candidate in either party, was midway through his first term as a U.S. senator from Illinois after eight years in the Illinois Senate.

Edwards, considered a fresh face in 2004 when he first sought his party's presidential nomination, attempted to move to the left in 2008 with an economic populist message. Although he initially amassed a sizeable campaign war chest and significant national support, he could not compete at the level of Obama and Clinton for money or attention.

Much of the discussion about Edwards focused on distracting issues concerning his personal wealth and spending habits. Details about his new 10,000-square-foot home in North Carolina and reports that he had charged two $400 haircuts to his campaign took the edge off his antipoverty message—even though the details of these issues revealed little or nothing of what he would have tried to do about poverty as president. He also faced repeated questions about whether he should continue running for president after his wife Elizabeth was diagnosed with an untreatable, though not immediately life-threatening form of cancer. He withdrew from the race at the end of January after suffering several primary defeats.[15]

That left Clinton and Obama in a four-month battle of attrition. Clinton, who would have been the first female president, compared her governmental experience favorably with Obama's. Not only had she been in the Senate longer, Clinton argued, but she also had been an active partner to her husband, Bill Clinton, during his eight years as president and twelve years as governor of Arkansas. But the nature and value of experience as a first lady were hard to define. Clinton had co-chaired a 1993 task force on health care reform that produced a costly and complex presidential proposal, which died an ignominious death in Congress—a lone and unsuccessful venture into presidential policymaking. She had traveled the world on state visits. Most important, as contemporaneous reports had often described, she was President Clinton's most trusted adviser on a wide range of issues; she was at the center, therefore, of a generally popular two-term presidency. For whatever reason, however, Clinton did not highlight her role as adviser to her husband in her own presidential campaign. As a result, what was by far the most substantial, directly relevant experience of any of the candidates was not a factor in the campaign's debate about qualifications.[16]

At the end of February, the Clinton campaign produced a memorable television spot featuring a ringing phone on a bed stand and asking voters which of the Democratic candidates they would rather have respond to a foreign policy crisis at 3:00 a.m.[17] That did not stop Obama from dismissing Clinton's years as first lady, when he remarked dryly, "My understanding is she wasn't Treasury secretary in the Clinton administration."[18]

Obama had little to point to as concrete accomplishments in the Senate at least in part because of the brief and peculiar trajectory of his senatorial career. In 2004, the year he was elected to the Senate, Obama gave an electrifying keynote address at the Democratic National Convention that immediately placed him in the running for the 2008 presidential nomination. As a result, he was likely contemplating a run for the White House before he was even sworn in as a senator, and in any case was never genuinely engaged in the work of the Senate. He spent much of his time as a senator away from Washington campaigning for president.

Obama's success in the primaries rested largely on his compelling personal story, exceptional rhetorical gifts, and aptly chosen campaign themes. Like Clinton, he was a pathbreaking candidate, bidding to be the first African American president. He came from humble origins: After his parents' divorce when he was two years old, Obama was raised first by his mother and later by his grandparents. As a scholarship student, he studied at Occidental College, Columbia University, and Harvard Law School; became president of the *Harvard Law Review;* and taught constitutional law at the University of Chicago—evidence of exceptional intellectual talent and accomplishment. On the campaign trail, he demonstrated a mastery of policy issues. Former Bush administration official Peter Wehner said, "He radiates good judgment."[19] Obama used his rhetorical skills to project an appealing message of change, future-thinking, idealism, racial healing, and bipartisanship.[20]

Some of Obama's best qualities only became apparent after he had largely locked up the nomination in the early primaries and, with economic conditions and other electoral fundamentals pointing to a strong Democratic year, become the favorite to win the presidency. Analysts cited his unflappable temperament as an important strength for the presidency. He maintained composure in response to Clinton's sharpened rhetoric as the nomination contest continued through the spring.[21] One commentator noted that "by the end of the campaign he didn't look green at all. He seemed fully in command of his campaign and his own emotions."[22] Obama exploited the newfound praise in his acceptance speech to the Democratic National Convention: "If John McCain wants to have a debate about who has the temperament and judgment to serve as the next commander in chief, that's a debate I'm ready to have."

***Republicans.*** John McCain emerged as the Republican nominee from a field that long lacked a clear frontrunner and was burdened by mixed messages about positioning and qualifications. Mitt Romney had an estimable record of achievement as governor of Massachusetts, but he chose to downplay his policies and accomplishments in the liberal state and instead stressed conservative positions on moral issues that were better suited to winning votes in the Republican primaries. Former New York mayor Rudolph Giuliani touted his experience leading the city through the 9/11 crisis. But needing to soft-pedal his liberal stances on abortion and homosexuality among Republican voters, Giuliani had no coherent message apart from advocating strong defenses against terrorism. He also disastrously underestimated the consequences of bypassing several early primaries.[23] Arkansas governor Mike Huckabee gained sudden prominence by winning the Iowa caucuses. He combined executive experience, conservative social positions, and an appealing personal style, but he emerged from obscurity too late to raise sufficient funds and form an effective national organization.

McCain, whose campaign appeared moribund as late as summer 2007, built an insurmountable lead with major primary wins in New Hampshire, South Carolina, and Florida. A veteran member of Congress, McCain pointed to his extensive legislative experience along with a personal story of heroic bravery as a prisoner of war in North Vietnam. The legislative record was indeed impressive. McCain had been a leading, independent-minded voice on foreign policy—criticizing both Republican and Democratic administrations when he felt they had taken ill-advised military action,[24] and yet providing the Clinton administration with Republican cover when it established diplomatic relations with Vietnam. He claimed credit for showing good judgment about the war in Iraq when the Bush administration in fall 2007 implemented a troop "surge," which he had advocated for several years, with apparent positive results. "The rest of the world takes John McCain more seriously because he is more serious," said one supporter.[25] McCain also had strong credentials as a reformer on domestic policy—particularly on campaign finance, but also on measures that took on the telecommunications and tobacco industries, defense contractors, and lobbyists.[26] *New York Times* columnist David Brooks summarized McCain's recent legislative efforts by remarking, "I don't think any senator had as impressive a few years" as McCain's during the George W. Bush presidency.[27]

The prisoner-of-war story, repeated endlessly by McCain's supporters, was profoundly moving but, in the cold light of day, was tangential to his capability for the presidency. No American president has ever been captured by the enemy. More to the point, it is far from clear that the physical courage needed to endure years of torture and danger of death has much to do with, for example, the political courage needed to adopt an unpopular policy for the sake of principle. President John F. Kennedy, who performed heroically during World War II in the PT109 incident, reportedly postponed withdrawing U.S. forces from Vietnam to avoid suffering the political consequences of foreign policy embarrassment in the 1964 election. Not surprisingly, however, no rival candidate or prominent commentator challenged the pertinence of McCain's heroism as a prisoner of war to the presidential campaign.

Other concerns about McCain's competence as a political leader did hamper his candidacy throughout the campaign. One problem was policy vision: McCain had a hard time weaving his record as a maverick reformer, which appealed to moderate voters, together with his positions on policies like taxes and the budget, which he had adjusted to the right to appeal to the conservative base of the Republican Party.[28] Economists generally preferred Obama's economic plan to McCain's and found the Democrat better informed on the subject. Erik Brynjolfsson of the Massachusetts Institute of Technology noted, "John McCain has professed disdain for 'so-called economic experts,' and the feeling is becoming mutual."[29]

Another problem was McCain's age—he turned seventy-two shortly before the Republican National Convention and would have been the oldest person ever to begin a first term as president. No doubt to avoid offending older voters, McCain's opponents in both the nomination and general-election campaigns refrained from mentioning the subject—rendering it no more than a minor issue. But the issue of his age was occasionally discussed in the media, often in connection with his treatments, between 1993 and 2002, for a dangerous form of skin cancer.[30] The issue deserved attention, in any case, because of the relatively high likelihood of significant health problems and disability, at some point within the next four years, for a person of his age.

Most important in any assessment of McCain's qualifications for the presidency, he was inclined to angry outbursts and impulsive actions. Thad Cochran, a longtime Republican senator from Mississippi, called him "erratic. He is hotheaded. He loses his temper, and he worries me."[31] This reputation stemmed partly from his response to goading by Bush during the 2000 nomination fight, but it was underscored in mid-September following the bankruptcy of Lehman Brothers. McCain swung from reassurance to anger. He blamed the economic crisis on "crooks," and advocated the firing of the chair of the Securities and Exchange Commission, whom he described as "asleep at the switch." He then called for the first presidential debate, scheduled for later that week, to be postponed while Congress dealt with the crisis, declaring, "If we do not act, every corner of our country will be impacted."[32] McCain suspended his campaign and flew to Washington to attend a meeting with congressional leaders at the White House. Then, anticlimactically, he did not speak at the meeting.[33] In the end, he decided to participate in the presidential debate after all, and the campaign resumed, but his seemingly erratic behavior damaged his prospects, especially when contrasted with Obama's measured tones on the same issue.

The most severe weakness of McCain's candidacy, from the standpoint of qualifications for the presidency, was his choice of Alaska governor Sarah Palin as his running mate. Widely described as a desperate "Hail Mary" gamble, the choice undercut one of the main rationales for McCain's candidacy. After campaigning against Obama in large part on a credible claim of superior experience, McCain chose a candidate to be his successor in the event of death or disability who had less experience than Obama. Palin had been mayor of Wasilla, Alaska (population, 6,300) before being elected governor in 2006 on themes of social conservatism and reform, and was little known outside the state. Republicans defending her nomination essentially mocked the very concept of qualifications. They pointed out that Palin had more executive branch experience than Obama and Biden combined; they touted her submitting balanced budgets as governor (a constitutional requirement in a majority of other states, and facilitated in Alaska by oil revenue); and they argued for her foreign policy experience on the basis of Alaska's proximity to Russia and Palin's titular position as head of the Alaska National Guard.

Few people took these claims any more seriously than they took a joke by Sen. Fred Thompson of Tennessee, who proclaimed Palin the only candidate who knew "how to field-dress a moose."[34] A number of conservative commentators broke ranks and pronounced the Palin selection cynical, pandering for popular support without regard to the well-being of the country. Clearly, the McCain campaign staff presumed that experience, as conventionally defined, did not matter to the voters. Initially, they were right: Palin's humorous remarks and physical attractiveness made her popular among the general public, and social conservatives were drawn to her devout evangelical Christianity, opposition to abortion (symbolized by her infant son, who has Down Syndrome), and support for gun rights.[35]

Palin's star faded rapidly, however. The few media interviews that she gave after the convention were disastrous. Televised interviews with Charles Gibson of ABC News and Katie Couric of CBS News showed Palin to be deeply uninformed about national issues and unable to explain her own qualifications. In answering questions, she would change topics two or three times within meandering, wildly ungrammatical sentences that left listeners completely confused. In what was probably the most important intervention of entertainment television in any presidential campaign, Palin's flubs were magnified by devastating imitations on NBC's *Saturday Night Live* by comedian Tina Fey, who not only captured Palin's voice and speech patterns but bore an uncanny physical resemblance to her. Fey's tremendously popular spots, viewed by millions on YouTube and other video Web sites in addition to their initial broadcasts on NBC, drew vast attention to Palin's failings. Although Palin retained strong support among social conservatives, her overall approval rating plummeted, contributing to a decline in McCain's standing in September and October. McCain's selection of Palin, reportedly made after minimal discussion within the campaign, was widely seen as exhibiting poor judgment on his part, particularly in view of his age and previous health problems.

Typical of contemporary political discourse, much of the discussion of the candidates focused on a seemingly endless variety of titillating but meaningless or nearly meaningless matters. The election season featured breathless debate about, among other things, Hillary Clinton's inaccurate statement that she had been fired upon by snipers on a state trip to Bosnia;[36] Obama's relationship with his former pastor, Jeremiah Wright, who was prone to inflammatory rhetoric attacking the United States;[37] Obama's occasional contact with a Chicago education activist who had participated in violent resistance to the Vietnam War in the 1960s; accusations that Obama was secretly Muslim; a Fox News correspondent's speculation that Obama's celebratory "fist bump" with his wife Michelle represented some sort of terrorist code; McCain's inability to recall the exact number of houses he and his wife own; a McCain advertisement comparing Obama's celebrity status to that of entertainment personalities Paris Hilton and Britney Spears; all the major candidates' disavowals of various politically incorrect statements by their supporters; and the Republicans' purchase of expensive clothes for Palin to wear on the campaign. Ill-advised offhand comments by both McCain and Obama were taken out of context and discussed prominently. McCain had stated early in the year that "the fundamentals of the economy are strong."

This conventional remark, presumably intended to promote confidence in the economy, was used by Democrats to claim that McCain was out of touch with the economic distress of ordinary Americans.[38] At a small gathering in April, Obama attributed the social conservatism of working-class Americans to their being "bitter" about their economic circumstances, which he said led them to "cling to guns and religion . . . or anti-immigrant sentiment." A flurry of media stories branded him "elitist," and Republicans continued to use the line against him throughout the fall campaign.[39] A voter who followed the campaign casually might have inferred that the election was mainly about which was worse—having too many houses or associating with a radical.

Overall, Obama made significant gains during the course of the fall campaign with respect to voters' relative assessments of the two candidates' qualifications for the presidency. In a CNN/Opinion Research Corporation poll in early September, McCain had a 19 percentage point advantage on leadership, and he and Obama broke even on the question of who had a clear plan for solving the country's problems. Obama gained decisively on both dimensions during the final weeks of the campaign. A week before the election he drew almost even with McCain in the CNN/Opinion Research Poll on "personality and leadership qualities," and an ABC News/*Washington Post* poll gave Obama a 17-point edge on temperament and a 32-point edge on optimism.[40] Despite his nearly complete lack of experience in national office, by election day Obama had won over many skeptics by displaying impressively steady competence in the campaign itself.

## Governance

All presidencies are not created equal. Rather, presidents have widely varying opportunities to shape public policy according to their preferences. One ingredient of success is the effectiveness of their White House staff, cabinet secretaries, and other top-level administration officials in formulating workable, politically feasible policies and promoting their adoption. That effectiveness in turn depends heavily on presidents' decisions on appointments and organization during the transition period. Even more important, however, presidents' opportunities to shape policy reflect the relative strengths of the political parties and ideological groups in Congress produced by the most recent congressional election—and how these conditions relate to the president's goals. In his transition, Obama's appointment decisions signaled that he intended to follow through on his promise of a centrist administration. Although he would have the benefit of large Democratic majorities in both the House and the Senate, he faced potential difficulty building the coalitions to support such an agenda.

### The Transition

Obama quietly formed a transition planning team, headed by a former chief of staff in the Clinton White House, John Podesta, in late summer—an unusual commitment of time and talent to the transition during a period when the candidates normally give undivided attention to winning the election. The secrecy of Obama's planning effort was undoubtedly intended to avoid any appearance of taking victory in the election for granted. In any case, the early organizing demonstrated a sophisticated approach to government and policy—a recognition of the importance of "hitting the ground running."[41]

After the election, Obama moved in a rapid, yet orderly manner to name the top people in his administration. In doing so he emphasized talent, experience, and diversity of perspective, with a distinctly centrist tendency overall. A remarkable number of Obama's appointees had Ivy League degrees, had worked in the Clinton administration, or both. Nearly all were people of independent stature, widely respected prior to their appointments. For White House chief of staff, Obama chose Rahm Emanuel, a member of the Democratic House leadership from Chicago who had also worked in the Clinton White House staff. Obama then assembled what the *Economist* magazine called a "star-studded economic team," led by three distinguished economists and the president of the New York Federal Reserve Bank, and a set of foreign policy and national security advisers noted for their "pragmatism and flexibility."[42] The economic appointments—central banker Timothy Geithner as secretary of the Treasury, Harvard economist and former Treasury secretary Lawrence H. Summers as director of the National Economic Council, economist and former Congressional Budget Office director Peter Orszag as director of the Office of Management and Budget, economist Christina Romer as chair of the Council of Economic Advisers, and former Federal Reserve chair Paul Volcker as chair of the new Economic Recovery Advisory Board—emphasized economic expertise rather than liberal ideology. (By contrast, only one of the four Bush administration officials they replaced had a Ph.D. in economics.) Obama's foreign policy and national security appointments—Hillary Clinton as secretary of state and Gen. James Jones as National Security Adviser, with Bush appointee Robert Gates remaining as secretary of defense—had been in varying degrees more supportive of U.S. military engagements during the Bush administration than had Obama.[43]

The appointments pleased conservatives and puzzled liberals. David Corn of *Mother Jones* magazine reported that "progressives are—depending on whom you ask—disappointed, irritated or fit to be tied."[44] The appointments ensure that Obama will have access to highly expert advice from a variety of perspectives. A reasonable concern is whether an administration populated with so many individuals of diverse views, who do not owe their stature to Obama, will pull together as a team.

## Election Results and the New Congress

In most respects, the results of the election enhanced Obama's opportunity to set policy. One factor, though easily overrated, is that his own victory was decisive. Obama won 28 states and 365 electoral votes, along with 53 percent of the popular vote. He received the largest share of the popular vote since George H. W. Bush's victory over Michael Dukakis in 1988. Obama's presidency will not be hampered by concerns about the legitimacy of his victory such as those that hung over Bill Clinton, who won only 43 percent of the popular vote in a three-way race in the 1992 election, or George W. Bush, who narrowly lost the popular vote to Al Gore in 2000.

As systematic research has shown, however, members of Congress look mainly to their own constituencies and policy preferences in making decisions on legislation.[45] The president's preferences are distinctly secondary to them, and the level of generalized public support for the president is, therefore, tertiary. Presidents can induce the public to pressure Congress on their behalf mainly if the public already agrees with their policies.[46] George W. Bush's aggressive and largely successful promotion of his 2001 legislative program, after losing the popular vote and winning the Electoral College only through the halting of a disputed recount in Florida by the U.S. Supreme Court, illustrates the limited significance of the size of the president's electoral mandate.[47]

What is far more important is the partisan and ideological make-up of the new Congress, which indicates how many members are predisposed to agree with the president's policy goals. In partisan terms, Obama occupies a commanding position. The Democrats will have a 59–41 majority in the Senate and a 257–178 advantage in the House.[48] These are large majorities by recent standards: the last time one party had as many members in both branches at the same time was 1979–1980. In general, party strength in Congress has been a powerful predictor of a president's legislative success.[49]

But the ideological makeup of Congress offers mixed benefits and costs for Obama, given his objectives. To a great extent, ideology and not party is the real force driving presidential support by Congress.[50] The difference was especially important during the long mid-twentieth century era when the Democrats were internally divided between northern liberals and southern conservatives. "We've only got 150 Democrats," said Lyndon Johnson, dismissing the Democrats' 258–176 advantage in the 88th Congress (1963–1964). "The rest of 'em are Southerners."[51] In fact, the Kennedy-Johnson administration had very limited success passing liberal programs, until the landslide 1964 election gave liberal Democrats a strong majority. Conversely, Ronald Reagan won an ambitious round of tax and budget cuts in 1981, despite nominal Democratic control of the House of Representatives, because enough conservative Democrats joined with the Republican minority to defeat the House Democratic leadership's alternative plans.

But as Figure 4-1 shows, there has been a strong trend since the 1970s toward greater ideological separation between the two parties, in both chambers.[52] This polarization has reflected basic forces in American politics. One is the realignment of the party system that has severely reduced the number of conservative southern Democrats and virtually eliminated liberal northeastern Republicans (remarkably long-lived relics of the Civil War). Another is the increasingly influential role played by ideologically motivated activists

**Figure 4-1** Democratic and Republican Party Mean Ideology Scores, House and Senate, 1879–2008

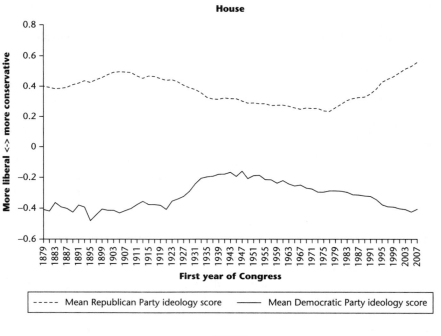

**House**

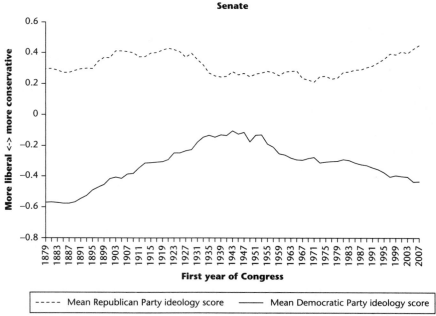

**Senate**

*Source:* Data are party means, based on Poole and Rosenthal's, DW-NOMINATE liberalism-conservatism scores. Available at http://voteview.com.

in the politics of congressional nominations.[53] Recent Congresses have been the most polarized in more than a century—with even the most conservative Democrat in the House more liberal than any Republican.[54]

Most important, there has been a steep decline in the size of the centrist group. To assess this decline, we used Keith Poole and Howard Rosenthal's measures of Congress members' voting records to identify the ideologically most moderate 218 members (a bare majority) of the House in the 100th Congress (1987–1988). We then calculated the difference in ideology scores between the most liberal and most conservative members of that centrist group. Finally, we looked at the data on the 110th Congress (2007–2008) to see how many of its members fell within the same ideological range. The size of the comparable centrist group had declined by 60 percent, to eighty-five members.[55] The new Congress has more Democrats and fewer Republicans than other recent ones, and although we will not know the ideology of the new members until they establish a record of roll-call votes, the parties will undoubtedly remain just about as sharply polarized.[56]

If Obama decides to pursue a conventional liberal Democratic agenda, the partisan and ideological makeup of Congress will work strongly in his favor. Although the Democrats fell one seat short of a "filibuster-proof," sixty-seat partisan majority in the 2008 Senate elections, they have sizable, ideologically cohesive majorities in both chambers. Senate Democrats should be able to negotiate for a few Republican votes to invoke cloture and end filibusters when they need to. As commentators have pointed out, there are two likely candidates for the role of Republican defector on cloture votes: Susan Collins and Olympia Snowe, both of Maine (where Obama won 58 percent of the vote), and the most moderate Republicans in the Senate.[57]

But speculation about whether Collins and Snowe will be willing to split with the Republicans and vote with the Democrats to end filibusters misses the point. If Obama continues to pursue a centrist course, Collins, Snowe, and the few other moderates in both parties will represent his precariously small base of support, with most of the uncertainty concerning his ability to attract sufficient support from strong liberals and conservatives. Congress members on both sides of the ideological spectrum, for example, criticized Obama's $825 billion economic stimulus proposal soon after he took office. Republicans charged that the package called for too much government spending and offered too little in tax cuts, while Democrats complained the plan missed a once-in-a-lifetime opportunity to advance long-term priorities such as environmentally friendly energy development and health care reform.[58] In such cases, Obama may struggle to find votes to end filibusters among conservative Republicans and liberal Democrats at the same time.[59]

In fact, presidents who have appealed to congressional moderates as their base of support have often found hard going. President George H. W. Bush paid a heavy price for promoting a centrist deficit reduction bill in 1990. To make a bipartisan measure possible, Bush agreed to break a 1988 campaign promise and accept tax increases as part of a balanced deficit-reduction package. Administration officials and Democratic congressional leaders worked out a compromise measure. But in a politically embarrassing episode for the administration, the bill was defeated in the House of Representatives by a coalition of conservatives opposed to tax increases and liberals opposed to spending cuts.[60] After running a centrist campaign, similar to Obama's, in 1992, Bill Clinton proposed an ideologically integrated deficit reduction package that included tax increases for corporations and the wealthy, spending cuts for some domestic programs, and redirection of other spending toward long-term domestic investments. He was barely able to win passage of a scaled-back version of his proposal, without a single Republican vote in either chamber, and at substantial political cost to himself and his party in Congress.[61] Clinton's centrist, "New Democratic" leadership largely degenerated into a habit of pandering to public opinion, issue-by-issue—blocking cuts in popular middle-class entitlement programs, but accepting draconian cuts in unpopular welfare programs.[62] Obama's plan for a post-partisan agenda raises the question, "Can the center hold?" when, in Congress, at least, the center has faded to a mere shadow of its former self.

## Issues and the Agenda

Even more fundamental than the skillfulness of the administration or the balance of power in Congress, the president's opportunities for success depend on the nature of the national agenda. This agenda comprises the problems and issues that the president faces, the amount of support for alternative courses of action, and the likelihood of these actions accomplishing their purposes if adopted. The rhetoric of the election campaign can be a significant constraint. Obama has become president in a time of extraordinary threats to the nation's well-being—the danger of economic collapse, potentially calamitous climate change, and war and terrorism—along with other pressing issues. He will have broad scope to define a course of action in some areas. The major uncertainty is whether his administration can identify politically feasible policies that have a good chance to succeed.

### Economic Crisis and Domestic Policy

The *New York Times* fittingly entitled its preview of Obama's domestic policy agenda, "A Towering To-Do List."[63] The state of the economy, officially declared to be in recession shortly after the election, topped the list. Signs of economic weakness had been accumulating for many months, but when the Lehman Brothers investment firm declared bankruptcy in September 2008, credit markets went into free fall. By year's end, unemployment had reached 7.2 percent, stock market averages had fallen 40 percent from their peak a year earlier, bankruptcies and foreclosures were occurring at staggering rates, and the Big Three Detroit automakers had joined state governments and financial firms in petitioning the federal government for relief.

The lame-duck Bush administration and Congress responded with every tool at their disposal, mounting the largest government intervention in the economy since the Great Depression, with no sign of effectively turning the economy around. In the process, the government in Washington was effecting major changes in the country's economic institutions. The financial bailout, enacted in early October, authorized purchases of up to $700 billion in bad assets, with the government acquiring equity in the companies it helped. Policymakers adopted a similar, though considerably smaller program to prevent a collapse of domestic auto manufacturers. Government mortgages were offered to homeowners struggling against foreclosure. Recognizing the implications of these actions, President Bush promised, "The government intervention is not a takeover." Nevertheless, the government was becoming the part-owner of banks, houses, and auto manufacturers, dramatic changes in the structures of American capitalism.[64] At the same time, the Federal Reserve Board repeatedly cut interest rates to spur a resumption of lending until, in December, it set the federal funds rate at 0.00–0.25 percent, as low as it could possibly go.[65]

From one perspective, these harrowing developments represented opportunity for Obama. Erwin Hargrove and Michael Nelson suggest that a system-threatening crisis such as the Great Depression can facilitate the sudden appearance of a "presidency of achievement," featuring "great bursts of legislative activity." The opportunity for achievement in such a crisis, they argue, depends on the president's skill and the availability of ideas that can yield popular and effective policy change.[66]

On the other hand, however, the economic crisis could undermine Obama's presidency. In the current crisis, an anxious public is likely to support whatever strategies the Obama administration chooses to adopt.[67] But the availability of workable ideas is much in doubt. There is no consensus, for instance, on how to restore the health of the financial services industry, which did not respond to the fall bailout, and faced at least $1 trillion in additional losses at the start of 2009. It was broadly conceded that any approach, from federal guarantees against financial losses to nationalization of the banks, came with the potential of failure and might only make matters worse.[68] Similarly, there are no fiscal measures that can pump money into the economy quickly and efficiently.[69] No matter what Obama and Congress try to do about the economy, the country may suffer a deep recession lasting several years and then recover only slowly. It may then prove impossible to remove the clumsy hand of government from the banking, automobile, housing, and perhaps several other industries. Obama could end up a failed president, overseeing a period of national decline.

Even if the recession is mercifully brief, it will likely preclude serious attention to other domestic issues for at least a number of months. Among Obama's most frequent campaign promises were the reform of the nation's health care system and an investment of $150 billion in clean energy technologies that will help control climate change.[70] Despite concerted prodding by the moderator in each of the three presidential debates, Obama refused to say that he would put any of his issues on the back burner.[71] Shortly after the election, Obama indicated that he would postpone health care reform, but Sen. Edward M. (Ted) Kennedy unveiled his own plan and called for immediate action.[72] Obama's lack of candor in the campaign, unexceptionable from the standpoint of election strategy, will make it harder to say *no* to impatient constituencies.

## International Issues and the Presidency

The international "to-do list" for the new president is also daunting, especially when it comes to dealing with the wars in Iraq and Afghanistan. During the campaign, Obama distinguished himself from McCain by proposing a sixteen-month timetable for withdrawing U.S. troops from Iraq, a position popular with Democratic constituencies.[73] His national security appointments, however, particularly Secretary Gates and General Jones, point toward a more cautious approach. Such an approach is bound to generate pressure from liberal Democrats to withdraw more quickly.[74] Obama also advocated increasing the U.S. military presence in Afghanistan, where the initial success of the U.S. invasion has given way to increasing disorder. In his acceptance speech to the Democratic National Convention, he drew the linkage between the two wars.

> When John McCain said we could just "muddle through" in Afghanistan, I argued for more resources and more troops to finish the fight against the terrorists who actually attacked us on 9/11, and made clear that we must take out Osama bin Laden and his lieutenants if we have them in our sights. . . . I will end this war in Iraq responsibly, and finish the fight against al-Qaida and the Taliban in Afghanistan.

But an increased commitment in Afghanistan would entail great risk. As Paul R. Pillar, a former national intelligence officer with the CIA, said, "We're trying to fend off security challenges to the government of Afghanistan from a collection of loosely-allied groups, chiefly of the Islamic militant variety. . . . [W]e have assumed the place of the Soviets."[75] In much the same way that the Iraq War destroyed the Bush presidency, two wars could destroy the Obama presidency.

On trade policy, the Obama administration will face heavy pressure from labor unions and congressional Democrats to further compromise the nation's openness to international trade. Economists agree that trade restrictions, in general and over the long run, harm consumers, slow economic growth, and reduce employment—all considerations that Obama, formerly a professor at the famously free market–oriented University of Chicago Law School, undoubtedly understands.[76] But free trade has become a bogeyman of Democratic constituencies, and Obama was forced to evince support for their objectives during the primaries. Criticizing the operation of the 1993 North American Free Trade Agreement (NAFTA) with Canada and Mexico, he pledged to renegotiate the agreement "and figure out how we can make this work for all people."[77] After the election, a National Association of Manufacturers spokesperson seemed certain that the new president would back away from his antitrade posture: "He parsed his answers [in the primary debates] in a way that suggests he understands the importance of global trade."[78] At a minimum, however, trade joins health care, energy, climate change, the two wars, and a number of other issues on which Obama may come under attack from congressional Democrats, liberal activists, and other Democratic constituencies. If that occurs, the Republicans will not rush to replace the missing political support.

Finally, and crucially for the long-term integrity of the constitutional system, Obama will need to address the role and authority of the presidency. Encouraged by Vice President Dick Cheney, Bush set aside long-established constitutional procedures to assert novel, unilateral powers in four areas: denying writs of habeas corpus to "enemy combatants," suspending the Geneva Conventions and allowing torture of terrorism suspects, conducting warrantless surveillance of U.S. citizens' phone records, and issuing more than one thousand signing statements declaring his intention not to enforce parts of certain laws.[79] Although Bush initially cited the urgency of acting in the immediate aftermath of the 9/11 attacks, he continued to exercise these dubious powers for the remainder of his term, appealing to a recently invented constitutional theory of "the unitary Executive."[80] For the most part, the Republican Congress declined to defend the constitutional prerogatives of the institution, and instead offered Bush its implicit consent.

Obama and the Democrats severely criticized the Bush administration for upsetting the constitutional balance of power. But the issues may look different to Obama from the perspective of the White House—much as they did when the formerly strict constructionist President Thomas Jefferson purchased the Louisiana Territory and imposed an embargo on goods from Great Britain. In view of his former employment as a professor of constitutional law, Obama may be eager to restore more traditional doctrines. But he also may find it convenient to retain some or all of the questionable authority, and the Democratic congressional majority may be inclined to defer to a Democratic president, much as the Republicans were willing to defer to Bush.[81] Presidents seldom yield power voluntarily, nor do Congresses controlled by their party often seize it from them.

## Conclusion

In the 1970s, Jimmy Carter promised the country "a government as good as its people."[82] In Barack Obama and his appointees, the country appears to have acquired a presidential administration that, however it compares with the people, is better than the electoral process that produced it. The Obama administration promises to be more moderate, experienced, and substantively competent than that process systematically selects for—or even prefers.

Although other recent presidents have also campaigned as moderates, including George W. Bush in 2000, presidential elections and especially the nomination process have offered increasingly important advantages to strongly liberal or conservative candidates, as opposed to centrists. Under the tutelage of political strategist Karl Rove, Bush abandoned the moderate strategy in his 2004 reelection campaign. In 2008, McCain, who had been a prominent centrist on some issues as a senator, played to the Republican base by taking consistently conservative positions on issues and choosing Sarah Palin as his running mate. For the most part, Obama's nomination appeared to fit the trend toward candidates with strong ideological positions. He was able to compete effectively for the Democratic nomination largely because his voting record in the Senate and his campaign positions—on Iraq, taxes, health care, and other issues—easily passed muster with liberals. Indeed, the Republicans accused him—on reasonable grounds, although incorrectly—of being the most liberal member of the Senate, and in a more desperate tactic even called him a "socialist."[83] Liberals were not put off by Obama's promise to overcome partisan conflict. (They may have dismissed it as campaign puffery.) In any case, when Obama demonstrated by his appointments to the White House staff, the cabinet, and other top positions that he was serious about governing from the center, most observers were surprised.[84]

By and large, the electorate assigns only modest value, if any, to a presidential candidate's having relevant experience. Candidates can even make a virtue of their lack of experience by calling themselves "outsiders"—a supposed credential that one can hardly imagine being cited for professional or managerial occupations outside of politics. The voters' tolerance for novices worked to Obama's advantage: he had quite limited experience and, in particular, had a good deal less of it than either Clinton or McCain. Yet, while the voters largely overlooked that deficiency, Obama himself evidently did not. Having given virtually no hint of such intentions during the campaign, he installed in senior positions numerous individuals who had served in the Clinton administration, along with a few from the Bush and Reagan administrations. If Obama invests trust and authority in these appointees, rather than bypassing them, his administration will have the benefit of an extraordinary amount of pertinent experience.

Finally, the generally superficial discussion of issues in the campaign creates no compelling requirement for a candidate to know or care a great deal about substantive matters of government or policy. Like other recent candidates, for example, both Obama and McCain ran on budget plans that did not add up, promising more spending, lower taxes, and smaller deficits than comported with simple arithmetic. Yet Obama deviated from the practice of most presidential candidates, showing both substantive concern and sophistication about government, by conducting extensive early planning for the transition. His pre-election transition planning process was so far from being required for electoral success that he felt compelled to keep it secret. During the transition, his major appointments were skewed sharply toward individuals with strong substantive expertise and primary orientations toward policy rather than politics and public relations. Such appointees will powerfully resist any impulse within the White House to sacrifice policy goals to political expediency.

Rather than being consciously chosen by the electorate or otherwise favored by the electoral process, in other words, a moderate, experienced, and substantively competent presidential administration has taken over Washington as if by stealth. Obama will encounter resistance on some issues as he attempts to push a centrist policy agenda through a Congress that has virtually no center. If he encounters too much resistance from liberal Democrats, and picks up too little compensating support from Republicans, he may eventually abandon the attempt. He would then have no choice but to govern largely as a conventional partisan Democrat.

In dealing with the most threatening problems facing the country—the economic crisis and the perilous issues of war and national security—Obama will have a great deal of leeway. The crucial challenge of the Obama presidency, therefore, will not be to get his proposals adopted and implemented but rather, in circumstances of enormous difficulty, to find workable strategies to propose.

# Notes

1. "'We Are Better than These Last Eight Years': Prepared Remarks of Barack Obama to the Democratic National Convention," MSNBC, August 28, 2008, www.msnbc.msn.com/id/26446638.
2. "Obama Victory Sparks Celebration, Praise around Globe," CBC News, November 5, 2008, www.cbc.ca/world/usvotes/story/2008/11/05/obama-reaction.html.
3. Elizabeth Drew, "The Truth about Obama," *New York Review of Books,* December 18, 2008, www.nybooks.com/articles/22170.
4. "Poll Finds Faith in Obama, Mixed with Patience," *New York Times,* January 18, 2009, A1; *New York Times*/CBS News Poll, January 11–15, 2009, http://graphics8 .nytimes.com/packages/pdf/politics/20090118_poll_results.pdf; see also *Los Angeles Times*/Bloomberg press release, "Transition to the Obama Presidency: Good Will toward President-Elect Barack Obama," National Political and Economic Survey, December 9, 2008.
5. Fred I. Greenstein, *The Presidential Difference: Leadership Style from FDR to George W. Bush* (Princeton, N.J.: Princeton University Press, 2004); and Paul J. Quirk, "Presidential Competence," in *The Presidency and the Political System,* 8th ed., ed. Michael Nelson (Washington, D.C.: CQ Press, 2006), 136–169.
6. Drew, "Truth about Obama."
7. See, in particular, Greenstein, *Presidential Difference,* chaps. 1, 14; and Greenstein, *Inventing the Job of President: The Presidential Difference from George Washington to Andrew Jackson* (Princeton, N.J.: Princeton University Press, forthcoming 2009). We also draw on Quirk, "Presidential Competence."
8. Quirk, "Presidential Competence."
9. The chief of staff was Mack McLarty. See Paul J. Quirk and Joseph Hinchcliffe, "Domestic Policy: The Trials of a Centrist Democrat," in *The Clinton Presidency: First Appraisals,* eds. Colin Campbell and Bert A. Rockman (Chatham, N.J.: Chatham House, 1996), 284–285.
10. The Shadow Cabinet is a group of minority party members with special responsibility to play a leadership role for their party in parliamentary debate.
11. Stephen Hess, *The Presidential Campaign: An Essay* (Washington, D.C.: Brookings Institution, 1988).
12. Note that they are sometimes employed by policymakers, including presidents, mostly to work on issues of public support.

13. Paul J. Quirk and Sean Matheson, "The Presidency: Elections and Presidential Governance," in *The Elections of 1996,* ed. Michael Nelson (Washington, D.C.: CQ Press, 1997), 127–128; and Colin Campbell, "Managing the Presidency or the President? Raising Some Issues Concerning the Bush II Administration's Approach to Executive Leadership," in *The George W. Bush Presidency: Appraisals and Prospects,* eds. Colin Campbell and Bert A. Rockman (Washington, D.C.: CQ Press, 2004), 1–2.
14. Capsulized profiles of the candidates are available at http://projects.washingtonpost.com/2008-presidential-candidates.
15. Peter Whoriskey, "Edwards Exacts Pledge as He Leaves," *Washington Post,* January 31, 2008, A11.
16. We suspect that the Clinton campaign doubted that the public would grasp the significance of a role as behind-the-scenes adviser, or did not want to remind voters of the health care fiasco or possibly of the Monica Lewinsky scandal.
17. Anne E. Kornblut and Perry Bacon Jr., "Obama, Clinton in Key Face-Off," *Washington Post,* March 4, 2008, A1.
18. Peter Nicholas, "Crisscrossing Iowa, Clinton and Obama Argue Experience," *Los Angeles Times,* November 20, 2007, A16.
19. Stuart Taylor Jr., "Cheering Obama, with Doubts," *National Journal,* January 12, 2008, 10.
20. Charlie Cook, "The Chemistry Experiment," *National Journal,* April 19, 2008, 46.
21. William Schneider, "Clinton's Many Messages Fall Flat," *National Journal,* March 1, 2008, 38.
22. Joel Achenbach, "In a Heated Race, Obama's Cool Won the Day," *Washington Post,* November 6, 2008, A47.
23. Matthew E. Berger, "The Big Fizzle," *National Journal,* February 2, 2008, 24.
24. David Brooks, "Tested over Time," *New York Times,* March 28, 2008, www.nytimes.com/2008/03/28/opinion/28brooks.html?_r=1.
25. "No Surrender," *Economist,* August 30, 2008, 27–29.
26. David Brooks, "The Real McCain," *New York Times,* February 26, 2008, www.nytimes.com/2008/02/26/opinion/26brooks.html; and Jonathan Rauch, "For the GOP, a Tonic Named McCain," *National Journal,* February 16, 2008, 10.
27. David Brooks, "Thinking about McCain," *New York Times,* September 25, 2008, A25.
28. Jonathan Rauch, "The 20 Percent Solution," *National Journal,* May 10, 2008, 19; "The Man with Half a Plan," *Economist,* April 19, 2008, 40–42; and Brooks, "Thinking about McCain."
29. "Examining the Candidates," *Economist,* October 4, 2008, 29–30.
30. Joe Neel, "McCain Cancer-Free and Healthy, Records Show," National Public Radio, May 23, 2008, www.npr.org/templates/story/story.php?storyId=90781894.
31. Kirk Victor, "The Right Stuff," *National Journal,* February 9, 2008, 12.
32. "The Candidates Intervene," *Economist,* September 27, 2008, 37–38.
33. Michael D. Shear, "For McCain, Days of Chaos, Improvisation and Drama," *Washington Post,* September 28, 2008, A10.
34. "The Maverick and the Hockey Mom," *Economist,* September 6, 2008, 33–34; Maureen Dowd, "Life of Her Party," *New York Times,* September 2, 2008, A25; and Julian E. Barnes, "An Important Job, but Focused on Alaska Policy," *Los Angeles Times,* September 6, 2008, A13.
35. "Maverick and the Hockey Mom."
36. Michael Dobbs, "Clinton Appears Weary of Taking 'Sniper Fire,'" *Washington Post,* March 26, 2008, A8. It was inconceivable that Clinton was intentionally lying, if only because there would have been no chance of getting away with such a lie.
37. Kirk Victor, "Can Obama Take a Punch?" *National Journal,* April 26, 2008, 9.

38. Mark Halperin, "McCain: Fundamentals of Economy ARE Strong," Time.com, September 15, 2008, http://thepage.time.com/2008/09/15/mccain-fundamentals-of-economy-are-strong.

39. Ronald Brownstein, "Not in Kansas Anymore," *National Journal*, April 19, 2008, 37; and "A Bitter Pill," *Economist*, April 19, 2008, 44.

40. "Campaign 2008," *Polling Report*, www.pollingreport.com/wh08.htm. In terms of qualifications to deal with specific issue areas, CNN/Opinion Research found the public gave the edge to McCain on terrorism and the Iraq War, and to Obama on energy, health care, and all economy-related issues.

41. James P. Pfiffner, *The Strategic Presidency: Hitting the Ground Running* (Lawrence: University Press of Kansas, 1996).

42. "Off to Work They Go," *Economist*, November 29, 2008, 31–32.

43. Ibid.

44. Peter Baker, "Liberals Wondering When Obama's Team Will Reflect Them," *New York Times*, December 9, 2008, A25.

45. Jon R. Bond and Richard Fleisher, *The President in the Legislative Arena* (Chicago: University of Chicago Press, 1990); George C. Edwards III, *At the Margins: Presidential Leadership of Congress* (New Haven, Conn.: Yale University Press, 1989); and Brandice Canes-Wrone, *Who Leads Whom? Presidents, Policy, and the Public* (Chicago: University of Chicago Press, 2006).

46. Canes-Wrone, *Who Leads Whom?* and George C. Edwards, *On Deaf Ears: The Limits of the Bully Pulpit* (New Haven, Conn.: Yale University Press, 2003).

47. Jacob S. Hacker and Paul S. Pierson, *Off-Center: The Republican Revolution and the Erosion of American Democracy* (New Haven, Conn.: Yale University Press, 2006).

48. The totals count independents with the party they caucus with—including, most importantly, two independent senators who caucus with the Democrats.

49. Andrew Rudalevige, "The Executive Branch and the Legislative Branch," in *The Executive Branch*, eds. Joel D. Aberbach and Mark A. Peterson (Oxford, UK: Oxford University Press, 2005), 433. Rudalevige also cites Paul C. Light, *The President's Agenda*, 3rd ed. (Baltimore: Johns Hopkins University Press, 1999), 281; Edwards, *At the Margins*, 172–173; Bond and Fleisher, *President in the Legislative Arena*, chap. 4; Steven A. Shull and Thomas C. Shaw, *Explaining Congressional-Presidential Relations: A Multiple Perspective Approach* (Albany: State University of New York Press, 1999), 84ff.; and George C. Edwards III and Andrew Barrett, "Presidential Agenda Setting in Congress," in *Polarized Politics: Congress and the President in a Partisan Era*, eds. Jon R. Bond and Richard Fleisher (Washington, D.C.: CQ Press, 2000), 128.

50. Rudalevige, "Executive Branch," 434. Rudalevige also cites Bond and Fleisher, *President in the Legislative Arena*, 87; Richard Fleisher and Jon R. Bond, "Partisanship and the President's Quest for Votes on the Floor of Congress," in *Polarized Politics*, 154–185.

51. *Taking Charge: The Johnson White House Tapes, 1963–1964*, Michael Beschloss, ed. (New York: Simon & Schuster, 1997), 84. Quoted in Rudalevige, "Executive Branch," 434.

52. Data available at Web site: ftp://voteview.com/junkord/hmeans3.txt; and ftp://voteview.com/junkord/smeans3.txt (see Figure 4-1 in text).

53. Richard Fleisher and Jon R. Bond, "The Shrinking Middle in the U.S. Congress," *British Journal of Political Science* 34, no. 3 (July 2004): 429–451.

54. Paul J. Quirk, "The Legislative Branch: Assessing the Partisan Congress," in *A Republic Divided*, Annenberg Democracy Project (Oxford, UK: Oxford University Press, 2007), 121–156.

55. Authors' calculations, based on Poole and Rosenthal's data set, "Common Space DW-NOMINATE Scores 1st to 110th Congresses," file HL010010C21_PRES.xls, accessed at www.voteview.edu. These ideology scores are designed to permit valid

comparisons over fairly lengthy periods of time. For details on the measurement, see Keith T. Poole, *Spatial Models of Parliamentary Voting* (New York: Cambridge University Press, 2005); Keith T. Poole and Howard L. Rosenthal, *Congress: A Political-Economic History of Roll-Call Voting* (New York: Oxford University Press, 1997).

56. The states and districts that see turnover in party control of congressional seats are among those more likely to send moderate members of either party. If relative moderate Republicans lose their seats to relatively moderate Democrats, there is likely to be little effect on the overall level of polarization.

57. Nate Silver, "Who Are the Swing Senators?" www.fivethirtyeight.com; and www.fivethirtyeight.com/2008/12/who-are-swing-senators.html.

58. Alec MacGillis, "Democrats Among Stimulus Skeptics," *Washington Post*, January 28, 2009, A1.

59. Spatial theories of Congress do not contemplate filibusters by combinations of liberals and conservatives (see Krehbiel, *Pivotal Politics: A Theory of U.S. Lawmaking* [Chicago: University of Chicago Press, 1998]). But such filibusters will be quite likely during the Obama administration. Considering the conservative status quo in most areas of policy, after the Bush administration, strong conservatives may oppose the direction of policy changes that Obama proposes; strong liberals may oppose the same changes as insufficient, attempting to hold out for larger ones.

60. Paul J. Quirk, "Domestic Policy: Divided Government and Cooperative Presidential Leadership," in *The Bush Presidency: First Appraisals,* eds. Colin Campbell and Bert A. Rockman (Chatham, N.J.: Chatham House, 1991), 69–92; Barbara Sinclair, "Governing Unheroically (and Sometimes Unappetizingly): Bush and the 101st Congress," in *Bush Presidency,* 155–189; Howard E. Shuman, *Politics and the Budget: The Struggle between the President and Congress,* 3rd ed. (Englewood Cliffs, N.J.: Prentice-Hall, 1992), chap. 10; and Daniel P. Franklin, *Making Ends Meet: Congressional Budgeting in the Age of Deficits* (Washington, D.C.: CQ Press, 1993), chaps. 3 and 4.

61. Barbara Sinclair, "Trying to Govern Positively in a Negative Era: Clinton and the 103rd Congress," in *The Clinton Presidency,* eds. Campbell and Rockman, 102–107; I. W. Morgan, *Deficit Government: Taxing and Spending in Modern America* (Chicago: Ivan R. Dee, 1995), 189–191; and George Hager and Eric Pianin, *Mirage: Why Neither Democrats nor Republicans Can Balance the Budget, End the Deficit, and Satisfy the Public* (New York: Times Books, 1997), 23.

62. Paul J. Quirk and William Cunion, "Clinton's Domestic Policy: The Lessons of a 'New Democrat,'" in *The Clinton Legacy,* eds. Colin Campbell and Bert A. Rockman (New York: Chatham House, 2000), 205–213; R. Kent Weaver, *Ending Welfare as We Know It* (Washington, D.C.: Brookings Institution, 2000).

63. "A Towering To-Do List," *New York Times,* November 6, 2008, B1, 5.

64. Lori Montgomery and Dan Eggen, "Spending Surge Pushing Deficit toward $1 Trillion," *Washington Post,* October 18, 2008, A1; and Dan Eggen, "Bush Defends Rescue Plan," *Washington Post,* October 18, 2008, A8.

65. Neil Irwin, "Fed Cuts Key Rate to Record Low," *Washington Post,* December 17, 2008, A1.

66. Erwin C. Hargrove and Michael Nelson, *Presidents, Politics, and Policy* (Baltimore: Johns Hopkins University Press, 1984), 67–68, 75–78.

67. "Business Issues in the News," *Polling Report,* www.pollingreport.com/business.htm; "Economic Outlook, Personal Finances, Consumer Behavior," *Polling Report,* www.pollingreport.com/consumer2.htm; and Michael A. Fletcher and Jon Cohen, "New Poll Shows 63% Are Already Hurt by Downturn," *Washington Post,* December 17, 2008, A7.

68. David Cho, "Treasury Weighs Hard Choices to Save Banks," *Washington Post,* January 28, 2009, A1.

69. David Leonhardt, "A Stimulus With Merit, And Misses," *New York Times*, January 28, 2009, B1; MacGillis, "Democrats Among Stimulus Skeptics."

70. "A Towering To-Do List."

71. "Debate Transcript: The Third McCain-Obama Presidential Debate," Commission on Presidential Debates, www.debates.org/pages/trans2008d.html.

72. Jeffrey Young, "Baucus-Kennedy Healthcare Powwow Set," *The Hill*, November 17, 2008, http://thehill.com/leading-the-news/baucus-kennedy-healthcare-powwow-set-for-tuesday-2008-11-17.html.

73. "The War for the White House," *Economist*, June 14, 2008, 34.

74. One open question is whether, after the 2007 "surge" in American troop presence, Iraq has been stabilized or is still a powder keg, and whether either outcome would be helped or hindered by American withdrawal. See Peter Galbraith, *Unintended Consequences: How War in Iraq Strengthened America's Enemies* (New York: Simon and Schuster, 2008), for an argument that the "surge" merely delayed the inevitable collapse of the Iraqi government beyond the end of the Bush administration.

75. Greg Miller, "Behind Afghanistan's Rising Attacks, 3 Men," *Los Angeles Times*, October 1, 2008, A1.

76. The efficacy of free-trade is widely argued among economists. See Lael Brainard and Robert Litan, "A Global Economic Agenda for the United States," in *Agenda for the Nation*, eds. Henry J. Aaron, James M. Lindsay, and Pietro S. Nivola (Washington, D.C.: Brookings Institution, 2003), 345–357.

77. Nina Easton, "Obama: NAFTA Not So Bad after All," *Fortune*, June 18, 2008, http://money.cnn.com/2008/06/18/magazines/fortune/easton_obama.fortune/index.htm.

78. "A Towering To-Do List," 5; see also "It's the Economy Again, Stupid."

79. James P. Pfiffner, *Power Play: The Bush Presidency and the Constitution* (Washington, D.C.: Brookings Institution, 2008).

80. John Yoo, *The Powers of War and Peace: The Constitution and Foreign Affairs after 9/11* (Chicago: University of Chicago Press, 2005); Sidney M. Milkis and Michael Nelson, *The American Presidency: Origins and Development, 1776–2007*, 5th ed. (Washington: CQ Press, 2008), chap. 15.

81. Joel D. Aberbach, Mark A. Peterson, and Paul J. Quirk, "The Contemporary Presidency: Who Wants Presidential Supremacy? Findings from the Institutions of American Democracy Project," *Presidential Studies Quarterly* 37, no. 3 (September 2007): 515–530.

82. Jimmy Carter, *A Government as Good as Its People* (New York: Simon and Schuster, 1977).

83. Obama was indeed the most liberal senator in 2007 according to ratings by *National Journal* that were based on a fairly small number of key votes, many of which Obama had missed. Brian Friel, Richard E. Cohen, and Kirk Victor, "Obama: Most Liberal Senator in 2007," nationaljournal.com, January 31, 2008, http://nj.nationaljournal.com/voteratings. In the comprehensive analysis of all roll calls by Poole and Rosenthal, Obama was more liberal than about 80 percent of the Democratic senators (Royce Carroll, Jeff Lewis, James Lo, Nolan McCarty, Keith Poole, and Howard Rosenthal, "Who Is More Liberal, Senator Obama or Senator Clinton?" voteview.com, April 18, 2008, http://voteview.ucsd.edu/Clinton_and_Obama.htm).

84. David Brooks, "The Insider's Crusade," *New York Times*, November 21, 2008, A35; David Corn, "This Wasn't Quite the Change We Pictured," *Washington Post*, December 7, 2008, B1.

# 5

# Congress:
# The Second Democratic Wave

Gary C. Jacobson

The Democrats' victory in the 2008 House and Senate elections was at least as impressive as Barack Obama's victory in the presidential race, and it was considerably less uncertain as election day approached. The results are summarized in Table 5-1. Democrats won twenty-one additional seats in the House, and eight in the Senate. These victories came on top of major Democratic gains in 2006; in the elections held during Bush's second term, the Democrats added a total of fifty-five House seats and fourteen Senate seats, giving them majorities in the 111th Congress of 257 to 178 in the House and 59 to 41 in the Senate. The two elections effectively reversed the verdict of 1994, leaving the partisan balance in Congress as solidly Democratic as it was before that year's Republican takeover.

There is no mystery about the Democrats' success in 2008. Aggregate congressional election results always reflect, among other things, the public's assessment of the president's performance and the state of the national economy—both of which are also closely related to one another. The president's party's fortunes rise or fall with his public standing and with the performance of the economy. Any election is more than a simple referendum, of course, but these fundamentals are always important, and when they hugely favor one party over the other, they are decisive. The same basic conditions also shape presidential elections, as they did in 2008. But the idiosyncrasies associated with the presidential candidates, such as John McCain's image as a maverick and Barack Obama's race and thin political résumé, render their effect less certain than in congressional elections.

## The Bush Legacy in 2008

The public's disenchantment with the Bush administration was without question the main source of the strongly pro-Democratic congressional tide in 2008, as it had been in 2006.[1] In the month after the attacks of September 11, 2001, Americans' views of Bush's performance were overwhelmingly positive, and he received the highest approval ratings of any president since polling began in the 1930s. Seven years later, Bush was suffering nearly the lowest approval ratings (and, unambiguously, the highest disapproval ratings) ever recorded for any president. As Figure 5-1 shows, Bush's approval ratings,

**Table 5-1**  Membership Changes in the House and Senate in the 2008 Elections

|  | Republicans | Democrats | Independents |
|---|---|---|---|
| *House of Representatives* | | | |
| At the time of the 2008 election | 199 | 236 | |
| Elected in 2008 | 178 | 257 | |
|    Incumbents reelected | 156 | 224 | |
|    Incumbents defeated | 14 | 5 | |
|    Open seats retained | 17 | 7 | |
|    Open seats lost | 12 | 0 | |
| *Senate* | | | |
| At the time of the 2008 election | 49 | 49 | 2* |
| After the 2008 election | 41** | 57 | 2* |
|    Incumbents reelected | 13 | 12 | |
|    Incumbents defeated | 5 | 0 | |
|    Open seats retained | 2 | | |
|    Open seats lost | 3 | | |

*Source:* Compiled by the author.

*The two independents caucus with the Democrats.

**These and other summary Senate results reported in this chapter will change by one seat in the Republicans' favor if Norm Coleman's pending court challenge to Al Franken's narrow victory succeeds in reversing the Minnesota results.

a little above 50 percent at the time of his second inauguration in January 2005, sank into negative territory and remained there for his entire second term. They were about 37 percent at the time of the 2006 midterm election, fell to the low 30s in 2007, and finally dropped to the low 20s just before the 2008 elections.

The reasons for Bush's declining approval ratings changed during the course of his second term. His administration's mishandling of the aftermath of Hurricane Katrina in September 2005 was an early factor, but popular disaffection with the Iraq War was Bush's main problem through 2007.[2] By the time the "surge"—the additional troops Bush ordered to Iraq to try to reverse the deteriorating situation there—succeeded by the only metric most Americans care about, a dramatic decline in American casualties, the shaky economy had eclipsed Iraq as the nation's dominant issue. A steep decline in housing prices began in late 2006. Falling prices and rising interest rates led to foreclosures that left many mortgages worthless, wiping out financial institutions that had invested heavily in mortgage-backed bonds and leading credit markets to freeze up. By summer 2008, the effects had spilled over into the stock market, driving share prices down more than 30 percent for the year and sharply reducing the wealth and retirement funds of millions of Americans. By election day, economists were virtually unanimous in predicting a deep recession, with massive job losses, perhaps the worst since the Great Depression of the 1930s. Not surprisingly, the public's view of the economy turned decisively negative (see Figure 5-2).

The Bush administration responded to the linked economic crises with massive bailouts and a partial government takeover of some financial institutions.

**Figure 5-1**   Approval of George W. Bush's Job Performance, 2001–2008

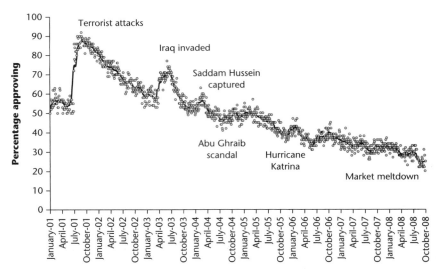

*Source:* 1,004 national polls taken by 14 major media polling organizations, reported at www.pollingreport.com.

**Figure 5-2**   Public's Net Rating of the Economy, 2001–2008

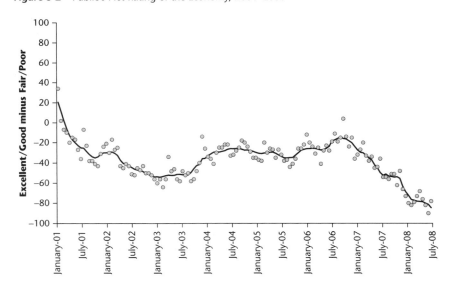

*Source:* "Consumer Views of the Economy," Gallup Polls, available online at www.gallup.com/poll/1609/Consumer-Views-Economy.aspx.

But these responses failed to reassure the public, and whatever benefit Bush might have gotten from success of the surge in Iraq was more than offset by negative views of his economic performance. Approval of Bush's handling of the

**Figure 5-3**    Public Dissatisfaction with United States, 2001–2008

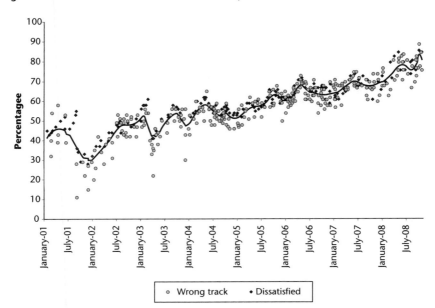

*Source:* "Direction of the Country: Right Track/Wrong Track," PollingReport.com (Gallup poll, November 13–16, 2008), available online at www.pollingreport.com/right.htm.

Iraq War actually rose between early 2007 and the last half of 2008—on average, from 28 percent to 34 percent—while the average approval of his handling of the economy fell steeply from 42 percent to 21 percent.[3]

Growing public disenchantment with Bush and the economy fed an increasing sense of dissatisfaction among voters with the overall direction of the country. As Figure 5-3 shows, the proportion of Americans saying they were dissatisfied or that the country was moving in the wrong direction grew steeply during Bush's second term, and by the beginning of 2008 exceeded 70 percent. Just when it seemed the numbers could not get any worse, the economy took its sharp downward plunge, pushing dissatisfaction rates as high as 90 percent in some October polls. The crisis cost Bush another seven or so percentage points in his approval rating, driven largely by a decline in support among Republicans. His numbers among Democrats and independents were already so low that they could not drop much further.

## Damage to the Republican Party

The downward trends in public opinion during Bush's second term contributed to the Democrats' success in the 2008 congressional elections in three distinct, mutually reinforcing ways. First, Bush's unpopularity tarnished the Republican Party's image and sapped its popular appeal. As approval of

**Figure 5-4**   Republican Share of Major Party Identifiers, 1990–2008 (Annual Averages)

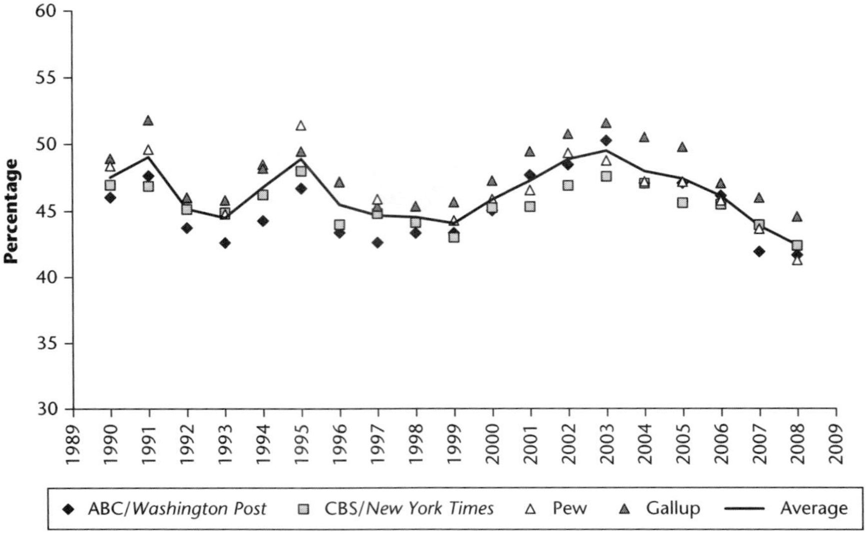

Bush's performance declined, so did the public's ratings of the Republican Party; specifically, every ten-point drop in approval of Bush reduced the party's favorable or positive rating by about five points.[4] During Bush's first term, the public rated the parties about equally; by 2008, Democrats enjoyed an average fifteen-point favorability advantage, 55 percent to 40 percent.[5]

More important, the distribution of self-identified partisans, which was nearly even in 2003 and 2004, had by 2008 shifted decisively in the Democrats' favor. This is clear from the annual averages among partisan respondents in four major national polls taken over the past two decades (Figure 5-4). The polls show slightly different results but identical trends: on average, the Democrats' advantage in party identification went from 51–49 in 2003 to 59–41 in 2008, the widest gap in two decades.[6] The Democrats' advantage grew most among younger voters. People who entered the electorate during the Bush years are currently the most Democratic of any age cohort.[7] In 2008 this shift in support for the two parties contributed crucially to both the congressional and presidential election results. The exit polls indicated that party line voting in House elections was nearly as high in 2008 as it was in 2004.[8]

## Strategic Politicians in 2008

Public dissatisfaction with the Bush administration and, consequently, the Republican Party continued to grow even after the Republican losses in 2006, laying the groundwork for further House and Senate losses in 2008. The prevalence of these sentiments in 2007, along with the Republicans' loss of control of Congress, became the second important source of the pro-Democratic tide in 2008 because it shaped potential candidates' always consequential decisions about whether to run for office in that year's elections. The Democrats' takeover of the House and Senate in 2006 immediately made service in Congress less satisfying to Republicans. Just as the Republican takeover of Congress in 1994 elections had prompted a larger than usual Democratic exodus from Congress in 1996, the insults of minority status made retirement more attractive to Republicans in 2008. The desire to "spend more time with the family" was reinforced by a recognition that the conditions that had made 2006 such a tough year for Republicans had only deteriorated, meaning that a quick recapture of majority status was not in the cards. The loss of three additional Republican seats in special elections held in early 2008—including the seat vacated by former Speaker Dennis Hastert of Illinois—was indicative of how bad conditions were for the GOP. As a result, five Republican senators and twenty-six Republican representatives decided not to seek reelection. Of the latter, only three left to pursue higher office (none succeeded); the remaining twenty-three retired from electoral politics.

Among Democrats, in contrast, not a single senator and only six House members retired, and three of the six left to run for the Senate (two succeeded). After primary defeats and a death further reduced the ranks of reelection-seeking incumbents, Republicans were left defending twenty-nine open House seats to the Democrats' seven, and five open Senate seats to the Democrats' none. By anticipating a bad year for their party, departing Republican incumbents helped to bring it about, for it is much easier to take an open seat from a party than to defeat an incumbent. As Table 5-1 shows, Democrats won twelve of the twenty-nine open Republican seats (41 percent) but only fourteen of 170 (8 percent) of the House seats defended by Republican incumbents. They also picked up three of the five open Senate seats (60 percent) compared to five of the eighteen (28 percent) defended by Republican incumbents. The imbalance of open seats between the parties thus both reflected and contributed to the Republicans' woes.

The same conditions that inspired Republican incumbents to retire helped Democrats to attract capable candidates and finance their campaigns. This was essential to their success. Elections are still fought at the local level, and the quality of the candidates and the vitality of their campaigns remain crucial determinants of success or failure. Favorable national conditions do not automatically deliver victories to the favored party; national issues, no matter how potent, need effective local sponsors to have their full electoral effect. Voters rarely expel an incumbent unless they regard the challenger as qualified, and even taking an open seat from the rival party usually requires a top-tier candidate and a full-scale campaign. Thus the effects of national political forces are mediated by the strategic decision of potential candidates whether to run and by the people who control campaign resources whether to donate. The effects of a national partisan tide will be muted if the party's leaders and activists do not make the strategic investments necessary to exploit it.[9]

Leading up to 2008, Democratic leaders, potential candidates, and associated activists recognized early that conditions were as conducive to success as they had been in 2006 and acted accordingly. The Democrats fielded high-quality candidates for most of the potentially vulnerable Republican seats and generously funded the great majority of their campaigns. One simple measure of candidate quality is previous electoral success. Career politicians tend to be selective about running, entering a race when the prospects of winning are promising and avoiding long-shot races for fear of ending or damaging a career. They also are typically more effective candidates when they do run. Current or former Democratic officeholders competed for seventeen of the twenty-nine open Republican House seats and all seven of the open Democratic House seats. Eleven of the seventeen experienced Democratic candidates for open Republican seats were successful, compared to only one of the twelve inexperienced Democrats. Because all seven of the experienced Democrats running for Democratic open seats also won, the overall success rate of experienced Democratic candidates for open seats was 75 percent. Twelve of the seventeen Republicans who managed to retain Republican open seats—all but two in overwhelmingly Republican districts—also had previously held elective public office.

## The Balance of Campaign Resources

Democrats also fielded a disproportionate share of experienced challengers against potentially vulnerable Republican incumbents in 2008. Twenty-six percent of the Republican House incumbents who won with less than 55 percent of the major party vote in 2006 faced experienced Democrats in 2008, compared with 12 percent of the Republicans in safer seats. But the most important evidence of strategic investment in Democratic challenges appears in the campaign finance data. Party fund raising in 2008 reflected the prevailing pro-Democratic national political conditions as well as the eagerness of ordinary Democrats—among whom Bush's approval ratings reached an astonishing record low of 3 percent in several pre-election Gallup polls—to effect wholesale national regime change. The same sentiment, of course, fueled Obama's prodigious fund raising.

Preliminary data indicate that the Democratic Congressional Campaign Committee (DCCC) and the Democratic Senatorial Campaign Committee (DSCC) substantially outraised and outspent their Republican counterparts, the National Republican Congressional Committee (NRCC) and the National Republican Senatorial Committee (NRSC). Most of the money donated to party campaign committees is now spent on supposedly independent campaigns on behalf of candidates. The Democrats' financial advantage is clear from Table 5-2, which displays the independent spending totals of these committees reported through election day.

For a party, distributing money efficiently is as important as raising it in the first place, although an abundance of funds makes it easier to risk investing

**Table 5-2**    Independent Party Spending in Congressional Campaigns through November 3, 2008

| Committee | Independent spending |
|---|---|
| Democratic Congressional Campaign Committee | $75,254,290 |
| National Republican Congressional Committee | $22,778,080 |
| Democratic Senatorial Campaign Committee | $70,077,697 |
| National Republican Senatorial Committee | $36,151,471 |

*Source:* Campaign Finance Institute, "A First Look at Money in the House and Senate Elections," November 6, 2008, available online at www.cfinst.org/pr/prRelease.aspx?ReleaseID=215.

in the kind of long-shot races that can produce surprise victories. In 2008 the DCCC spent more than $1 million on thirteen of the sixteen candidates for open seats who won at least 45 percent of the vote and thus could be considered at least potentially competitive; these candidates also were abundantly funded by individual donors and political action committees. The other three spent more than $1 million in money they raised for their own campaigns. The Democrat won eleven of these sixteen races, and none of the losers could blame the defeat on a shortage of funds.

The DCCC also spent more than $1 million on behalf of fourteen challengers and between $298,000 and $1 million on another seven. All fourteen successful Democratic challengers were among these beneficiaries of the party's independent spending. Another nine unsuccessful Democratic challengers won more than 45 percent of the vote without significant financial help from the party. Three of them were well funded from other sources, but the remaining six were not, and at least a couple of them must be considered missed opportunities.[10] On the whole, however, the DCCC invested wisely, keeping pace with a field of opportunities that kept expanding during the campaign (a phenomenon discussed below).

For Democratic challengers, the party's help—along with the substantial sums raised directly by the candidates—seems to have been effective. The mean shift in the major-party vote between 2006 and 2008 to the twenty-eight Democratic challengers helped by independent party spending was 4.2 percentage points. Other, less well-funded Democratic challengers ran on average slightly worse (-0.7 percentage points) than the 2006 candidate. The eighteen Democrats running for open Republican seats who received party help ran an average 9.6 percentage points ahead of the 2006 candidate, compared to 3.7 points for those not aided by party spending. And most of the Democratic takeovers required such greater-than-average vote swings. Only five of the Democrats' twenty-six pick-ups would have been achieved with only the national average 1.3-point swing to the party's House candidates; eleven of them required swings of five or more points.

The NRCC did not have the money to keep up with the DCCC, which heavily outspent it in all but one of the thirty-seven Republican-held districts where the Democrat won at least 45 percent of the vote.[11] Most of the money the NRCC did spend was spent defensively; 76 percent of its independent expenditures were aimed at holding Republican seats, whereas 79 percent of the DCCC's much larger independent spending budget was invested in taking such seats away from the GOP. Republican incumbents facing serious challenges were, as is almost invariably the case, amply funded[12]; for example, all but one of the fourteen losers received more than $2 million in contributions and independent expenditures.[13] Republican losses, then, could not be attributed to a shortage of campaign funds.

The NRCC invested in independent campaigns for only eight Republican challengers (sums ranging from $381,401 to $979,480), five of whom were trying to take back seats the Republicans had lost in 2006 or in subsequent special elections. All eight targeted freshman Democrats were among the twenty from districts where Bush had won more than 53 percent of the vote in 2004. The Republican challenger succeeded in winning three of the reddest of these districts (Kansas 2nd and Louisiana 6th, where Bush had won 60 percent of the vote in 2004, and Texas 22nd, where he won 65 percent) as well as retaking Florida's 16th district from a freshman Democrat undone by a sex scandal and winning Louisiana's 2nd district in a December runoff against incumbent William Jefferson, under federal indictment for corrupt activities. The NRCC also spent substantial sums against two senior Democratic incumbents from Pennsylvania, John Murtha and Paul Kanjorski, who were thought to be vulnerable for personal reasons. Both Republican challengers lost.

## Senate Campaigns

Democrats were equally aggressive in mounting Senate campaigns. Experienced Democratic candidates flocked to contest every potentially winnable Republican Senate seat. The roster of Democratic contenders for the twelve Republican seats that were listed at any time during the election year as being in play by the authoritative Cook Political Report (see Figure 5-5 and the discussion on p. 110) included two governors, a former governor, two U.S. representatives, three state legislators, and the mayor of a state's largest city. Only two of the twelve were novices, one of whom was comedian Al Franken, bare victor in Minnesota. Other Democratic victors included governors Mark Warner (Virginia) and Jeanne Shaheen (New Hampshire), U.S. Representatives (and cousins) Mark Udall (Colorado) and Tom Udall (New Mexico), state legislators Kay Hagen (North Carolina) and Jeff Merkley (Oregon), and Anchorage mayor Mark Begich (Alaska). In contrast, nine of the twelve Senate Democrats seeking reelection faced Republicans who were political novices, as did five of the eleven Republicans whose states were never listed as in play.

As usual, the competitive Senate candidates of both parties were amply funded, but Democrats enjoyed an advantage because the DSCC raised so much more money than the NRSC. In contests for the eleven seats listed as

**Figure 5-5**   Senate Seats at Risk in 2008 According to the Cook Report

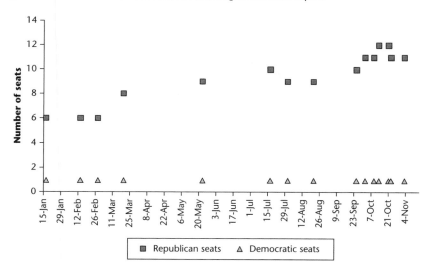

Source: "2008 Senate Race Ratings," Cook Political Report, November 3, 2008, www.cookpolitical.com/charts/senate/raceratings_2008-11-03_13-29-13.php.

competitive in the final Cook assessment (ten held by Republicans, one by Democrat Mary Landrieu of Louisiana), the receipts reported by the candidates through October 18 showed that the campaigns of both parties were on average equally well funded, with the Republican candidate having a fund-raising advantage in six and the Democrat in five. (On average, the Republican candidate had raised about 3 percent more money than the Democrat.) But once party independent spending is added to the mix, the Democratic candidates were better funded in eight of the eleven contests and, on average, had about 24 percent more campaign money from all sources than their Republican rivals. Both parties concentrated their efforts in these eleven contests, which absorbed 98 percent of the DSCC's independent expenditures and nearly 100 percent of the NRSC's. The difference was that the DSCC had nearly twice as much cash to spend (see Table 5-2).

In short, the party operatives who control campaign resources skillfully followed strategies that reflected the political conditions prevailing in 2008. Money flowed to Democrats competing to take House and Senate seats away from Republicans. Democratic committees and candidates were able to raise unprecedented sums because their activists were eager to change the national regime and optimistic about their chances of doing so. Republican committees and candidates faced bleak prospects at the polls and discouragement at the grass roots; they spent their money largely in defense of threatened incumbents and seats opened by Republican retirements. The best such a strategy can accomplish is to limit the damage.

## The Economic Crisis

Taken as a whole, the parties' strategic distribution of campaign resources reinforced the effects of the national conditions that had shaped those strategies and helped to make the 2008 congressional elections into a second consecutive referendum on Bush's second term. They also positioned the Democrats to take advantage of the third source of the pro-Democratic tide, the financial meltdown that hit the economy full force in mid-September 2008. As noted earlier, the economic crisis pushed down Bush's already dismal approval ratings even lower (Figure 5-1) and strengthened the consensus among voters that the country was on the wrong track (Figure 5-3).

The crisis, and Obama's politically effective response to it, gave the Democratic presidential nominee a solid lead in the national polls that he never relinquished. It also shifted the congressional battlefield further in the Democrats' favor. Figures 5-5 and 5-6 display the number of House and Senate seats at risk (that is, the number of races rated as toss-ups, leaning to one of the parties, or likely to go to the rival party) according to the Cook Report's periodic pre-election assessments of House and Senate races. On the House side, the number of seats in play grew gradually from January through the end of August, with Republicans always defending the larger number. After that, however, the number of at-risk Republican seats grew steeply, rising from thirty-six in August to fifty-one by election day, while the number of Democratic seats at risk dropped from twenty to thirteen. Democrats ended up winning twenty-six of the at-risk Republican seats—more than were classified as being at risk at the beginning of the election year. Republicans took four of the at-risk Democratic seats plus Jefferson's which, because of its overwhelmingly Democratic makeup (Kerry won 75 percent of the vote in the district in 2004), had not been considered in play.

A similar pattern is evident in the Senate races. Among Democrats, only Landrieu's seat was ever considered at risk. But the number of Republican Senate seats in play rose from six to as high as twelve before ending up at eleven just before the election, with a noticeable bump upward in the wake of the economic meltdown. On election day Democrats won eight of those seats. The full Senate election results are listed in Table 5-3.

It is impossible to determine precisely how many additional seats the September economic events handed to the Democrats, but a standard regression equation estimating House seat changes based on presidential approval and other variables suggests that for every one percentage-point drop in the president's approval ratings, his party loses about one House seat.[14] Thus, Bush's approximately seven-point decline in approval in the wake of the economic meltdown may well have cost the Republicans an additional seven House seats. The same conditions probably added to the Democrats' Senate total as well. State polls in Oregon, North Carolina, and Minnesota showed the Democratic challenger moving into the lead after mid-September, while the other successful Democrats were already leading in the polls by then.[15]

**Figure 5-6**    House Seats at Risk in 2008 According to the Cook Report

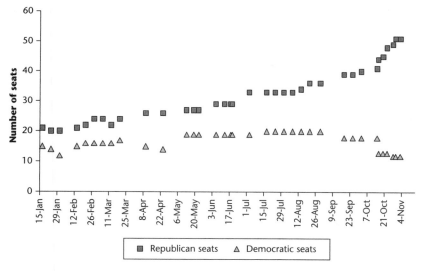

*Source:* "2008 Competitive House Race Chart," Cook Political Report, November 3, 2008, www.cookpolitical.com/charts/house/competitive_2008-11-03_17-12-33.php.

## An Obama Effect?

Barack Obama won the White House by carrying all of the states that voted for Kerry in 2004 plus nine that voted for Bush. To a remarkable degree, Democratic gains in the 2008 congressional elections coincided with Obama's victories, as Table 5-4 illustrates. In the House elections, Democrats picked up three seats in states won by McCain but lost four, for a net loss of one. They picked up ten seats in states that were blue in both presidential elections but did even better in states that switched from Bush to Obama, netting twelve seats (their only loss in any of these states resulted from a sex scandal in Florida). The Democrat took all four Republican Senate seats in states that switched from Bush to Obama and three of the four seats in the consistently blue states. Their only victory in a consistently red state came in Alaska, where Senator Stevens's felony conviction for corrupt behavior no doubt made the difference.

Why this connection between the presidential and congressional election results? On its face, it looks like a classic coattail effect, with the victorious presidential contender pulling his party's down-ticket candidates into office on the strength of his popularity. On the other hand, Obama ran behind the successful Democratic Senate candidates in Alaska, North Carolina, New Mexico, and Virginia and ran clearly ahead only in New Hampshire and Minnesota. Future studies based on complete electoral data and the major academic surveys should clarify the relationship between the vote for president and the vote for House and Senate candidates in 2008. It seems likely at

**Table 5-3**  Senate Election Results, 2008

| State | | Vote total | Percentage of major party vote |
|---|---|---|---|
| *Alabama* | | | |
| Vivian Figures | D | 752,391 | 36.6 |
| *Jeff Sessions | R | 1,305,383 | 63.4 |
| *Alaska* | | | |
| Mark Begich | D | 151,767 | 50.7 |
| *Ted Stevens | R | 147,814 | 49.3 |
| *Arkansas* | | | |
| Mark Pryor | D | 804,678 | 100.0 |
| *Colorado* | | | |
| Mark Udall | D | 1,230,981 | 55.4 |
| Robert Schaffer | R | 990,751 | 44.6 |
| *Delaware* | | | |
| *Joe Biden | D | 257,484 | 64.7 |
| Christine O'Donnell | R | 140,584 | 35.4 |
| *Georgia* | | | |
| James Martin | D | 908,222 | 42.5 |
| *Saxby Chambliss | R | 1,226,238 | 57.5 |
| *Idaho* | | | |
| Larry LaRocco | D | 219,903 | 37.2 |
| James Risch | R | 371,744 | 62.8 |
| *Illinois* | | | |
| *Dick Durbin | D | 3,616,210 | 70.4 |
| Steve Sauerberg | R | 1,520,896 | 29.6 |
| *Iowa* | | | |
| *Tom Harkin | D | 941,665 | 62.7 |
| Christopher Reed | R | 560,006 | 37.3 |
| *Kansas* | | | |
| Jim Slattery | D | 441,399 | 37.8 |
| *Pat Roberts | R | 727,121 | 62.2 |
| *Kentucky* | | | |
| Bruce Lunsford | D | 847,005 | 47.0 |
| *Mitch McConnell | R | 953,816 | 53.0 |
| *Louisiana* | | | |
| *Mary Landrieu | D | 988,298 | 53.3 |
| John Kennedy | R | 867,177 | 46.7 |
| *Maine* | | | |
| Tom Allen | D | 279,500 | 38.6 |
| *Susan Collins | R | 444,300 | 61.4 |
| *Massachusetts* | | | |
| *John Kerry | D | 1,959,843 | 68.0 |
| Jeff Beatty | R | 922,727 | 32.0 |
| *Michigan* | | | |
| *Carl Levin | D | 3,038,386 | 64.9 |
| Jack Hoogendyk Jr. | R | 1,641,070 | 35.1 |
| *Minnesota* | | | |
| Al Franken | D | 1,212,431 | 50.005 |
| *Norm Coleman | R | 1,212,206 | 49.995 |
| *Mississippi* | | | |
| Erik Fleming | D | 480,915 | 38.6 |
| *Thad Cochran | R | 766,111 | 61.4 |
| *Mississippi* | | | |
| Ronnie Musgrave | D | 560,064 | 45.0 |
| *Roger Wicker | R | 683,409 | 55.0 |

*(Continued)*

**Table 5-3** (Continued)

| State | | Vote total | Percentage of major party vote |
|---|---|---|---|
| *Montana* | | | |
| *Max Baucus | D | 348,289 | 72.9 |
| Bob Kelleher | R | 129,369 | 27.1 |
| *Nebraska* | | | |
| Scott Kleeb | D | 317,456 | 41.1 |
| Michael Johanns | R | 455,854 | 58.9 |
| *New Hampshire* | | | |
| Jeanne Shaheen | D | 357,153 | 53.3 |
| *John Sununu | R | 312,601 | 46.7 |
| *New Jersey* | | | |
| *Frank Lautenberg | D | 1,951,218 | 57.2 |
| Dick Zimmer | R | 1,461,025 | 42.8 |
| *New Mexico* | | | |
| Tom Udall | D | 505,128 | 61.3 |
| Steve Pearce | R | 318,522 | 38.7 |
| *North Carolina* | | | |
| Kay Hagan | D | 2,249,311 | 54.4 |
| *Elizabeth Dole | R | 1,887,510 | 45.3 |
| *Oklahoma* | | | |
| Andrew Rice | D | 527,736 | 40.9 |
| *James Inhofe | R | 763,375 | 59.1 |
| *Oregon* | | | |
| Jeff Merkley | D | 864,382 | 51.8 |
| *Gordon Smith | R | 805,159 | 48.2 |
| *Rhode Island* | | | |
| *Jack Reed | D | 320,644 | 73.4 |
| Robert Tingle | R | 116,174 | 26.6 |
| *South Carolina* | | | |
| Robert Conley | D | 790,621 | 42.3 |
| *Lindsey Graham | R | 1,076,534 | 57.7 |
| *South Dakota* | | | |
| *Tim Johnson | D | 237,889 | 62.5 |
| Joel Dykstra | R | 142,784 | 37.5 |
| *Tennessee* | | | |
| Robert Tuke | D | 765,876 | 32.8 |
| *Lamar Alexander | R | 1,571,584 | 67.2 |
| *Texas* | | | |
| Richard Noriega | D | 3,389,365 | 43.9 |
| *John Cornyn | R | 4,337,469 | 56.1 |
| *Virginia* | | | |
| Mark Warner | D | 2,369,327 | 65.8 |
| James Gilmore | R | 1,228,830 | 34.2 |
| *West Virginia* | | | |
| *John Rockefeller | D | 447,560 | 63.7 |
| Matthew Wolfe | R | 254,629 | 36.3 |
| *Wyoming* | | | |
| Chris Rothfuss | D | 60,631 | 24.3 |
| *Michael Enzi | R | 189,046 | 75.7 |
| *Wyoming* | | | |
| Nick Carter | D | 66,202 | 26.6 |
| John Barrasso | R | 183,063 | 73.4 |

*Source:* See Green Papers, www.thegreenpapers.com.

*Indicates incumbent senator.

**Table 5-4**    Democrats' Success in Campaigns for Republican-Held Seats, 2008

*House*

| Election results, 2004 and 2008 | Number of states | Number of Republican districts | Taken by Democrats in 2008 | Net | Percentage |
|---|---|---|---|---|---|
| Won by Bush and McCain | 22 | 75 | 3 | −1 | −1.3 |
| Won by Kerry and Obama | 19 | 70 | 10 | 10 | 14.3 |
| Won by Bush and Obama | 9 | 54 | 13 | 12 | 22.2 |

*Senate*

| Election results, 2004 and 2008 | Number of states | Republican Senate seats up | Taken by Democrats in 2008 | Percentage |
|---|---|---|---|---|
| Won by Bush and McCain | 22 | 15 | 1 | 6.6 |
| Won by Kerry and Obama | 19 | 4 | 3 | 75.0 |
| Won by Bush and Obama | 9 | 4 | 4 | 100.0 |

*Source:* Compiled by the author.

this point, however, that the coincidence of Democratic successes in various states mainly reflects two related phenomena: voters responding to the strongly pro-Democratic national conditions described earlier on both their presidential and congressional ballots, and the extensive work the Democratic campaign did to register and turn out new voters in the battleground states.

## Continuity and Change in the Electoral Landscape

Overall, the results of the 2008 congressional elections showed far more continuity than disjuncture with previous voting patterns, providing little evidence of any major shake-up of partisan alignments. For example, Table 5-5 displays the correlations between district-level presidential voting in 2000 and 2004 and House voting in 2004, 2006, and 2008. The table shows that the 2008 House vote was as closely related to the underlying district partisanship, represented by the presidential vote in 2000 or 2004, as it had been in 2004 or 2006. The 2008 House vote was also strongly related to the 2004 and 2006 House votes, particularly the latter. The district-level presidential vote in 2008 is not yet available, but it will be quite surprising if it is not also very highly correlated with these other variables.

Democrats added seats in the 2006 and 2008 congressional elections in all regions of the country (Figures 5-7 and 5-8), but their largest proportionate gains came in the Mountain West, and their smallest on the West Coast, where they already dominated.[16] After the 2004 election, Democrats held only 28 percent of the House seats in the Mountain West; after 2008, they held 59 percent of them, and their share of the region's Senate seats had grown from 22 percent to 44 percent. Despite these regional variations, the

**Table 5-5**   Correlations between Presidential and House Voting at the District Level

| House vote | Presidential vote | | House vote | |
|---|---|---|---|---|
| | 2000 | 2004 | 2004 | 2006 |
| 2004 | .84 | .83 | | |
| 2006 | .83 | .84 | .93 | |
| 2008 | .85 | .86 | .90 | .94 |

*Source:* Compiled by the author.

**Figure 5-7**   Partisan Distribution of House Seats by Region, 2004–2008

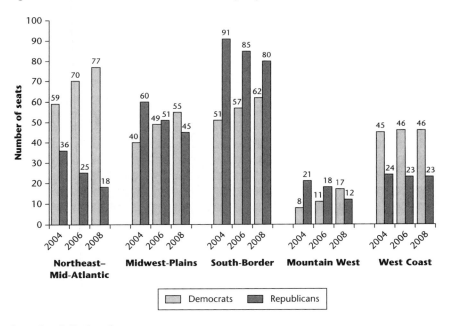

*Source:* Compiled by the author.

electorate's response to the performance of the president and the Republican Party during Bush's second term was broadly national.[17]

The 2008 Senate election results also indicate continuity with recent political trends. As Figure 5-9 shows, states went consistently blue or red in the 2008 presidential and Senate elections at the same high rate typical of recent years. And in the 111th Congress, the number of senators representing states won by their party's most recent presidential candidate reached its highest point in the past half century (Figure 5-10). Thus the trend toward greater partisan coherence in voting for president and Congress that was observed during the Clinton and Bush administrations was not reversed in 2008, a sign

**Figure 5-8**    Partisan Distribution of Senate Seats by Region, 2004–2008

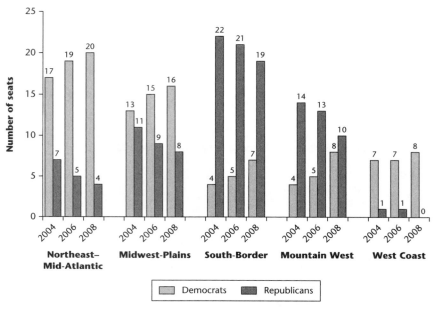

**Figure 5-9**    States Won by Same Party in Senate and Presidential Elections, 1952–2008

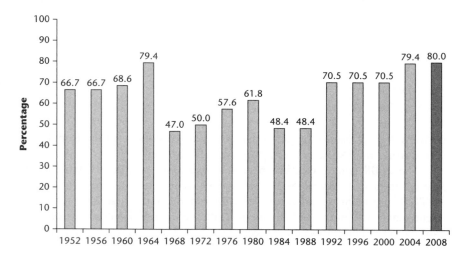

**Figure 5-10**    Senate Seats Held by Party Winning the State in the Most Recent Presidential Election

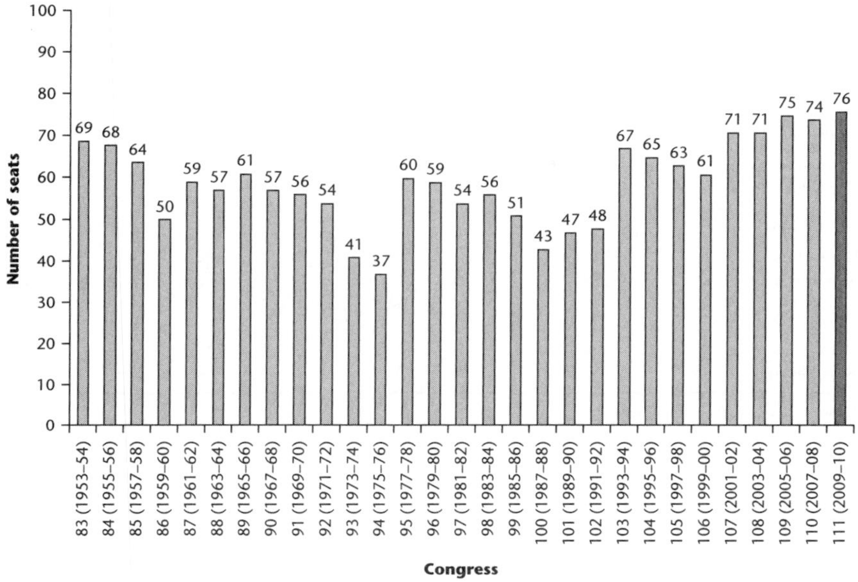

*Source:* Compiled by the author.

that, although the relative strength of the two parties has shifted, the pattern of partisan division characteristic of the last two decades remains in place.

## The New Congress and Prospects for the 2010 Midterm Election

Barack Obama and the Democrat-controlled 111th Congress take office under the most difficult circumstances faced by any new government since the 1930s: unresolved wars in Iraq and Afghanistan; a severe economic downturn; serious challenges involving health care, the environment, energy, and entitlement programs; and a huge and growing budget deficit. It is not clear how President Obama or Congress will try to deal with this daunting agenda. One thing is certain, however: despite full Democratic control of the government, a lurch to the political left is unlikely and would almost certainly fail if it were attempted. In the House, the median member of both parties' caucuses will be more conservative (although, with the influx of new Democrats, the chamber's median will be more liberal). According to Poole and Rosenthal's standard measure of ideology (the DW-NOMINATE score, based on roll-call votes and scaled to a range of 1 for most conservative to -1 for most liberal), the Republican representing

**Table 5-6**    2004 Presidential Vote and the Distribution of House Seats, 2004–2008

| | John Kerry's share of the major party vote in the district, 2004 | | | |
|---|---|---|---|---|
| | < 47%<br>(206) | 47%–53%<br>(55) | > 53%<br>(154) | Total<br>(435) |
| *After 2004* | | | | |
| Democrats | 29 | 26 | 147 | 202 |
| Republicans | 197 | 29 | 7 | 233 |
| *After 2006* | | | | |
| Democrats | 47 | 34 | 152 | 233 |
| Republicans | 179 | 21 | 2 | 202 |
| *After 2008* | | | | |
| Democrats | 63 | 42 | 152 | 257 |
| Republicans | 163 | 13 | 2 | 178 |

*Source:* Compiled by the author.

seats taken by Democrats in 2008 were more moderate (they had a median DW-NOMINATE score of .423) than those representing seats that the party retained (.534).[18] The last two elections have been hard on (relatively) moderate Republicans because they typically represent the kind of district a moderate Democrat can win, at least under favorable circumstances. And, of course, circumstances were very favorable to Democrats in the two most recent elections. Even eleven-term Connecticut representative Christopher Shays, with the least conservative voting record of any Republican in the House (.241), could not survive the Democratic tide in 2008. With his defeat, not a single Republican represents any of the twenty-two districts in New England, once the strongest Republican region in the country.

Going into the 2008 House elections, Democrats already held almost all of the districts whose underlying partisanship was Democratic. Just as in 2006, their gains in 2008 were concentrated in districts that leaned Republican, as Table 5-6 shows. District partisanship is estimated here by the districts' 2004 presidential vote, with districts sorted into three categories depending on whether John Kerry's share of the major-party vote was less than 47 percent (Republican-leaning districts), more than 53 percent (Democrat-leaning districts), or somewhere in between (balanced districts). Republicans held only seven seats in Democratic-leaning districts after 2004, and lost five of them in 2006 and one more in 2008. Aside from Joseph Cao, who took Jefferson's lopsidedly Democratic seat in Louisiana, only Mike Castle, who holds Delaware's single House district, continues to serve as a Republican in a Democratic-leaning constituency, winning 62 percent of the vote in 2008 while Obama was winning 63 percent.

Democrats added seventeen seats in the balanced districts in 2006 and 2008, with their share of these districts rising from 47 percent in 2006 to

76 percent in 2008. But even if Democrats won all of the Democratic-leaning districts and all of the balanced districts, they would still fall short of a majority (218 seats). They need to win Republican-leaning districts as well, because Republicans hold an important structural advantage in the competition for House seats: regular Republican voters are distributed more efficiently (from the party's perspective) across states and districts than are Democratic voters. Part of the reason for the Republicans' advantage is demographic: Democrats win a disproportionate share of minority and other urban voters, who tend to be concentrated in cities with lopsided Democratic majorities.[19] But it is also the effect of deliberate partisan gerrymanders conducted by the Republicans in states where they controlled redistricting after the 2000 census.[20]

Democrats have thus faced an uphill battle in trying to win and then increase their House majorities (Senate majorities, too—the same Republican efficiency advantage applies to states). It took two successive elections with strongly pro-Democratic national conditions for them to achieve their current majorities. Thirty-four of their net additional seats came from Republican-leaning districts in which Bush won more than 53 percent of the 2004 vote, and these districts now comprise a quarter of their total holdings. This will have the effect of moderating the Democratic caucus, because Democrats representing such districts are, of necessity, considerably more moderate than other Democrats; their median DW-NOMINATE score in the first session of the 110th Congress was −.230, compared to −.317 for Democrats from balanced districts and −.480 for Democrats from Democratic-leaning districts. Similarly, more than half of the Democratic senators who replaced Republicans in 2006 and 2008 are from states in the South or the Mountain West, and they, too, will have to compile moderate records or risk defeat.

Moderation, although essential, may not be enough to maintain the large Democratic majorities in future elections. Democrats have had the wind at their back in two successive elections, but now that they must take full responsibility for the government's performance in a time of serious crisis and widespread public discontent, they cannot expect political conditions to favor them a third time running; rather, the opposite is more likely. Much will depend on whether the economy improves and on the public's broader evaluation of the Obama administration's performance. The electoral future will also depend on the durability of the Democrats' recent gains in partisan identification, which remains in doubt. The set of seats up in 2010 should help them retain their Senate majority because only two of the sixteen seats Democrats will be defending are in states won by John McCain, whereas Republicans must defend nineteen seats, six in states that went to Obama. On the House side, however, Democrats will have to defend seats in sixty-three Republican-leaning districts (Table 5-5), including sixteen that gave Bush more than 60 percent of the vote in 2004. The Republicans' structural advantage in House elections—even greater now than it was back in 1994—provides the foundation for a major Republican comeback should the Democratic regime falter.

# Notes

1. Gary C. Jacobson, "Referendum: The 2006 Midterm Congressional Elections," *Political Science Quarterly* 122 (Spring 2007): 1–24.

2. Gary C. Jacobson, "The Effects of the George W. Bush Presidency on Partisan Attitudes," presented at the Annual Meeting of the Midwest Political Science Association, Chicago, April 3–6, 2008.

3. The relevant data may be found at www.pollingreport.com.

4. Jacobson, "Effects of Bush Presidency on Partisan Attitudes." The equation is: View of Republican Party Favorable/Positive = 24.99 + .49 Presidential Approval (0.88) (.02) Adjusted R2 = .79 N = 172; Standard errors in parentheses.

5. See "Political Parties: The Republicans" data, available at www.pollingreport.com/institut2.htm#Republicans; and "Political Parties: The Democrats" data, available at www.pollingreport.com/institut2.htm#Democrats.

6. Partisan leaners—people who call themselves independents but who say they lean toward a party—are not included as partisans in these data.

7. Based on Pew Research Center for the People and the Press data compiled by Michael Dimock from surveys from January through October 2006 (number of cases = 17,599).

8. See exit poll data reported by CNN at www.cnn.com/ELECTION/2008/results/polls/#val=USH00p1.

9. Gary C. Jacobson and Samuel Kernell, *Strategy and Choice in Congressional Elections* (New Haven, Conn.: Yale University Press, 1981); and Gary C. Jacobson, "Strategic Politicians and the Dynamics of House Elections, 1946–1986," *American Political Science Review* 83 (September 1989): 773–793.

10. William Hendrick won 48.5 percent of the vote against Ken Calvert in California's 44th district despite raising only $155,553 through October 15; Joseph Larkin won 46.9 percent of the vote against Thaddeus McCotter in Michigan's 11th district despite raising only $23,432 through October 15; neither benefited from any independent party spending.

11. By a ratio of 4:1 in open seats, more than 3:1 in incumbent-held seats; data are from the Campaign Finance Institute, "A First Look at Money in the House and Senate Elections," at www.cfinst.org/pr/prRelease.aspx?ReleaseID=215.

12. Gary C. Jacobson, *The Politics of Congressional Elections,* 7th ed. (New York: Pearson Longman, 2008), 46–51.

13. The remaining Republican incumbent's funds were listed at $1.6 million in the preliminary report.

14. Jacobson, *Politics of Congressional Elections,* 160.

15. Click on the charts in "The Polls: 2008 Senate Elections" at www.pollster.com/polls/2008senate.

16. Northeast–Mid-Atlantic includes Maine, New Hampshire, Massachusetts, Rhode Island, Connecticut, Vermont, New York, Pennsylvania, New Jersey, Maryland, Delaware, and West Virginia; Midwest-Plains includes Ohio, Michigan, Wisconsin, Illinois, Indiana, Iowa, Nebraska, North Dakota, South Dakota, Kansas, Missouri, and Minnesota; South-Border includes Florida, Georgia, North Carolina, Virginia, Alabama, Louisiana, Mississippi, Kentucky, Tennessee, Texas, Oklahoma, South Carolina, and Arkansas; Mountain West includes Idaho, Montana, Colorado, Nevada, New Mexico, Arizona, Alaska, Utah, and Wyoming; West Coast includes California, Washington, Oregon, and Hawaii.

17. The West Coast, which saw a minimal seat change (largely because California's fifty-three districts were gerrymandered to eliminate all competitive seats after the 2000 census), nonetheless produced the largest Democratic vote share gain for Democrats of any region, 3.2 percentage points.

18. Data for the first session of the 110th Congress are available at http://voteview.com/dwnomin.htm, courtesy of Keith T. Poole. For an account of the methodology

for DW-NOMINATE see Keith T. Poole and Howard Rosenthal, *Congress: A Political-Economic History of Roll Call Voting* (New York: Oxford University Press, 1997), 3–57.

19.  For example, according to the CBS News/*New York Times* Poll of August 20–25, 2004, Democratic identifiers outnumber Republicans nearly five to one in New York City. See "New York City and the Republican Convention," November 6, 2004, at www.cbsnews.com/htdocs/CBSNews_polls/nyc.pdf.

20.  Gary C. Jacobson, "The Congress: The Structural Basis of Republican Success," in Michael Nelson, ed., *The Elections of 2004* (Washington, D.C.: CQ Press, 2005), 163–186.

# 6

# The Media:
# Coloring the News

## Marjorie Randon Hershey

"My, I felt this thrill going up my leg," said MSNBC anchor Chris Matthews in February 2008, a feeling he described as "an objective assessment" of a Barack Obama speech.[1] On another network a few months later, Fox News host E. D. Hill searched for a way to characterize a fond fist bump between Barack and Michelle Obama and came up with "a terrorist fist jab?"[2] Rush Limbaugh referred to the Democratic candidate as "Obama Osama."[3]

Advocates of objective journalism might turn pale at these commentaries on major broadcast and cable networks, especially if they compared media reports in 2008 with those of a generation ago. In 1970, 80 percent of all television viewing was captured by CBS, NBC, and ABC,[4] and the network news anchors, commentators, and journalists of that time were seen by most Americans as nonpartisan and unbiased. As late as 1987 political scientists were able to conclude that "the national news media in the U.S. . . . all tend to report the same kinds of messages concerning public policy, from the same sources."[5]

If the shift from more homogenized, neutral coverage to more inflammatory, "niche" news is alarming to some, however, it would be familiar to Americans in the early years of our history. From the revolutionary period through the first part of the nineteenth century, most press coverage in the United States was overtly partisan, designed to mobilize support for a cause, a party, or a political leader.[6] Dueling Federalist and Republican newspapers vilified opposition leaders, accusing them of everything from immorality to treason,[7] and shocking the famous observer of American life, Alexis de Tocqueville, who wrote in the 1830s that American printers had a "vulgar turn of mind" and the newspapers they produced made "open and coarse appeals to the passions of their readers."[8] Throughout much of the 1800s and into the next century, sensationalism and "yellow journalism"—exaggerations, bias, and scandal-mongering—characterized much of the news coverage available to Americans.

Efforts to meet the ideal of professional, objective journalism are more recent. The growing concentration of media ownership during the 1900s meant that more and more cities had only a single daily newspaper serving their readers and only a small number of radio and television outlets. To maintain a large audience in a geographic area containing a great diversity of views and interests, print and broadcast media worked to keep the news neutral in tone and therefore broadly acceptable, as well as to confine opinions to the editorial pages and broadcast segments labeled as "commentary."

In the past two or three decades, however, the media world has taken another dramatic turn. With the rise of cable television's vast array of broadcast frequencies, viewers are no longer confined to the offerings of ABC, CBS, and NBC. The audience for nightly news on network stations has plummeted to less than 20 percent of all viewers.[9] Others who wish to find out what's happening can choose from among a super-abundance of niche news sources, often slanted toward particular points of view, from MSNBC on the left to Fox on the right. The explosion of Internet sites that deal with politics, ranging from the online outlets of major newspapers and broadcast stations to individual blogs offering unique (and often intense) opinions, further expands the set of choices.[10] In this new media environment, if Americans prefer to learn about the presidential candidates from an evangelical Christian perspective, or through the satire of Jon Stewart or Stephen Colbert, then all they need is Internet access or a remote control.[11]

In fact, even the remaining bastions of the mainstream media—mass-circulation newspapers and the traditional TV and radio networks, which aspire to an objective portrayal of events—cannot simply provide their audiences with a serving of raw news that contains all of the happenings of the day. No matter how exciting and important the events they are portraying, the "newshole" of the daily paper or news broadcast is very limited, and there will be time and space for just a few aspects of a few stories or features. As businesses that hope to make a profit, these prominent news organizations need to offer what their readers and viewers find interesting. So the mainstream media, which often serve as signals to the rest of the media world about what was important in the day's events, tend to boil down a campaign to a fairly small set of themes or "frames,"[12] reflecting both the emphases of the candidates and the medium's need to attract an audience.

This chapter begins by discussing the mainstream press's coverage of the 2008 presidential race. Most of this coverage focused on the "game" aspect of the campaign: the most recent poll numbers, showing who was ahead at the time and who was gaining or losing, and the campaigners' tactical and strategic moves.[13] Such "horse race coverage," devoid of issues, has consistently characterized election reporting in recent decades,[14] because it serves up the simple story lines of conflict, drama, and excitement that lead people to buy and read newspapers.

Looking beyond the horse race, what did the mainstream press's audience (and the audience for other media that take their cues about what's newsworthy from the mainstream outlets) learn about the presidential candidates in 2008? To identify the main non–horse race themes to which large numbers of Americans were exposed, I examined all of the stories containing the names Obama or McCain in four major opinion-leading newspapers—the *New York Times,* the *Wall Street Journal,* the *Los Angeles Times,* and the *Washington Post*—during three two-week periods of the campaign. These were the two parties' national convention weeks (August 25–September 7), the period encompassing three of the four candidate debates (September 27–October 10), and the two weeks surrounding election day (October 26–November 9). I created a census of the most common themes appearing in the coverage, and then I coded whether each of these themes was mentioned in each story, opinion column, or editorial.

## What Did the Mainstream Media Emphasize?

As might be expected from the mainstream press, with its emphasis on objective reporting, journalists did not present their own, independent portrayals of the candidates. Rather, their coverage closely reflected the main ideas promoted by the campaigns' own advertising and press releases and the candidates' speeches. This, of course, meant that these journalists had to choose among the contending images provided by each campaign, because there was not enough room in these newspapers to present all the talking points promoted by both campaigns. Which campaign was better able to get its preferred portrayal of its candidate, and of his opponent, carried in the mainstream press? Table 6-1 shows these media choices during each week of the coding period.

### McCain: McSame or Maverick?

Overall in these six campaign weeks the most common theme in McCain's coverage reflected an argument pressed consistently by the Obama campaign: that McCain's approaches to issues so closely resembled those of President George W. Bush that a McCain victory would be like a third Bush administration (listed as "Same as Bush" in Table 6-1).[15]

For example, former vice president Al Gore received "a stadium-rattling ovation when he likened McCain to a Bush clone. 'I believe in recycling,' the environmental-minded Gore quipped, 'but that's ridiculous.'"[16] Especially in the early weeks of the fall campaign, the idea that the Republican candidate was "McSame" appeared in almost one of every ten articles about the campaign (see Figure 6-1)—a substantial proportion, given the large number of images of the candidates presented in the press coverage.

Another of the four most commonly reported themes about McCain was also drawn from the Obama campaign's claims: that McCain made reckless or rash decisions ("Reckless" in Table 6-1). As one columnist put it, "McCain, once the candidate of tested experience, must now battle the perception that he has become the riskier choice, a man too given to rash moves under pressure."[17] As Figure 6-1 shows, this theme gained in prominence during the debate weeks. It helped undercut McCain's assertion that his long service in government gave him the experience to be an effective president. This assertion was further weakened by his choice of Alaska governor Sarah Palin as his running mate: Palin's governmental experience was even more limited than Obama's. In these ways,

**Table 6-1**    Main Themes in Mainstream Press Coverage of the Presidential Race,
August–November 2008

| McCain | Obama |
|---|---|
| *August 25–31 (n = 856)* | |
| Same as Bush (68) | Conflict with Hillary Clinton (136) |
| Maverick (36) | Lacks experience (72) |
| Trying to appeal to women, Clinton voters (29) | First black American nominee (44) |
| Old (25) | Celebrity, lacks substance (37) |
| Out of touch, e.g., on economy (22) | Will bring change (28) |
| *September 1–7 (n = 706)* | |
| Maverick (77) | Lacks experience (53) |
| Same as Bush (59) | Conflict with Hillary Clinton (34) |
| Trying to shore up conservative base (53) | Higher taxes, more spending (27) |
| Patriotic (41) | Will bring change (21) |
| Reckless/Will bring change (37 each) | Celebrity, lacks substance (16) |
| *September 27–October 3 (n = 454)* | |
| Taxes, cut wasteful spending (52) | Higher taxes, more spending (58) |
| Reckless (36) | Lacks experience (33) |
| Same as Bush (31) | Mentions of race, race as an issue (18) |
| Maverick (30) | Will bring change (14) |
| Supports the war in Iraq (23) | Conflict with Hillary Clinton (14) |
| *October 4–10 (n = 547)* | |
| Taxes, cut wasteful spending (70) | Associates with radicals (77) |
| Reckless (34) | Higher taxes, more spending (67) |
| Same as Bush (27) | Lacks experience (27) |
| Maverick (18) | Racism among voters (26) |
| Supports the war in Iraq (15) | Conflict with Hillary Clinton/Not "one of us" (18 each) |
| *October 26–November 2 (n = 843)* | |
| Taxes, cut wasteful spending (71) | Higher taxes, more spending (126) |
| Same as Bush (56) | Mentions of race, race as an issue (53) |
| Maverick (25) | Will bring change (48) |
| Media unfair to McCain/Palin (21) | Racism among voters (47) |
| Iraq/Patriotic/Reckless (17 each) | Associates with radicals (46) |
| *November 3–9 (n = 986)* | |
| Same as Bush (43) | First black American president (91) |
| Taxes, cut wasteful spending (30) | Higher taxes, more spending (91) |
| Maverick (28) | U.S. is post-racial (71) |
| Experienced (22) | Racism among voters (58) |
| Patriotic (18) | Conflict with Hillary Clinton (58) |
| Total number of themes: 4,392 | |

*Note: (n = #)* is the total number of mentions of Obama-related and McCain-related themes in that week's coverage. The number in parentheses after each specific theme is the number of times that theme was mentioned during that week.

the Obama forces helped to define McCain for the media audience, especially in turning one of McCain's biggest selling points—that his years of service had produced sound judgment and superior leadership—into a weakness.

McCain did succeed in getting several of his own talking points incorporated into much of the mainstream press coverage. One was that he would continue the tax cuts started by the Bush administration and add spending cuts ("Taxes, cut wasteful spending" in Table 6-1). McCain was also successful in

**Figure 6-1**  Most Frequent McCain Themes in 2008 Campaign Coverage

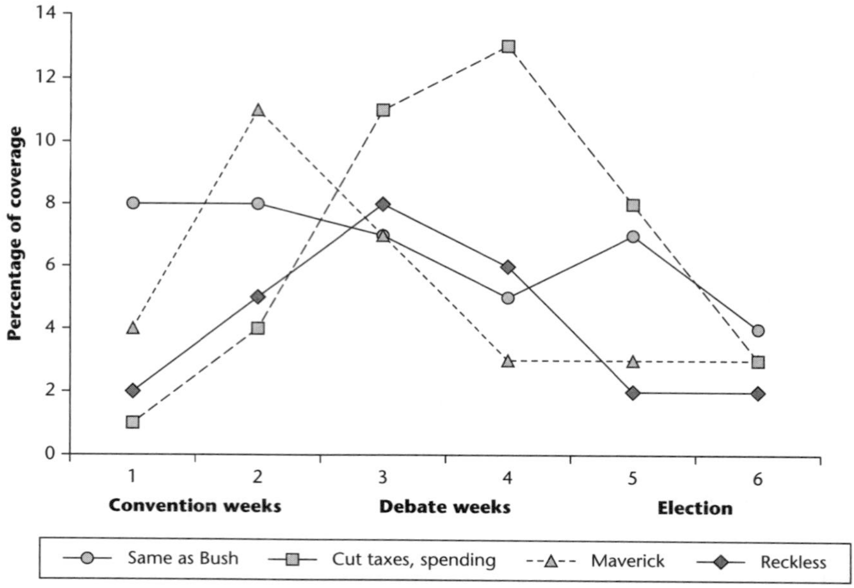

*Source:* Compiled by the author.

promoting his image as a "maverick," independent of his party and of any other outside pressures. The maverick theme was most common during the Republican convention but declined during the debate weeks; the image of McCain as a tax- and spending-cutter grew in strength during the debates but faded as election day approached.

A number of other themes appeared to a lesser extent in McCain's coverage. In descending order of frequency, these were: that his campaign reached out to the conservative Republican base ("Trying to shore up conservative base" in Table 6-1); that McCain was a great patriot ("Patriotic" in Table 6-1); that he aimed for victory in Iraq ("Supports the war in Iraq" or "Iraq" in Table 6-1); that he tried to win the support of women voters who had previously backed Sen. Hillary Clinton's bid for the Democratic nomination ("Trying to appeal to women, Clinton voters" in Table 6-1); and that he was experienced, stood for change ("Will bring change"), and was bipartisan.

All of these themes were consonant with the messages promoted by the McCain campaign. The only dissonant theme in this group involved references to McCain's age, a criticism emphasized, at least in subtle ways, by the Obama campaign.

In short, although the two most frequent themes in McCain's coverage—the "McSame" and "reckless" themes—offered negative information about him, most of the other images of McCain in the mainstream press were positive, reflecting talking points stressed by his campaign. Until later in the race, when his falling poll numbers led to a much more negative tone in media reports, McCain's campaign had some success in getting its definition of his strong points accepted by leading news outlets.

The large number of themes in McCain's coverage, however—the wide scatter of images—mirrored a complaint often voiced by campaign insiders as well as by other conservative groups: the Republican campaign lacked a unified, consistent message. Instead, many suggested that the campaign appeared to respond to daily targets of opportunity, when it should have been connecting all of its communications to an overarching rationale for McCain's candidacy. In the eyes of many journalists, this reflected ongoing leadership changes in the campaign, especially prior to the Republican convention. The people closest to McCain did not always agree on how the campaign should be run.[18]

After the McCain campaign announced a major shake-up on July 1, in which Steve Schmidt, who had been a principal of the 2004 Bush reelection team, took control of most aspects of the McCain organization, there was more of an attempt at message discipline. By late July the *New York Times* reported that "John McCain is beginning a newly aggressive campaign to define Mr. Obama as arrogant, out of touch and unprepared for the presidency."[19] The campaign unleashed a rapid-fire series of attacks. A new slogan, "Country First," was introduced to emphasize McCain's long military service and heroism. An ad called "Troops" charged that when Obama visited Europe in July, he chose not to visit wounded U.S. soldiers because he wasn't allowed to bring cameras into the hospital, limiting the political profit he could get from a visit. The McCain campaign posted an ad on YouTube mocking Obama as "The One," the messianic figure in *The Matrix* films, closing with a clip of Charlton Heston as Moses parting the Red Sea. Another well-publicized ad, linking the Democratic candidate with Britney Spears and Paris Hilton, sought to portray Obama as merely a "celebrity," a lightweight out of his league in presuming to run for president.

Again, however, the McCain campaign's frequent change of subject muddled the impact of all these efforts. As one reporter noted in September,

> There is nothing orderly about what [the campaign's leadership is] doing, just a relentless barrage of statements, e-mails, conference calls, Internet ads, cable interviews and political chaff designed to batter Obama and feed the media's insatiable appetite for combat and conflict, the more outrageous the better.[20]

## Obama: Friend of Taxes and Terrorists?

Although Barack Obama often received more press coverage than did McCain, much of that coverage featured themes promoted by the Republicans. In fact, all but one of the five most frequent themes in Obama's coverage could be seen as critical of the Democrat. The single most common image, which appeared frequently during the debate and election weeks, dealt with Obama's tax plan ("Higher taxes, more spending" in Table 6-1). Obama was

**Figure 6-2**    Most Frequent Obama Themes in 2008 Campaign Coverage

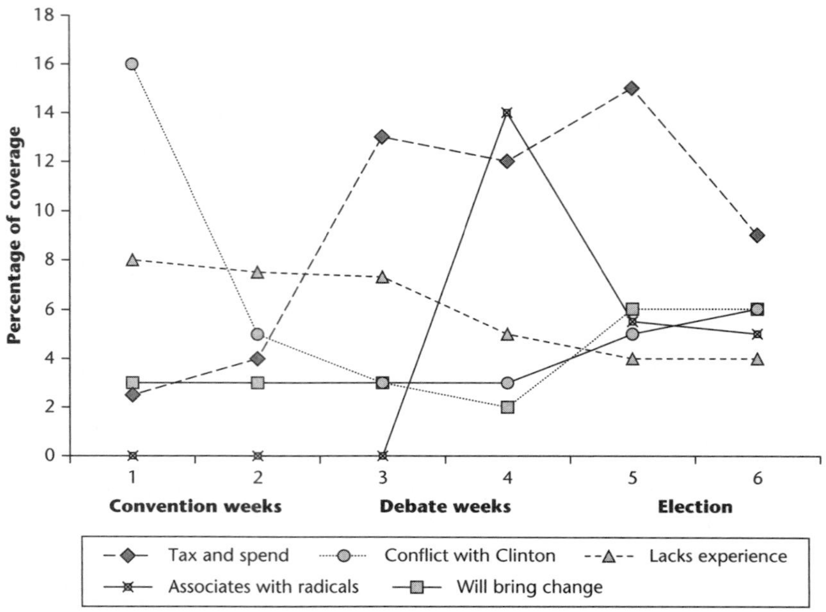

*Source:* Compiled by the author.

referred to as the "tax and spend" candidate (see Figure 6-2). Here, McCain's focus was uncharacteristically clear: "My opponent will raise your taxes. My tax cuts will create jobs. His tax increases—increases, he wants to increase your taxes!—he'll eliminate 'em!"[21] The emphasis on taxing and spending increased greatly when, after the financial disaster on Wall Street in September, the condition of the economy, which had been the focus of no more than about five percent of campaign coverage for months, suddenly rocketed to become the major topic of 43 percent of the coverage.[22]

The second most frequent theme in Obama's press coverage was the continuing story of conflict between him and his former primary opponent, Hillary Clinton. It is understandable that the bulk of these stories appeared during the week of the Democratic convention, even though several observers reported that the extent of the conflict was overblown in media reports even at this time: "The amount of media attention on extremist Clinton-supporters seemed oddly disproportionate to the actual numbers on the ground."[23] Yet, as Table 6-1 shows, no other theme received as much attention during the Democratic convention, in part because the conflict between the two candidates was such a colorful story. Consider the words of one die-hard Clinton supporter interviewed just after Obama accepted the party's nomination: "'I hate Obama so much that I'm going to devote as much time to McCain as I did to Hillary,' said Adita Blanco, a Democrat from Edward, Okla., who has never voted for a Republican. 'Obama has nothing. He has no experience. The Democratic Party doesn't care about us. You couldn't treat [Clinton] any worse.'"[24]

Even after the conventions ended, however, references to the conflict between Obama and Clinton remained frequent, as Figure 6-2 shows, all the way through the post-election coverage. In contrast, very few stories or commentaries referred to Mitt Romney or Mike Huckabee, McCain's main primary opponents, at any point during the fall campaign. Granted, the Republican primary race ended two months before the Democrats' race did. But the extended run of the Obama-Clinton conflict theme probably had more to do with how well it fit the prevailing definition of "news."[25] It involved the exceptional event of a race between a black man and a white woman married to a controversial former president; it was dramatic and conflict-filled; and it enabled reporters to tap into the Clinton Saga, a seemingly never-ending story of power, sex, and money, three of the forces best able to draw an audience. In recent years, journalists have been especially likely to apply this "conflict and drama" frame to coverage of the Democratic Party,[26] perhaps because the Democrats are so much more open about their internal disputes than are the Republicans.

Obama's inexperience and lack of readiness for the presidency ("Lacks experience" in Table 6-1), a major emphasis of the McCain campaign, was the third most frequent frame in Obama's coverage. The proportion of these references declined somewhat over time, just as the mentions of McCain's recklessness began to increase. Next most common was the coverage of McCain and Palin's claim that Obama associated and continued to associate with radicals and terrorists ("Associates with radicals" in Table 6-1). This charge, which had a meteoric rise when the Republican campaign began to emphasize it during the debate weeks, carried intense emotions. As an example, "'Barack Obama's friend tried to kill my family,' said John M. Murtagh in a statement released by McCain's campaign, the latest attempt to link Obama to Vietnam-era radical William Ayers, now a Chicago academic who has served with Obama on various boards and organizations."[27] Governor Palin put particular effort into keeping this theme alive, often referring to Obama "palling around with terrorists."

Only one of the five themes most common in Obama's coverage reflected an image that his campaign was trying to stress. That was the message that Obama stood for change ("Will bring change" in Table 6-1), the theme with which he had begun his primary campaign in February 2007 and which his ads and other communications promoted consistently. Yet even in the face of this heavy emphasis, media coverage during the conventions and the debates devoted less attention to this image than to Obama's conflicts with Hillary Clinton. Finally, at the end of the campaign, the Obama organization was able to recapture attention to the "Obama will bring change" theme. It showed up in the coverage of the last two weeks of the race more often than any other frame discussed up to this point, except for references to the Democrat as a tax-and-spend liberal and to the conflict with Clinton.

The next most common theme in Obama's coverage also reflected McCain's criticisms of the Illinois senator: that Obama was exotic or "different," might not share voters' values, and was "not one of us" ("Not one of us" in Table 6-1). Articles in October began to sprout quotations from suspicious citizens, such as that Obama "just doesn't seem like he's from America,"[28] and "I just hope and pray that the man has not been planted here by a foreign country. I just hope he is not the kind who flew those planes into those towers."[29] After this, the next most frequent frames were mixed: that Obama was a celebrity without real substance (an emphasis to which McCain returned at times) and discussions about Obama's bipartisanship and his emphasis on hope, both promoted by the Obama campaign. Also prevalent, however, were mentions of rumors that Obama was a Muslim and lacked patriotism, as evidenced by false claims that he had been sworn in as senator with his hand on the Koran and refused to salute the American flag or say the pledge of allegiance.

## Race: The Elephant in the Room

Throughout much of the campaign, media coverage seemed to ignore the elephant in the room: Obama was the first black presidential nominee of a major party (see Figure 6-3). One main reason, of course, was that neither the Obama nor the McCain campaign was discussing the issue openly. So as not to make whites uneasy, Obama offered appeals to voters that transcended race. His advertising portrayed him interacting with a lot of white citizens and a few black citizens, the same way most other presidential candidates advertise themselves. Black faces were not prominent among the supporters standing behind the candidate at campaign events. Photos of Obama's white mother and grandparents appeared in several of his television ads. Close to the election, the campaign ran ads in which Obama spoke directly to the camera for long periods—a "talking head" approach that may have seemed old-fashioned to some, but could make the darker skin tones of Obama's face more familiar and reassuring to whites unaccustomed to the sight of a black man running for the nation's highest elected office.

At the same time, the McCain campaign feared a backlash if it referred explicitly to race. As a Democratic strategist commented, "When race gets injected, given the 200-year history of this country, it is really fraught with peril."[30] Both campaigns were in uncharted territory with respect to race as the fall campaign began, as were voters and journalists, and they all responded with caution. At the close of the Democratic National Convention, for example, a reporter noted, "Obama is the first African-American to be nominated for the White House by a major party, a fact that, for all its significance, has been barely mentioned over the course of this four-day gathering."[31]

**Figure 6-3**   Explicitly Racial Themes in 2008 Campaign Coverage

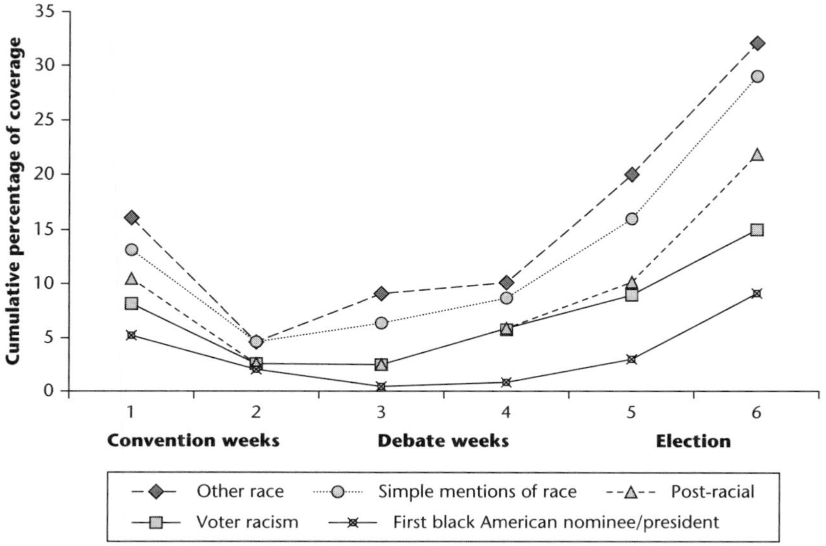

*Source:* Compiled by the author.

The challenge for both campaigns was that racism in the United States is an issue deeply layered with emotion, even rage; it does not often lend itself to calm discussion. Although only a small percentage of the American people is willing to express overt racism, social psychologists argue that a substantially larger proportion holds racially biased attitudes of which they may be barely conscious: what some sociologists term "racism without racists."[32] These subtle forms of prejudice, in which individuals may not see themselves as bigoted but do feel misgivings or fears about people of other races, are said to operate especially in ambiguous situations in which there are competing claims and no clear-cut rules—in short, in situations such as political campaigns.[33]

In this unique campaign environment, overt mentions of race by either campaign might produce unpredictable responses. Yet the elephant in the room could not be ignored completely. Race seemed to be the subtext—the unstated message—of several themes in Obama's media coverage. The emphases on his associations with radicals or terrorists and the suggestion that he might be disguising Muslim roots; that his background was "exotic" or "different," and that he was "not one of us"; that he "doesn't share our values"; that he was lacking in patriotism; that he was "presumptuous" in running for president; and that he was simply a celebrity with no real substance—all had an ambiguous quality. They could be seen as standard questions of trust and honesty, raised in virtually all presidential campaigns, but they could also elicit the unconscious biases that some students of racial attitudes posit.

How could journalists portray the ambiguity of the situation: the possibility of unstated but powerful messages about race? In many cases, they quoted extensively from white Democrats showing signs of this struggle. One Pennsylvania Democrat was reported describing his concern about other people's feelings toward Obama: "Some people are prejudiced and don't want to vote for him, for one thing, because he's black and for another, because they feel he's a Muslim. . . . I think for some people saying Obama is a Muslim is their way of getting around the black issue."[34] A reporter described a white West Virginia truck driver, a self-identified Democrat who had not been able to feel comfortable supporting Obama: "It's not race, [he] said. Something he cannot quite put his finger on is holding him back. 'I would probably go toward Obama. But I'm scared. . . . You know what I mean?'"[35] This "something he cannot quite put his finger on" was not lost on the McCain campaign. The Republican's slogan in mid-summer was "An American President for America." Presuming the campaign did not believe that large numbers of voters were geographically challenged, this appeared to be an effort to remind voters that Obama was "different," to the point of raising suspicion about his loyalties.

More explicit references to race increasingly found their way into the mainstream media as the campaign wore on. One way to raise the issue without getting blamed was to blame the other candidate for raising the issue. In July, Obama accused the Republican campaign of trying to scare voters by emphasizing that he "doesn't look like the other presidents," has a "funny name," and would be a risky choice. The McCain camp took the opportunity to do the same. Shortly after Obama's comment, a McCain spokesperson was widely quoted as saying, "Barack Obama has played the race card, and he played it from the bottom of the deck. It's divisive, negative, shameful and wrong."[36]

As in the case of coded racial remarks, reporters wrote about outright racism largely by quoting individuals. A *Washington Post* reporter offered the tale of a white-collar worker who had been laid off three times in the past year but who said, "We're not ready for a black guy."[37] A columnist quoted a union political director saying in frustration, "We've been talking with staff in different parts of the Midwest . . . and we're all struggling to some extent with the problem of white workers who will not vote for Obama because of his color. There is no question about it. It's a very powerful thing to get over for some folks."[38] Not surprisingly, some of the most blatant uses of the race issue came from independent political groups in targeted, "narrowcast" media, which were sometimes picked up by the mainstream press. In one such case, a chain e-mail message reached national prominence when the mayor of a small southern town forwarded it to a list that eventually included a reporter. The e-mail claimed that "the biblical book of Revelation says the antichrist will be in his 40s and of Muslim ancestry." The mayor said he forwarded the e-mail because he was "just curious" about whether Scripture actually suggested that Obama is the Antichrist.[39]

As Figure 6-3 shows, overt mentions of race (including but not limited to racism) were most common during the Democratic convention and at the close of the fall campaign. References to racial themes declined markedly after the Democratic convention ended; very few such mentions were recorded during the Republican convention and the first debate week. References to voter racism, in particular, began to rise during the fourth week of the coding period. And of course, as election day drew near and the Democrat was running ahead in the polls, the theme of Obama's becoming the first black president became more frequent. Right after the election, the notion that the Obama candidacy demonstrated real improvement in race relations in the United States, indicating that American politics was "post-racial," also increased. In the words of a black delegate to the Democratic convention, "This is going to show that America's precepts are not just rhetoric."[40]

The patterns in Figure 6-3, and in particular the dearth of references to race in the middle of the campaign, though it was obviously on the minds of many strategists and voters, illustrate the real uncertainties both politicians and journalists feel about dealing with racial issues in American politics. The candidacy of the first black presidential nominee would naturally raise a lot of interesting issues for journalists: why it happened in this particular election year; how it affected the feelings of supporters, potential donors, and others; how it could influence the "horse race" of which the media are so fond. Yet aside from the week of the Democratic convention, Obama's race was rarely addressed as a theme in the coverage until the closing weeks of the campaign.

## Media Bias: Making Media Coverage the Issue

The last of the major themes in the coverage dealt with media bias. Throughout the nominating contest, McCain, other Republicans, and Hillary Clinton all charged that Obama was being covered more respectfully than other candidates and was even idolized by reporters. During the summer and fall, the charge that the media were "in the tank" with Obama became a central tenet of the McCain campaign. Republican spokespersons complained in late July that Obama's week-long visit to the Middle East and some European capitals was covered by a planeload of about forty reporters, including some media "stars," whereas McCain's previous visits to Iraq had met with much less media interest. Underscoring the point, his campaign posted a three-minute video on the Internet titled "Obama Love," beginning with a short clip of MSNBC host Chris Matthews saying that he felt a "thrill going up my leg" while watching Obama give a speech; in the background was a soundtrack of the old Frankie Valli love song, "Can't Take My Eyes Off You." The Republican National Committee followed quickly with an e-mail fundraising appeal designed to tap conservative discontent with the mainstream media. The e-mail referred to "the fawning coverage the liberal mainstream media gives Barack Obama," and asked for money to counteract the "lopsided media coverage."

At about the same time, an independent group of conservatives called Citizens United put up a thirty-second ad on Fox News advertising a film to be issued in September titled, *Hype: The Obama Effect.*" The Fox ad featured clips from several conservative political figures, including former Ohio secretary of state Ken Blackwell, a black American, charging the media with pro-Obama bias. McCain aides began calling NBC, which is MSNBC's parent company, the "National Barack Channel." McCain ads connected this charge of bias to the claim that Obama was "arrogant" about becoming president, and that his Middle Eastern and European tour was designed as a "victory lap."

Governor Palin carried the media bias theme further in her acceptance speech at the Republican convention, noting sharply that she wasn't going to Washington to seek the good opinion of the reporters and commentators. She quickly drew an enormous amount of media attention. Much of it was critical, which the McCain campaign and conservative commentators claimed was more evidence that liberal media elites viewed "average" Americans like Palin with disdain. The charge by conservatives was not surprising; it had been a central tenet of right-wing rhetoric for many years. But many reporters were taken aback by McCain's own use of this theme. During the primary campaign, as well as throughout his race for the 2000 Republican nomination, reporters' daily and unfiltered access to McCain on the bus he named the "Straight-Talk Express" had won him extensive—and what many regarded as favorable—media coverage. In fact, McCain had jokingly referred to reporters as his "base," and as late as March 2008, a *New York Times* reporter wrote, "It certainly is no secret that Sen. John McCain, the presumptive Republican nominee, is a darling of the news media. . . . The mainstream news media by and large don't cover Mr. McCain; they canonize him."[41]

What evidence is there of media bias in the 2008 campaign? One indicator is the amount of coverage each candidate received. The Pew Research Center's nonpartisan Project for Excellence in Journalism (PEJ) tracked the proportion of campaign coverage in which each candidate was a "significant presence"—that is, in which at least 25 percent of the story referred to that candidate. Until the Republican National Convention, Obama received substantially more press attention than McCain did (see Figure 6-4). After the conventions ended, however, so did Obama's advantage in coverage. Until the two weeks before election day, when most commentators were predicting a Democratic victory, the amount of news space the two candidates received was essentially equal.

There could be many reasons why Obama initially received more ink than McCain did. John McCain had been in Congress for twenty-six years. His history, from his days as a prisoner of war in Vietnam to his lengthy service in Washington, was well known. His previous candidacy for president had been reported extensively by the national media. In contrast, Obama was a political unknown, at least outside of Chicago, until 2004. Few Americans knew much about his background or his work in the Senate. When he became the first black candidate to have a real shot at his party's nomination, it is not surprising that he drew even more media attention than most other newcomers would. In every

**Figure 6-4**   Amount of Media Coverage of McCain and Obama, June–November, 2008

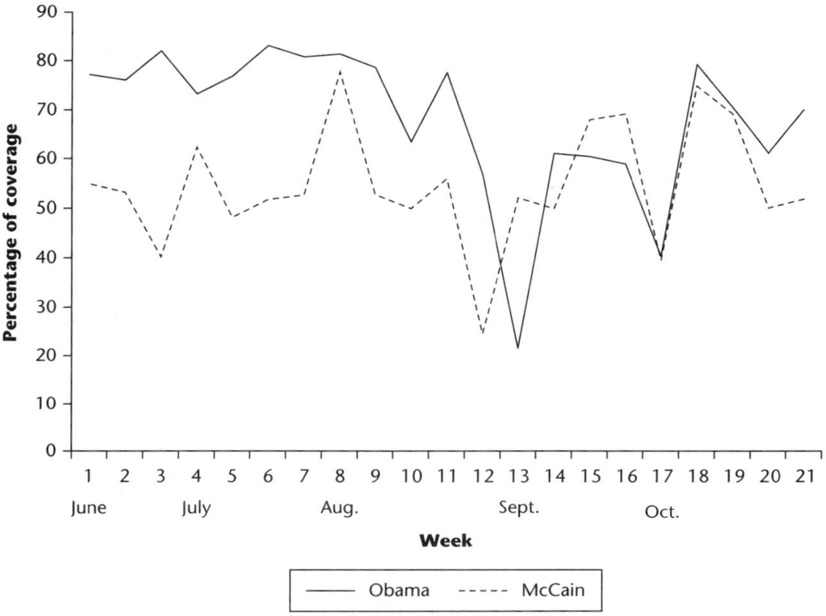

Source: Compiled by Pew Research Center Project for Excellence in Journalism (PEJ), on the Internet at http://journalism.org/node/13498.

Note: The PEJ's Campaign Coverage Index measured the number of stories out of all the presidential campaign coverage in which a candidate was a subject of at least 25 percent of the story. A story is considered to be about the presidential campaign if 50 percent or more of the content refers to the campaign.

sense of the word, Obama was "news." Yet the possibility that one candidate in a presidential election might find it more difficult than his opponent to get his name and ideas out to the public through media coverage is not encouraging, even if it does reflect the fact that, like McCain, the candidate had been covered more fully in the past.

PEJ analysts also measured the positive or negative tone of the coverage from September 8 to October 16,[42] and found that McCain was at a disadvantage. In the PEJ's coding period, the coverage of Obama was balanced, with almost equal amounts of positive, neutral, and negative coverage. In the case of McCain, however, there were almost four times as many negative stories as positive stories.

It didn't start that way. Early in the PEJ's coding period, right after the Republican convention, McCain's coverage was largely positive and Obama's coverage was more negative, according to the PEJ's analysis. Those patterns were reversed after the economic shocks of mid-September, when a giant Wall Street investment firm declared bankruptcy and several others followed. In part, the tone of the coverage at this time seemed to reflect the candidates' strategic choices in reaction to the Wall Street crash. McCain's response was to lurch from one move to another. First, he endorsed the proposed government bailout, then suspended his campaign, then associated himself with House Republicans' criticisms of the bailout, and finally returned to the campaign trail suddenly and without convincing evidence that his "rescue mission" to resolve the crisis had made a difference. Obama, in contrast, took a more measured approach.

When McCain attacked Obama in early October for his association with 1960s radical Bill Ayers, Obama's coverage trended strongly negative for a time, according to the Pew data. So the tone of the coverage seems to have been related to what was going on in the campaign at the time. Favorable poll data for a candidate, in particular, resulted in positive coverage, and attacks on the candidate gave his coverage a negative tone. At times, this became a self-reinforcing spiral, as it did late in the campaign for McCain. Because media coverage focused so heavily on the horse race, McCain's dropping poll numbers produced coverage that stressed these numbers and the strategic decisions intended to deal with them, which in turn further undermined his poll numbers.[43] At that point, McCain had little chance of recovery.

The tone of the coverage varied from one media outlet to another, however. According to Pew, MSNBC covered Obama less negatively, and McCain more negatively, than did the media as a whole. The opposite was true of Fox.[44] In the print press, front-page newspaper coverage in major newspapers was more negative toward McCain and more positive toward Obama than was broadcast coverage. And discussions of Obama on five major online news sites (AOL, Yahoo, Google News, CNN.com, and MSNBC.com) were similar in tone to media coverage overall, but McCain's online coverage was more negative. The diversification of media sites, then, gave viewers and readers a variety of perspectives to choose among.

The *Washington Post*'s ombudsman reported that her newspaper's coverage of the race advantaged Obama.[45] The *Post*'s editorial and op-ed pages ran substantially more positive pieces about Obama than about McCain during the year prior to the election, she found, and many more negative pieces about McCain than about Obama. On the news pages, Obama was featured in more stories and photos than was his opponent. The historic nature of Obama's candidacy helps to explain the Obama tilt in the *amount* of coverage, she wrote. But the pro-Obama tilt in the *tone* of coverage, at least on the op-ed page, was less justifiable. She concluded, "Obama deserved tougher scrutiny than he got."

According to most polls, citizens believed that media coverage was biased in favor of Obama. A Pew poll reported on October 22 that fully 70 percent of the sample (including 90 percent of the self-identified Republicans) thought the media wanted Obama to win, compared with just 9 percent who felt the media favored McCain and 13 percent who were not sure. Only 8 percent said that the media favored neither candidate.[46] Respondents might have been reporting their own observations of the coverage, or they might have been convinced by Republican charges of media bias, which went unanswered by the Obama campaign.

It is also plausible that the history-making nature of Obama's candidacy led journalists, at least in the mainstream media, to feel some sense of awe or protectiveness about the campaign or their experience with it. For example, when Barack Obama entered the room for his first press conference as president-elect, the members of the traveling press corps who had covered his campaign rose to their feet as a group.[47] Their personal attitudes may have affected the tone of their reporting, just as the sudden frost in McCain's approach to reporters may have influenced their coverage of him. But considering that the tone of both campaigns' coverage varied from one time to another, and from one news outlet to another, it seems just as likely that when a campaign is rising in the polls, its success lends a positive aura to the substance of reporters' stories, and when one candidate attacks another, coverage of the targeted candidate—and perhaps the attacker as well—becomes more negative.

## Media as Fact-Checkers

When reporters learn about a new campaign claim or attack, their traditional response is "two-handed journalism." The reporter presents the campaign's claim and then asks the opposing campaign for a rebuttal ("on the other hand, . . ."). But what do reporters do if they know that one of the claims is demonstrably false? Presenting both claims gives the reader or viewer no way to determine whether one claim is right or whether both are just "politics as usual." Editorial writers, columnists, and bloggers are not faced with this dilemma, as they are free to praise one claim and debunk the other. But reporters have typically avoided challenging a campaign directly in news reports, in their own voices, for fear of feeding citizens' suspicions that the news is biased.[48]

In the 2008 presidential race, however, reporters more frequently challenged what they believed to be false statements—directly, without attribution to other sources, in their news stories. Major media outlets issued "fact check" reports after each presidential debate, building on the "ad watches" used in prior campaigns. The spirit of these fact checks began to invade news stories as well. In a surprisingly frank example, an unsigned Associated Press story reported Palin's charge that Obama was "palling around with terrorists." The story continued, without attribution to any source,

> While it is known that Obama and Ayers live in the same Chicago neighborhood, served on a charity board together and had a fleeting political connection, there is no evidence that they ever palled around. And it's simply wrong to suggest that they were associated while Ayers was committing terrorist acts. Nonetheless, Palin made the comments at two appearances in separate states.[49]

What led some reporters to drop the "other hand" and rebut a candidate's claim themselves? McCain partisans might argue that this happened to McCain and Palin because journalists were pro-Obama. Obama supporters could say that although neither campaign was guiltless, the McCain campaign was responsible for most of the misinterpretations of the opponent's positions, and so, naturally, got corrected more often. On the other hand, media people may simply have learned that two-handed coverage wasn't providing audiences with the factual information they needed. In any case, many media sources began to take their work as fact checkers of campaign claims more seriously in 2008 than they had in recent years.

## Innovations in Use of the New Media

Fact-checking may have been even more necessary than usual in 2008 because the expanding variety of media led to a veritable monsoon of campaign-related information, characterized by varying degrees of accuracy. The 24/7 news cycle and the burgeoning number of Internet blogs were a gaping maw crying "Feed me!" to journalists and partisans of all kinds. Hoaxes, such as the claim that Governor Palin had been confused about whether Africa was a country or a continent, spread at warp speed to meet the voracious demand for content. Shrewd campaign staffers were able to feed this appetite for news and gain media attention as a result. In earlier elections, for instance, it was difficult for each party to make itself heard during the other party's national convention. But in 2008, with so many new media anxious for content, the McCain campaign received coverage during the Democratic convention by providing news feeds from its "Not Ready '08" headquarters. As McCain manager Steve Schmidt put it, "This new [media] environment . . . is easily manipulated because of round-the-clock thirst for news, increased competition, lowered standards created by the proliferation of outlets and hunger for the outrageous."[50]

One vital medium in 2008 was the video-sharing site YouTube. Not yet in existence in 2004, YouTube has become a regular news and entertainment source for millions of political aficionados. By October, 39 percent of registered voters reported having watched campaign videos online, and YouTube videos mentioning either Obama or McCain had been viewed 2.3 billion times.[51] This was a boon for the campaigns, which could post an ad on YouTube for free, rather than paying high rates to broadcast it on TV. At times, both campaigns called press conferences to announce a new ad, hoping that reporters would provide free coverage of the ad's message, even though the ad was rarely shown in paid media slots. This tactic, known as a "vapor," or "ghost" ad, was used more often in 2008 than in previous campaigns, partially because posting an ad on YouTube enhanced the campaign's claim that the ad was legitimate.

Once posted on YouTube, the campaign could give the ad widespread exposure by e-mailing its online address to millions of supporters, who in turn were asked to send the link to people in their own e-mail networks. The Obama campaign used this form of viral marketing to post Michelle Obama's speech to the Democratic National Convention on YouTube three hours after it was delivered and then urged supporters to forward the link to friends and family, so that Mrs. Obama's talk eventually reached tens of millions of people at no cost to the Obama organization.

Bloggers also played a major role throughout the campaign. Several Web sites, including Nate Silver's FiveThirtyEight.com (for election projections), Markos Moulitsas's Daily Kos and Arianna Huffington's Huffington Post (or HuffPo, for liberal commentary), and Michelle Malkin's Hot Air and the Drudge Report (for conservative commentary), were as central to many politically engaged people's daily lives as any newspaper or newscast. The blogosphere is often described as a democratizing force in politics. Although most influential bloggers could not easily be described as "grassroots," they did expand the information available to many citizens and, at times, even set the agenda for both campaigns. It was a blogger for the *Washington Post,* for instance, who reported that McCain was advertising his victory in the first presidential debate on the *Wall Street Journal* Web site—twelve hours before the debate was to take place.[52] The candidate's aim was to influence the post-debate commentary, and it certainly did, though not in the direction his campaign had hoped. Another "citizen reporter," though an Obama supporter, posted on HuffPo Obama's comment at a San Francisco fund-raiser that small-town people cling to their religion and their guns because they are bitter about the economy—a remark Obama later called "my biggest boneheaded move," and which dogged his steps in swing states for the rest of the campaign.

Although both campaigns had sophisticated Web sites and made extensive use of the Internet in other ways, Obama was light years ahead of McCain in exploiting new applications. The Obama Web site went up earlier, was more elaborate, and contained more tools for supporters to use. Through Barack-Obama.com, partisans not only could donate money, watch videos, and download music, but also could customize the site (MyBarackObama.com) to post their own blogs, locate groups of Obama supporters in their area, and make phone calls to undecided voters in other states using a script provided by the campaign. Through this means, individual supporters were able to update the campaign's database of likely voters. The campaign also developed an iPhone application that would rearrange an individual's cell phonebook to match the order of the campaign's targeting efforts, so that phone numbers in highly targeted states would show up first. After the supporter called those friends, he or she could communicate the canvassing results ("already voted," "undecided") into the Obama database. McCainSpace had several of the same features, but lacked the tools by which supporters could use the site to canvass and send the results to the campaign.

Because Obama's supporters were more likely than McCain's to be in the age and educational groups that tend to be "wired," the Obama Facebook site had attracted 2.3 million "friends" by a week before election day, almost four times as many as McCain's site had. This was another means by which the campaign could reach supporters and potential supporters directly, without having to rely on the traditional media to convey its message. The social networking phenomenon became so conventional in 2008, however, that even the more buttoned-up Republican National Committee (RNC) set up a Web site called BarackBook.com as a parody of Facebook, highlighting "friends" with whom the RNC felt Obama had questionable associations.

E-mail, now almost Stone Age in the toolkit of Internet applications, was used widely by both campaigns. The Democrats generated a huge e-mail list—more than thirteen million people, to whom the Obama campaign sent more than seven thousand different messages[53]—in part by asking people who wanted free tickets to rallies or other events to provide their e-mail address and other information in return. After the election, the campaign recontacted its e-mail list to add to its database—an unusually forward-looking move for a presidential campaign. To encourage supporters' feeling of ownership of the campaign and the administration, Obama's staff created a Web site for the post-election transition called Change.gov, asking people to "share your story and your ideas" with the transition team about what the incoming administration's priorities should be.

Obama's campaign also used text messaging extensively; McCain's did not. The Obama campaign organization collected a million cell phone numbers, initially by offering the chance to learn Obama's choice for vice president by text message prior to the official announcement. These numbers were later used to provide willing supporters with campaign updates, reminders to vote early, and other contacts, an especially useful connection with young people who lacked landlines. Many Obama rallies began by asking attendees to text friends and ask them to vote for Obama in November. Supporters who had signed up to receive text messages from the campaign got between five and twenty texts per month, and those in battleground states received at least three text messages on election day.[54]

In concert with the national parties' efforts to amass extensive information about every registered voter,[55] consultants in 2008 developed sophisticated strategies to track and profile individuals' patterns of Web surfing. One company created a system to plot the political leanings of Internet viewers by using a variety of data sets, including data on the sites each individual visited. It could then tell a campaign which visitors to a particular Web site trended Democratic or Republican and what specific concerns each visitor had. For each person who visited the site, then, the campaign could use this information to display an Obama (or McCain) pop-up ad, depending on the visitor's political leanings. If the voter's profile indicated that he or she has also visited sites dealing with energy issues, the pop-up could be further refined to provide Obama's (or McCain's) stand on energy policy.[56] Even domain names attracted the interest of both campaigns. Candidate organizations and other groups competed fiercely to register domain names that the opposition might want. At one point, for instance, those who clicked on Obama-Biden.org or Obama-Biden.com were redirected to a site put up by the American Issues Project, an anti-Obama group whose site harshly attacked the Obama campaign.

The Internet, in short, is no longer used by campaigns just to raise money. It has come to influence every aspect of presidential campaigning, from identifying supporters to communicating with them to entering their networks and talking to their friends. With new applications appearing regularly, political use of the Internet should continue to expand in 2010 and 2012. Because the Internet has become the main source of information for people younger than thirty about the presidential election,[57] any successful national campaign will need to bring Internet strategies into the core of its efforts. That, in turn, should increase the opportunities for younger and more Web-savvy people in running campaigns. The image of a campaign's Internet expert as a solitary techie in a remote basement is unlikely to survive in the wake of the 2008 election.

## How Well Did the Media Do Their Job?

Early in his political career, Thomas Jefferson famously said that if he had to choose between a government without newspapers or newspapers without a government, he would choose the latter. Two decades later, while serving as president, he had adjusted his thinking: "Nothing can now be believed which is seen in a newspaper. Truth itself becomes suspicious by being put into that polluted vehicle."[58] The role of the media in a democratic nation has always been both vital and challenging. How well did the media measure up in meeting their responsibilities to keep citizens informed about the candidates for president in 2008—their background, their character, and their proposals? And how have new media affected the media's ability to accomplish these goals?

Clearly, in 2008 there was abundant information available about Barack Obama and John McCain to any citizen who wanted it. But was the nature of the information helpful to voters? As always, media coverage put much of its effort into reporting the horse race—an emphasis that seems to have infected the tone of the coverage more generally, and which helps a voter make an informed choice in a general election about as much as would a two-headed coin. Journalists' coverage of the role of race in the campaign was another powerful example of a missed opportunity. Race is one of the most complex and challenging issues in American life, and its centrality has changed over time.[59] Although a political campaign is not the best venue in which to explore the richness of this question, media audiences deserved more than they received.

Was the information presented fairly? Most Americans thought not. Charges of pro-Obama media bias were commonplace in polling organizations' reports as well as by vocal McCain supporters. This perception is especially interesting in that, as we have seen, the most common themes in the coverage of Obama reflected talking points emphasized by the McCain campaign: that Obama was a tax-and-spend liberal, was locked in continuing conflict with Hillary Clinton, lacked experience, and was friendly with radicals. In contrast, although two of the most frequent themes in McCain's coverage ("same as Bush" and "reckless") came from the Obama playbook, most of the other themes used by the media to characterize McCain resembled the points his own campaign was trying to convey. Overall, Obama was the focus of more stories and commentaries than McCain was, in part because so much more about Obama's run for president met the media's standard definition of news. But when McCain's coverage turned negative, was that a reflection of reporters' excitement about Obama's candidacy, or of the Republican's declining poll numbers and the chorus of insider criticisms of his organization and its strategic choices?

Another real concern is that the partisan polarization of American politics has been reflected in many new media outlets, from bloggers to cable newscasts. Citizens who wanted to limit their information search to sources that confirmed their biases could certainly have done so in 2008. If so, then they could have been exposed to unchallenged falsehoods, such as that Obama was a Muslim or McCain was an unhinged risk-taker. Yet it is difficult to know how many voters did confine themselves to these partisan echo chambers. Perhaps Rush Limbaugh fans got an occasional whiff of Jon Stewart's comedy, or MSNBC devotees happened to see McCain videos on YouTube.

Ironically, then, the increasing diversity of opinionated media sources may be voters' best defense against media bias. The writer Joan Didion once criticized a presidential campaign as "a closed system staged by the candidates for the news media—one in which the media judged a candidate essentially by how well he or she manipulated them, and one in which the electorate were bystanders."[60] Such a campaign would seriously impoverish a democracy. In the chaos of the current media environment, however, that closed system is much more difficult to maintain. In this sense, the unruly new media are serving us well.

# Notes

1. Archived at www.youtube.com/watch?v=3m9Gbb6NSwM.
2. Archived at www.youtube.com/watch?v=G_vmQrTi3aM.
3. Tim Craig, "Remark About Bin Laden, Obama a Joke, Official Says," *Washington Post*, October 15, 2008, B2.
4. Markus Prior, *Post-Broadcast Democracy* (New York: Cambridge University Press, 2007), 1.
5. Benjamin I. Page, Robert Y. Shapiro, and Glenn R. Dempsey, "What Moves Public Opinion?" *American Political Science Review* 81 (March 1987): 39.
6. Richard Davis, *The Press and American Politics*, 3rd ed. (Upper Saddle River, N.J.: Prentice-Hall, 2000), chap. 2.
7. See Carol Sue Humphrey, *The Press of the Young Republic, 1783–1833* (Westport, Conn.: Greenwood Press, 1996), chaps. 4 and 5.
8. Alexis de Tocqueville, *Democracy in America* (New York: New American Library, 1956), 94.
9. Prior, *Post-Broadcast Democracy*, 1, 2.
10. See Matthew Robert Kerbel, "The Media: The Challenge and Promise of Internet Politics," in *The Elections of 2004*, ed. Michael Nelson (Washington, D.C.: CQ Press, 2005), 88–107.
11. Markus Prior, "News vs. Entertainment: How Increasing Media Choice Widens Gaps in Political Knowledge and Turnout," *American Journal of Political Science* 49 (July 2005): 577–592.
12. On the framing of political issues, see, for example, Thomas E. Nelson, Zoe Oxley, and Rosalee A. Clawson, "Toward a Psychology of Framing Effects,"

*Political Behavior* 19 (September 1997): 221–246, and Robert M. Entman, "Framing: Toward Clarification of a Fractured Paradigm," *Journal of Communication* 43 (Autumn 1993): 51–58.

13. "Winning the Media Campaign: Top Storylines," Pew Research Center's Project for Excellence in Journalism, October 22, 2008, available at http://journalism.org/node/13312.

14. Diana C. Mutz, "Effects of Horse-Race Coverage on Campaign Coffers," *Journal of Politics* 57 (November 1995): 1015–1042; and Marjorie Randon Hershey, "The Campaign and the Media," in *The Election of 2000,* ed. Gerald M. Pomper (New York: Chatham House, 2001), 55–56, 66.

15. Mentions of the frequency of these themes in the text refer to the overall number of mentions in the coverage. Table 6-1 lists only the five themes mentioned most frequently about each candidate in each particular week.

16. Mark Z. Barabak, "We Are a Better Country than This," *Los Angeles Times,* August 29, 2008, A1.

17. E. J. Dionne Jr., "McCain's Lost Chance," *Washington Post,* September 29, 2008, A19.

18. See, for instance, Patrick Healy, "Target: Barack Obama. Strategy: What Day Is It?" *New York Times,* July 4, 2008, A14.

19. Jim Rutenberg, "McCain Is Trying to Define Obama as Out of Touch," *New York Times,* July 31, 2008, A1.

20. Dan Balz, "Misunderestimating McCain," "The Trail," *Washington Post,* http://voices.washingtonpost.com/the-trail/2008/09/11/misunderestimating_mccain.html.

21. Michael D. Shear and Shailagh Murray, "Back on the Stump, Candidates Attack Each Other on Economy," *Washington Post,* September 6, 2008, A1.

22. "The Latest Campaign Narrative—'It's the Economy, Stupid',," Pew Research Center's Project for Excellence in Journalism, September 22, 2008, available at http://journalism.org/node/12900.

23. Megan Daum, "A Few PUMAs on the Loose," *Los Angeles Times,* August 30, 2008, A31.

24. Eli Saslow, "Many Clinton Supporters Say Speech Didn't Heal Divisions," *Washington Post,* August 27, 2008, A1.

25. Doris A. Graber, *Mass Media and American Politics,* 7th ed. (Washington, D.C.: CQ Press, 2006), chap. 4; and James T. Hamilton, *All the News That's Fit to Sell* (Princeton: Princeton University Press, 2004).

26. Marjorie Randon Hershey, "The Constructed Explanation," *Journal of Politics* 54 (November 1992): 943–976.

27. Robert Barnes and Michael D. Shear, "Battling through Battleground States," *Washington Post,* October 9, 2008, A10.

28. Quoted in Peter Wallsten, "Frank Talk of Obama and Race in Virginia," *New York Times,* October 5, 2008, A1.

29. Quoted in Kevin Merida, "North Carolina's New Blues," *Washington Post,* October 22, 2008, A1.

30. Chris Lehane, quoted in Michael Powell, "With Genie out of Bottle, Obama Treads Carefully on Race," *New York Times,* August 2, 2008, A1.

31. Adam Nagourney, "Framing Goals, Obama Takes the Fight to McCain," *New York Times,* August 29, 2008, A1.

32. See, for example, Eduardo Bonilla-Silva, *Racism without Racists,* 2nd ed. (Lanham, Md.: Rowman and Littlefield, 2006).

33. See Nicholas D. Kristof, "Racism without Racists," *New York Times,* October 5, 2008, "Week in Review," 10.

34. Jim Rutenberg and Marjorie Connelly, "Polls Show Obama Gaining among Bush Voters," *New York Times,* October 24, 2008, A18.

35. Lori Montgomery, "Economy May Not Influence Election as It Has in Past," *Washington Post,* August 31, 2008, A12.
36. Mark Z. Barabak, "'Race Card' Issue Lands Face-Up in the Spotlight," *Los Angeles Times,* August 1, 2008, A10.
37. Marc Fisher, "What's Real about the Split in Virginia," *Washington Post,* October 30, 2008, B1.
38. Bob Herbert, "The Dog that Isn't Barking," *New York Times,* August 26, 2008, A19.
39. There is no such scripture. Jonathan Allen, "Fort Mill Mayor's Obama E-Mail Causes Furor," *Fort Mill Times,* October 1, 2008, available at www.fortmilltimes .com/187/story/309384.html.
40. Quoted in Alec MacGillis, "Black Delegates Also Bask in Obama's Big Moment," *Washington Post,* August 28, 2008, A23.
41. Neil Gabler, "The Maverick and the Media," *New York Times,* March 26, 2008, 23; and Dana Milbank, "For Obama and McCain, the Bitter and the Sweet," *Washington Post,* April 15, 2008, A3.
42. "The Color of News," Pew Research Center's Project for Excellence in Journalism, October 29, 2008, http://journalism.org/node/13436.
43. "Winning the Media Campaign," Pew Research Center's Project for Excellence in Journalism.
44. "The Color of News."
45. Deborah Howell, "An Obama Tilt in Campaign Coverage," *Washington Post,* November 9, 2008, B6.
46. "Most Voters Say News Media Wants Obama to Win," Report, October 22, 2008, available at http://pewresearch.org/pubs/1003/joe-the-plumber.
47. Dan Balz and Shailagh Murray, "President-Elect Meets the Press, Cautiously," *Washington Post,* November 8, 2008, A1.
48. For evidence on the "hostile media hypothesis," see Jeanette Morehouse Mendez, "Killing the Messenger: An Experimental Analysis of the Hostile Media Effect," *Journal of Political Science* 35, no. 1 (2007): 31–62.
49. Associated Press, "Palin Says Obama 'Palling Around' with Terrorists," October 4, 2008, available at www.nytimes.com/aponline/washington/AP-Palin-Obama.html.
50. Jim Rutenberg and Adam Nagourney, "An Adviser Molds a Tighter, More Aggressive McCain Campaign," *New York Times,* September 7, 2008, A22.
51. David Carr and Brian Stelter, "Campaigns in a Web 2.0 World," *New York Times,* November 3, 2008, B1.
52. Jim Rutenberg, "A Day after McCain and Obama Face Off, a Debate over Who Won," *New York Times,* September 28, 2008, A26.
53. Jose Antonio Vargas, "Obama Raised Half a Billion Online," available at http://voices.washingtonpost.com/the-trail/2008/11/20/obama_raised_half_a_billion_on.html.
54. Ibid.
55. Marjorie Randon Hershey, *Party Politics in America,* 13th ed. (New York: Pearson, 2009), chap. 4.
56. Peter Whoriskey, "Candidates' Web Sites Get to Know the Voters," *Washington Post,* August 30, 2008, D1.
57. "Internet's Broader Role in Campaign 2008," Pew Research Center for the People and the Press, January 11, 2008, available at http://people-press.org/report/384/internets-broader-role-in-campaign-2008.
58. See Humphrey, *The Press of the Young Republic,* 72. Humphrey points out that Jefferson qualified his earlier remarks with, "But I should mean that every man should receive those papers, and be capable of reading them."
59. Paul M. Sniderman and Thomas Piazza, *The Scar of Race* (Cambridge, Mass.: Harvard University Press, 1994).
60. Gabler, "The Maverick and the Media."

# 7

# Voting Behavior:
# A Blue Nation?

## Nicole Mellow

The stakes in the 2008 presidential election were both high and unusual. Disillusionment with the sitting president, an economic crisis on par with the Great Depression, an unpopular war, the first major party African American candidate, the first nominating contest in which a woman was a viable candidate, and a perceived climate of hostility toward traditional partisanship lent an air of urgency and unpredictability to the election. Although horse-race style analysis of elections has long been an American pastime, 2008 produced an unparalleled cacophony of prognostication, with nearly as many postulates as there were queries: How would "Joe the Plumber" vote? What would young people do? What about African Americans? Who had the loyalties of the "pit bull hockey moms"?

When the returns rolled in, history had been made. Not only was Barack Obama elected the first African American president, the Democrat defeated his Republican rival, John McCain, with 53 percent of the popular vote. No Democrat since Lyndon B. Johnson routed Barry Goldwater in 1964 has had such a decisive popular victory. Democrats celebrated more than just Obama's election. Having won control of both houses of Congress in 2006 after twelve years as the minority party, Democrats increased their hold on Congress in 2008 with significant gains in both houses.[1] When Obama took office in January 2009, it marked the first time in fifteen years that the Democrats had full control of the national government.

Did this election signify a partisan or ideological "revolution" in American politics, as some were quick to claim?[2] Or was 2008 a deviating election, auguring that the country would return to partisan stalemate in short order? Determining whether 2008 was a significant turning point in the balance of power between the parties will only be possible with the hindsight of many more elections to come. Yet interpreting election night returns and exit poll data in the context of recent "red state versus blue state" dynamics and other national party coalition trends provides some insight into what obstacles and prospects are ahead for Democrats intent on becoming the new majority.

## Whose Majority Is It?

Scholars have long sought to make sense of the episodic shifts in political authority that have occurred throughout American history. The classic instance of this type of massive change in power is the New Deal. Spurred by the Great Depression, voters in 1932 rejected long-reigning Republican ideas of limited national government, laissez-faire capitalism, and voluntarism in favor of Democrat Franklin D. Roosevelt's calls for a greater government role in regulating the economy and ensuring the welfare of citizens. That landslide election gave Roosevelt 472 electoral votes to Hoover's 59, and 57 percent of the popular vote to Hoover's 40 percent. Roosevelt's victory was national in scope. He lost only six states, all of them in the Mid-Atlantic or New England, yet the most populous states in those regions, New York, New Jersey, and Massachusetts, supported him. Democrats also won sizeable majorities in Congress. In subsequent years, Roosevelt and his party enacted the host of social welfare and work programs associated with the New Deal; they also enhanced presidential authority, expanded the size of the bureaucracy, and legitimized an activist national government. Subsequently, during World War II and the Cold War, Democrats authored the shift from an isolationist foreign policy to one of liberal internationalism. The ideas, institutions, and political leaders of the New Deal were sufficiently coherent to constitute a new political regime, and a majority of voters regularly reauthorized this regime in elections through at least the 1960s.

The Democrats' New Deal victory in 1932 represents the archetype of a realigning election and the birth of a new political era. Realignment has a complex, even technical, definition, yet the general form involves significant political change that is electorally driven, substantive, and durable. Scholars have documented, and disagreed about, a number of such moments of change, including the elections of Andrew Jackson (1828), Abraham Lincoln (1860), and William McKinley (1896).[3] What is of signal importance, though, is that realignments represent a lasting shift in voter behavior and the emergence, often dramatic, of a new majority.

The elections of the past fifty years have not been as easy to classify. Some presidential contests, such as those of 1964, 1972, 1980, and 1984, resulted in landslide victories, with sizeable popular and electoral vote margins for the winner that dwarf Obama's. Yet any long-term "mandate" that might have resulted from those elections was quickly curbed. After electing Democrat Lyndon Johnson and fortifying Democratic control of Congress in 1964, the country was rent by social and political divisions and elected Republican Richard Nixon four years later. Nixon was reelected in 1972 by a landslide (losing only Massachusetts and the District of Columbia), yet he left office in disgrace two years later. In 1980, Ronald Reagan proffered a new public philosophy of limited government joined with military strength. His election and reelection in 1984 were followed, in 1988, by the election of his vice president, George H. W. Bush. This string of Republican victories seemed, at last, to be a repudiation of the New Deal, and recent works of political history tend to characterize the late twentieth century as a conservative, Republican era that began with Reagan, or possibly Nixon.[4]

But unlike the New Deal and earlier party eras, the Republican regime was embraced with ambivalence by voters. With the exception of the Senate from 1981 to 1987, Congress stayed under Democratic control throughout the 1970s and 1980s. When Republicans finally won control of both the House and Senate in 1994, Democrat Bill Clinton remained in the White House, and was reelected two years later. Indeed, divided party control has become the norm in Washington, with the same party ruling both Congress and the presidency for only ten of the last forty years. This is not just an artifact of the difficulty of dislodging congressional incumbents. No recent president has been able to secure a big win, or a significant electoral mandate. Pluralities prevailed in the two elections won by Clinton. In the 2000 election, George W. Bush won with fewer popular votes (but more electoral votes) than the losing candidate, and in 2004, Bush earned re-election with a very slim popular vote majority (50.73 percent). In short, voters stopped sending the type of clear messages to Washington that they had in earlier political eras.[5]

Part of the reason that neither party has been able to claim a clear mandate is that the parties in recent years have been geographically divided and have commanded the allegiances of opposing halves of the country. This division became apparent in the 2000 election and was quickly labeled the "red state/blue state" divide by the media. Red, or Republican, states in the South and interior West were those captured in 2000 and 2004 by Bush, whereas blue, or Democratic, states in the Northeast, Great Lakes region, and Pacific Coast were those captured by Democrats Al Gore and John Kerry in 2000 and 2004, respectively. Although this geographic division of the party system has only garnered media attention in the last three presidential elections, it is the result of nearly a half century of regional realignments within and between the parties.[6]

The current organization of the party system has its origins in the 1960s, when the New Deal Democratic Party still dominated national elections. The party's electoral strength since the 1930s had derived from an accord brokered between its regional halves in the North and South. The basis of this accord was that national policy would be tailored to accommodate the dominant interests in each region: organized labor and manufacturers in the North, agriculture and labor-intensive industry in the South. Issues that defied regional tailoring, such as civil rights for African Americans, were suppressed.

By the late 1960s and early 1970s, this accord was in jeopardy. Republican leaders were quick to exploit the emerging fissures in the New Deal coalition—most obviously, but not entirely, in the area of civil rights. During his presidency, Richard Nixon consistently promoted policies that split the New Deal Democrats' interregional alliance, even forgoing Republican unity at times to do so. The Republicans gained an advantage at this time by appealing to southern Democrats, not just on racial issues but on other social issues and economic and foreign policy matters as well.

The regional discord of this late New Deal era led to a dramatic reorganization of the geographic basis of the party system. The most transparent outcome of Republican efforts to destabilize the Democrats' geographical base was an acceleration of the GOP's capture of the South. But Republican Party leaders concentrated their attention on the West as well, a region that,

like the South, contained states with fast-growing economies and populations. Also, as in the South, the farming states of the West had a political history of antagonism toward a perceived domination by northern financial and
political elites. These economic, social, and symbolic similarities were fodder
for a growing Republican Party.[7]

With the regional crack-up of the Democratic Party, the New Deal
regime was revealed to be an ultimately unstable sectional fusion. Two new
versions of the Republican and Democratic parties replaced the New Deal
party system in the 1970s. One was an "emerging Republican majority" centered in the fast-growing suburbs and small towns of the South and West.[8]
The other was a refashioned Democratic Party with enhanced electoral muscle in the historically urbanized, densely populated, and commercially developed states of the North and the Pacific Coast. Just as Republicans displaced
Democrats in some regions, such as the South, Democrats, in turn, displaced
Republicans in other regions, such as New England, where the GOP had
historically reigned.

As the demands made by the South and West on the national government
began to clash with those of the North and Pacific Coast, the parties responded.
"Red versus blue" partisan conflict intensified as the parties' geographic bases
shifted. Less of a national realignment, the current party system—at least until
2008—had been one of partisan stalemate between two regionally centered
parties.

Although these regional differences produced a partisan standoff, both
parties claimed that the tides of national majority support were in their favor.
In the late 1960s, Kevin Phillips, a Republican strategist and campaign
adviser to Richard Nixon, sketched a description of "the emerging Republican majority," the electoral base of which, he said, would be not in the country's old industrial cities, but in suburbs and small towns, especially those in
the growing regions of the South and West. For Phillips and other Republican strategists, the formula for electoral success depended on the use of racial
and other social wedge issues to divide Democrats, populist appeals to reject
what Republicans described as an overweening federal presence in the lives
of ordinary citizens, and nationalist calls for a revitalized military to combat
the continuing threat of communism.[9] In the aftermath of the Republican
takeover of Congress in 1994, William Kristol claimed, "The nation's long,
slow electoral and ideological realignment with the Republican Party is reaching a watershed."[10] The electoral success of George W. Bush and Republicans
in Congress during the subsequent decade seemed to provide evidence for this
claim of a Republican realignment.

Yet, in 2002, at a high point of Republican popularity, Democratic strategists John Judis and Ruy Teixeira published their counter to Phillips's thesis in
the aptly named *The Emerging Democratic Majority*.[11] Judis and Teixeira saw
the prospects for a new national majority that combined Democrats' traditional appeals to working-class voters and ethnic and racial minorities with
appeals to young professionals working and living in "ideopolises." They

argued that cities like Seattle, Raleigh-Durham, and Austin, which are fast growing and information economy based, are likely to be especially receptive to the Democratic Party's social tolerance and environmental goals. Although the party came up short in 2004, Democrats regained Congress in the "blue sweep" midterm elections of 2006 with victories across the country.

After so many decades of divided party control, partisan stalemate, and regional realignment, and with each party claiming that political trends are in its favor, did the elections of 2008 represent a turning point? Have the winds of change driven Democrats to an enduring new majority? Or was this election merely a temporary corrective to the mistakes of Republican rule—especially in economic affairs—of the last eight years?

## "It's the Economy, Stupid"

James Carville, the political strategist who helped engineer Bill Clinton's 1992 victory, famously posted a sign in campaign headquarters stating that focusing on the economy ("It's the economy, stupid!") would bring victory to the Democrats. Although direct, this remark was less a brilliant insight than a timely reminder of what has historically been the Democrats' strong suit. Tough economic times tend to benefit the Democratic Party, and in 1992, Carville wanted to make sure that voters were reminded of the country's recent recession. No one needed reminding in 2008. Against a backdrop of home foreclosures, financial crises, corporate bankruptcies, and the failure of industrial giants, 63 percent of voters in 2008 said the economy was the number one issue facing the nation, and of these, 53 percent voted for Barack Obama.

Voters have evinced this degree of concern about the economy only twice since 1970. In 1976 and again in 1992, more than 60 percent of voters ranked the economy as their main concern.[12] In both of these elections, the Democratic challenger, first Jimmy Carter and then Bill Clinton, defeated a Republican president (Gerald R. Ford in 1976 and George H. W. Bush in 1992). Aside from Clinton's reelection in 1996, these were the only Democratic presidential victories in more than forty years. Ranked lower by the voters, the economy has been substantially downgraded compared with social policy and foreign affairs in most recent presidential elections, leaving Democrats with a seemingly insurmountable electoral challenge.

The irony of Democratic success appearing to hinge on widespread economic anxiety is that it was this party that helped minimize the vicissitudes of capitalism for working people and build the middle class in the first half of the twentieth century. In other words, the New Deal Democratic Party's success at economic management may have sapped some of the vitality from the animating issue for future generations of voters. Although low-income and working-class voters still regularly favor the Democrats, many middle-income voters have drifted away from the party since the 1970s, returning only when economic anxiety crests.[13]

The 2008 election illustrates the electoral boon that economic concerns bring to Democrats, as well as the limits of either generic pocketbook worries or the party as a solution to those worries. Winning the support of 60 percent of those making less than $50,000 annually, Obama increased the Democratic share of these low- and lower-middle-income voters over those of recent elections.[14] Voters with annual family incomes between $30,000 and $50,000 actually had divided evenly between the two parties in the last several elections, but in 2008, they swung solidly behind Obama, who received 55 percent of their support. Worrisome for Democrats is that Obama did not fare as well with solidly middle-class voters—those with annual family incomes between $50,000 and $75,000. He won just 48 percent of these voters, who make up slightly more than a fifth of the total electorate. This is a large group for whom the Democratic Party label, even in the current unstable economic environment, was not enough to win their support.

In addition to rising economic worries, Democrats were helped by the corresponding decline in voters' foreign policy concerns. Foreign affairs issues historically tend to benefit the Republican Party, and they were much lower in voter priority in 2008 than in other recent elections. For example, only 9 percent of voters cited terrorism as their top concern, down from 19 percent in 2004. Ten percent said that Iraq was the nation's top priority (down from 15 percent in 2004), but, as in 2004, a large majority of these voters preferred the Democrat. Even more challenging for John McCain and the Republican Party, voters were highly critical of President Bush. In the final months of the 2008 campaign, more than 70 percent of poll respondents disapproved of the job Bush was doing, making him the most unpopular president in modern times.[15]

In 2008 voters' priorities alone seemed destined to benefit the Democratic Party. They suggested a country that, far from being divided, was generally more united in its anxieties and its assessment of the existing administration than in recent years. In the context of media stories likening the current economic crisis to the Great Depression, this combination of significant economic worries and strong disapproval of the Republican administration should have led to a sweeping national Democratic victory. Yet Obama's popular vote margin, although substantial, was not the rout that history would lead us to expect. In fact, Obama won five fewer electoral votes than Bill Clinton won in 1992. One important reason is that, despite voters' relative unity on the country's ills, the red state/blue state regional axis that has divided the nation in recent years remained largely unchanged.

## A Red/Blue Nation

Despite significant changes in national politics from just four years before, the basic division of the country into "red" Republican and "blue" Democratic regions stayed the same in 2008. The muscle behind Obama's win was provided by the regions that have tended to vote Democratic in recent elections—the North (including the Great Lakes portion of the Midwest) and the Pacific Coast. Obama won every state in these regions,

**Figure 7-1**   Percentage of Major Party Voters Selecting Democratic Presidential Candidate, 1960–2008, by Region

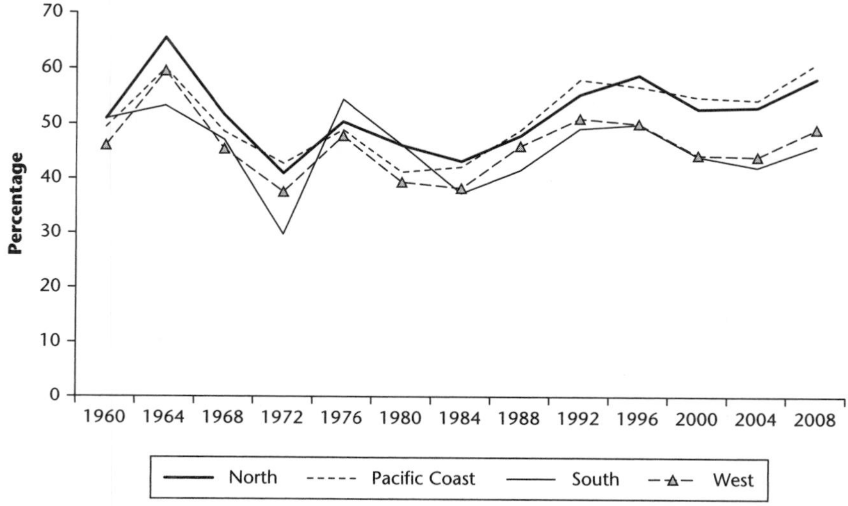

Source: Presidential Elections, 1789–2000 (Washington DC: CQ Press, 2002); CNN.com (2004 data); and David Leip, Atlas of U.S. Presidential Elections (2008 data), available at http://uselectionatlas.org. Regional calculations are the author's.

including states such as Ohio and Indiana that have eluded Democrats in recent presidential contests. The unified support of these traditionally blue regions, along with Washington, D.C., and Hawaii (both of which also are strongly Democratic) provided Obama with 273 electoral votes—three more than he needed to win. The continuity of general regional preferences is evident in Figure 7-1, which shows the percentage of major-party voters in each region who supported the Democratic presidential candidate from 1960 to 2008.[16]

In every election since 1960, major-party voters in the North and Pacific Coast regions have supported the Democratic presidential candidate to a greater degree than voters in the South and West. The exception is 1976, when Georgia's Jimmy Carter headed the Democratic ticket and won a higher proportion of voters in the South than elsewhere. The general partisan gap between voters in the North and Pacific Coast and voters in the South and West has widened over time and is especially evident in the last two decades.

This regional split stayed essentially the same in 2008. Although Obama gained a higher proportion of southern and western support than did Kerry in 2004 or Gore in 2000, he increased the Democratic share of northern and Pacific Coast support by similar margins. Clear majorities of major-party voters from the North and Pacific Coast supported all three recent Democratic candidates (Gore, Kerry, and Obama). In contrast, none of the three could garner more than 50 percent of the two-party vote in the South or West. Thus, although Obama fared better in all regions than his immediate Democratic predecessors, he did not do well enough to pull the red regions of South and West into the Democratic column.

**Figure 7-2**    Electoral Map of 2008, Obama Margin of Victory

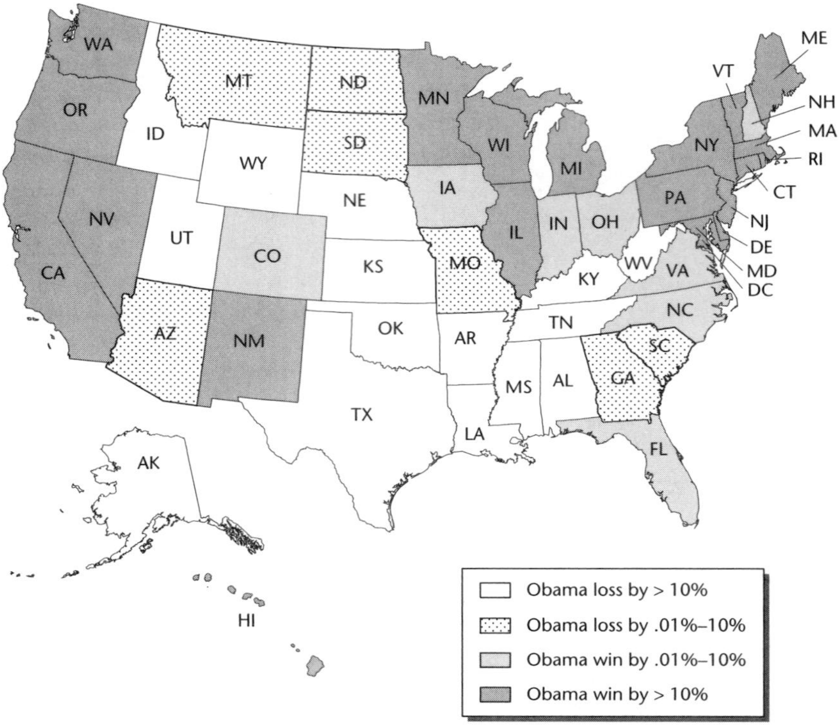

Obama loss by > 10%

Obama loss by .01%–10%

Obama win by .01%–10%

Obama win by > 10%

*Source:* David Leip's Atlas of U.S. Presidential Elections, available at http://uselectionatlas.org/RESULTS.

A closer look at the geography of the 2008 election reveals that Obama secured most of his greatest margins in states in the traditionally blue regions of the North and Pacific Coast. Figure 7-2 shows Obama's popular margin of victory in each state.

Obama won easily—by more than ten percentage points—throughout the older urban and industrial regions of the North and the Pacific Coast. His margin of victory was less than 10 percent only in the three states of those regions in which Republicans recently have been competitive—Ohio, Indiana, and New Hampshire. Conversely, McCain won a large majority of states in the South and West. The Republican fared best—winning by more than ten points—in much of Appalachia, the Deep South "cotton belt" states, and in the western farm states.

By winning every state in the North and Pacific Coast, Obama consolidated Democratic power in the regions that tend to be most supportive of his party. Although this victory alone would have been sufficient to win the presidency in 2008, it did not undo the recent red/blue divide nor produce a durable national Democratic majority. However, as Figure 7-2 also makes clear, Obama did poach into what has been reliably Republican territory in recent elections by picking up a number of electoral vote–rich states in the South and West. The states that voted against their regional tendencies in 2008 were all in the South and West: Florida, North Carolina, and Virginia in the Southeast; and Colorado, New Mexico, and Nevada in the Mountain West. In the West North-Central subregion of the Midwest, Iowa and Minnesota also defected from the regional tendency to vote Republican.

In winning these eight states, Obama built on ground that was already more receptive to Democratic advances than the rest of the South and West. In 2004 Democrats won one of the eight (Minnesota) and lost six of the remaining seven by less than 10 percent (Florida, Virginia, Colorado, New Mexico, Nevada, Iowa).[17] Of the eight, only North Carolina went Republican by more than 10 percent in 2004. Yet North Carolina, Virginia, and Colorado all went Democratic in 2008. These are states that have consistently gone Republican, even if sometimes by small margins, in recent presidential elections.

## Picking the Regional Lock: Opportunities for Democrats in the South and West

As noted earlier, the economy was a big part of the story of Obama's election in 2008, as it often has been for successful Democratic presidential candidates. Yet it is not the only story, or else Obama's victory would have been more geographically widespread. Consider a sector of the economy in which the downturn directly affected voters: the housing market. If Obama's victory was simply a response to a troubled economy, indications of homeowner distress would have foretold where he would be successful. But they did not.

One measure of homeowner distress is the condition of negative equity, or owing more on one's home than the house is currently worth. The percentage of mortgaged homes with negative equity was lower in some states, like New York and Pennsylvania, where Obama won, than it was in other states, like Texas and Kansas, where he lost. This was true even within the same region. The percentage of negative equity homes in Georgia, which Obama lost, was 23 percent, while in North Carolina, which Obama won, only 10 percent of homes had negative equity. The same was true to the west: the percentage of homes with negative equity in Texas (Obama loss) was 17 percent versus New Mexico's 8 percent (Obama win). Although home ownership reveals only one facet of economic stress, other economic indicators, such as state unemployment rates and changes in personal income by state, provide additional evidence that economic distress was not the whole story of Obama's victory.[18]

One of the more interesting shifts in voter loyalties in 2008 occurred among high-income earners. Historically, income has been strongly correlated with vote choice. Working-class and low-income voters tend to vote Democratic, and more affluent voters tend to vote Republican. In 2008, voters whose family income exceeded $100,000 annually split their vote evenly between McCain and Obama. The Democratic vote share of this group increased eight percentage points from 2004, from 41 percent to 49 percent. Even more pronounced was the change among voters whose family income was more than $200,000: in 2004, just 35 percent of these voters gave their support to the Democrats, whereas in 2008 the number jumped to 52 percent. Importantly, voters whose family income exceeded $100,000 made up more than a quarter of the electorate in 2008—and thus were critical to Obama's victory.

Democrats began attracting greater support from higher-income earners in the 1960s, as the party began to embrace a set of "post-material" goals, such as social equality, environmentalism, and opposition to war.[19] Researchers recently have demonstrated that there is a red/blue dimension to the change in traditional economic class loyalties. Although affluent voters still support Republicans at much higher rates than low-income voters in poor states, most of which are red, the correlation is very low in rich (mostly blue) states, where both low- and high-income voters support the Democratic Party.[20] This is one reason why support for Obama was so strong in the relatively wealthy, traditionally blue states of the North and Pacific Coast.

Democratic strategists Judis and Teixeira saw the party's emphasis on post-material concerns as a key element in building a national majority. In particular, they argued that this emphasis would attract highly educated professionals less likely to be swayed by the Democrats' traditional economic message. Thus, in 2008 although college graduates were closely split between the two candidates (Obama got 50 percent of their vote, McCain 48 percent), 58 percent of those with a post-graduate education supported Obama. This helps to account for Obama's success in the more-educated blue regions of the country, and it may help to explain why Obama captured the states that he did in the South and West. Figure 7-3 is a map showing where advanced-degree holders are concentrated.

With the exceptions of Kansas and Alaska, every state with a higher than average percentage of advanced-degree holders voted for Obama. Generally, in the continental U.S., these states are in the Pacific Coast and the North. However, outside of those regions, four of the eight states that voted for Obama (Minnesota, New Mexico, Colorado, and Virginia), have a higher than average percentage of advanced-degree holders. Put differently, four of the five states outside of the traditionally blue North and Pacific Coast regions with above average percentages of advanced-degree holders voted for Obama. Home to high-tech industries, they also have the type of metropolitan areas (ideopolises) that Judis and Teixeira identified as crucial to Democratic growth, places like Minneapolis/St. Paul, Albuquerque, Boulder/Denver, and the northern Virginia suburbs.

Although support from highly educated, high-income earning professionals was an important ingredient of Obama's success outside the blue regions, these voters still comprised a small minority of the entire electorate in 2008. Also helping to ensure Obama's win was the strong support of African American and Latino voters. African American support for the Democratic Party is nothing new. When the New Deal Democratic Party foundered in the 1960s, one of the deepest regional fissures was over the issue

**Figure 7-3**   Percentage of Population with an Advanced Degree

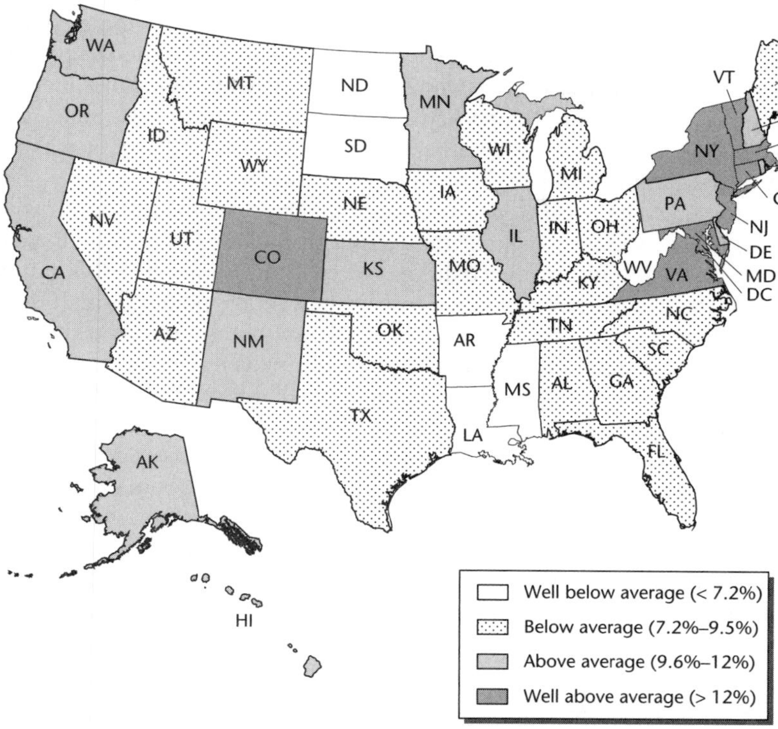

Legend:
- Well below average (< 7.2%)
- Below average (7.2%–9.5%)
- Above average (9.6%–12%)
- Well above average (> 12%)

*Source:* U.S. Census Bureau, 2007 American Community Survey.
*Notes:* Category breaks are based on mean +/–1 standard deviation. Data are from 2007.

of civil rights for African Americans. Northern Democratic support for civil rights, while alienating the South, helped secure the lasting support of African American voters for the Democratic Party. Since that time, Democrats have regularly earned more than 80 percent of the African American vote.

In 2008 Obama received the support of 95 percent of African American voters, a seven percentage point increase from 2004. Making this near-universal support more meaningful was the increase in turnout among African American voters, from 11 percent of the electorate in 2004 to 13 percent in 2008. Because of the high concentration of African Americans in the South, their increased participation and support for the Democrats helped shift states like Virginia and North Carolina away from Republicans. Indeed, although Democratic turnout increased in most states, Virginia and North Carolina were among the top ten states generating greater Democratic turnout.[21]

Even with the strong support of African American voters, however, Obama was unable to capture most other southern states, including the Deep South states from South Carolina to Louisiana in which African Americans make up a higher percentage of the population than anywhere else in the country. The main reason for this was the weak support for Obama among southern whites. Only 30 percent backed the Democrat, a substantially lower percentage than whites elsewhere. This continues a trend of the past two decades in which southern whites have been less receptive to the Democratic presidential candidate than other whites.[22] In short, while African American mobilization on behalf of Obama helped him to win states in the South that have recently become more sympathetic to the Democratic Party, it was not enough to trigger a broader realignment in the region.

In addition to increasing African American support, Obama succeeded in increasing Latino support, making the Democratic Party's ongoing efforts to build a multiracial, multi-ethnic coalition especially successful in 2008. Latino support for the Democratic candidate rose 14 percentage points from 2004 to 2008; 67 percent of Latino voters endorsed Obama on election day. This was in keeping with the level of support that this group has traditionally given the Democratic Party, but it is noteworthy because in 2004 President Bush attracted 44 percent of Latino voters—an all-time high for the Republican Party, and one that seemed to portend a possible shift in party loyalties among Latinos.

Strong support from the Latino community helped Obama capture an additional set of states—this time in the Mountain West. Figure 7-4 shows the percentage of each state's population that is of Latino origin. In addition to Florida, which has a large Cuban American population, states in the Southwest have the highest percentages of Latinos. All three Mountain West states that went to Obama—Colorado, New Mexico, and Nevada—are well above average in the proportion of Latinos in their states. Of the fifteen states with above-average percentages of Latinos, Obama won all but four: Texas, Idaho, Utah, and McCain's home state of Arizona. As with African American support, mobilizing Latinos was not sufficient to transform the Mountain West into a Democratic region, but in combination with other factors, the support of this voting bloc helped Obama break new ground in previously Republican territory.

## The Art of Redrawing the Map

An economy in crisis, an unpopular war, and a president with historically high disapproval rates came together in 2008 in a way that seemed to portend a national Democratic realignment. This did not happen. Instead, Obama succeeded in making America's blue regions bluer while poaching a number of red states from the Republicans. In short, the United States is still a divided nation. But the footholds Obama gained in the South and especially in the Mountain West indicate that there are opportunities on which the Democrats can build in their effort to construct a national coalition.

Two trends in particular favor the Democrats. One involves voter turnout. Overall, voters turned out at only a slightly higher rate, 62 percent of the eligible electorate, than in 2004. But that is because many Republicans stayed home. Democratic turnout surged in 2008. Indeed, when placed in historical perspective, it becomes clear that Democrats generally have been increasing their turnout in recent elections.

**Figure 7-4**   Percentage of Total Population Who Are of Hispanic or Latino Origin

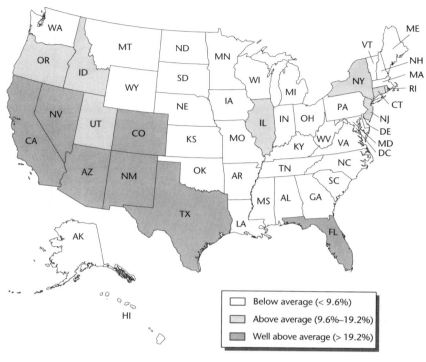

☐ Below average (< 9.6%)

▨ Above average (9.6%–19.2%)

▓ Well above average (> 19.2%)

*Source:* U.S. Census Bureau, May 2008, available at www.census.gov/popest/states/asrh/SC-EST2007-04.html.

*Notes:* Category breaks are based on mean +/–1 standard deviation. Data are from 2007.

Figure 7-5 shows Democratic and Republican voter turnout in each election since 1960. Republican turnout has fluctuated, spiking in 1972, 1984, and 2004—all years in which a Republican president was up for reelection—before dropping again. In comparison, Democratic turnout has increased with each election since 1980, whether the Democratic candidate won or lost. Although Obama brought more Democrats to the polls than Kerry, his success was not a radical departure from the pattern of the past. This suggests a degree of systematic coalition building that holds promise for Democrats in the future.

The other trend that portends good news for the Democrats is the youth vote. After years of declining youth turnout, young people voted in greater numbers in 2004 and in even greater numbers in 2008. About 53 percent of eligible youth voted in 2008, up five percentage points from 2004. This growth increased the youth share of the total electorate from 17 percent in 2004 to 18 percent in 2008.[23] And as Figure 7-6 shows, young voters tend to favor the Democratic candidate more than other age groups. In 2008, this tendency was especially pronounced.

Obama gained the support of 66 percent of voters between the ages of 18 and 29, an increase of twelve percentage points over these voters' support

**Figure 7-5**    Partisan Turnout Trends, 1960–2008

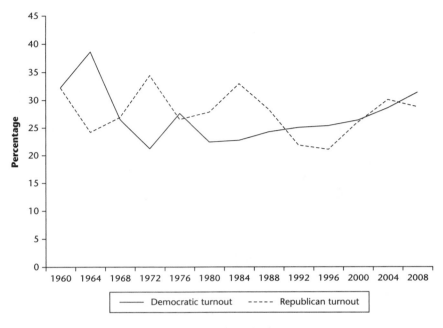

Source: Center for the Study of the American Electorate, American University.

for Kerry in 2004. Some of Obama's greater appeal may owe to his personal style, or to the celebrities who turned out to recruit young voters for the party, or even, perhaps, to the campaign's well-organized use of new technologies. But to the extent that young people are drawn to youthful ideopolises, this phenomenon likely helped Obama in states in the South and West where Democrats recently have struggled. More important, a person's first vote, especially in turbulent times, can be a good indicator of future party loyalty, and if this holds true, then Obama's success in attracting first-time voters may translate into a more enduring Democratic success.[24]

Aside from these promising trends, the 2008 election provides some lessons that the Democratic Party would do well to capitalize on as it tries to build an enduring national majority. The first and most general lesson is that economic distress, by itself, is not enough to substantially disrupt the Republicans' regional coalition. This may be because voters are not yet confident that Democrats can deliver on their economic promises. It also may be that voters simply have a broader set of concerns on which they make up their minds, and a declining economy alone is insufficient to change their party affiliation.

Second, common to several states that Obama captured in the South and West are concentrations of highly educated professionals, often living in ideopolises. This group's support for the Democratic Party has been growing

**Figure 7-6**   Percentage of Voters Selecting Democratic Presidential Candidate, 1972–2008, by Age

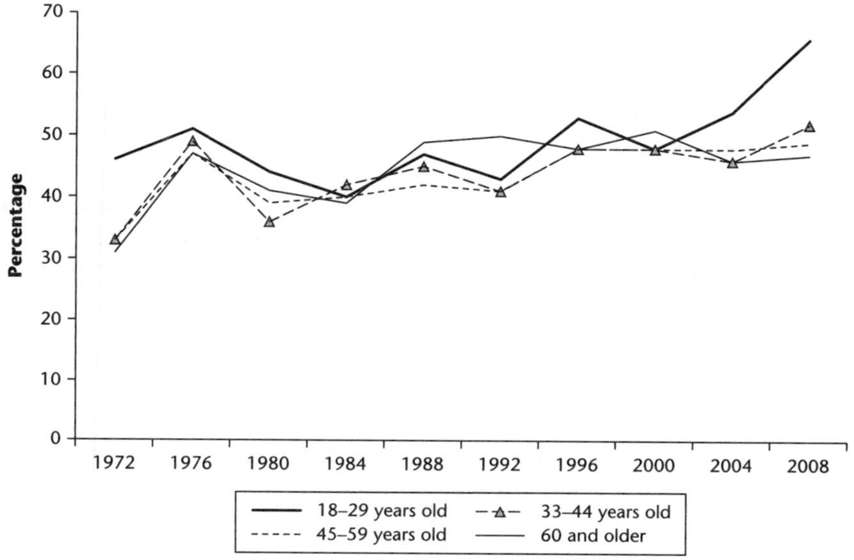

Source: New York Times National Exit Polls table.

in recent elections and was instrumental in making states like Virginia and Colorado receptive to Democratic advances in 2008. With their financial clout and their social and professional networks, these voters could become an important part of the Democratic coalition, especially if Obama delivers on issues of enduring concern to them, such as the environment.

Yet relying too heavily on the support of this group may not be the wisest strategy for Democrats to adopt. As with young voters, some of Obama's appeal to highly educated professionals may be idiosyncratic, owing to a shared sense of generational or social class sensibilities and "post-partisan" aspirations. To the extent that this is true, attachment to Obama may not translate into enduring loyalty to the Democratic Party. In addition, ideopolises alone generally are not large enough to transform entire states. Democrats currently fare well in Atlanta, Austin, and Salt Lake City but that has yet to translate into success in Georgia, Texas, and Utah.

Perhaps most important is that the voting bloc of educated professionals is still relatively small, and if current education and income trends continue, it is unlikely to grow. It may even shrink: the percentage of adults aged twenty-five to thirty-four who have an associate's degree or higher is smaller than the percentage of adults aged forty-five to fifty-four who have one. This relationship between the generations holds true for high school graduates as well in that a higher percentage of older adults have high school diplomas than younger adults.[25] Of course, if, once in power, Democrats are able to reverse these trends with programs that increase access to education and job promotion, they will likely succeed in building a much larger and economically diverse base, one that can perhaps rival the old New Deal coalition.

The other lesson to emerge from 2008 is the potential for Democrats to thrive in the Mountain West. States in this region have some of the fastest growing proportions of independent voters. Leading up to the 2006 midterm elections, Mountain West voters began to grumble about the Republican Party's deficit spending and encroachments on civil liberties.[26] Many of them supported Democratic candidates in 2006, and in 2008 many responded to Obama's message. Furthermore, the region is growing quickly with groups receptive to the Democratic Party: Latinos and white, college-educated professionals relocating from other regions.

In recent elections, both parties have competed for Latino votes, but draconian efforts at immigration reform by conservative Republicans in the mid-2000s severely hurt the GOP with this voting bloc. In contrast, Democrats have enjoyed Latino support because of the party's past efforts on behalf of working-class and minority constituents. If Democrats respond to recent Latino discontent with reform proposals that emphasize paths to citizenship for immigrants, the party may succeed in building even further on its success of 2008. Such an approach may engender backlash from non-Latinos in the region, yet another traditionally Republican constituency; however, regional businesses for whom having a larger cheap labor pool is advantageous, could be courted by the Democrats with a more generous immigration policy.

The states Obama won in the Mountain West and in the South reveal that the dominance the Republican Party has enjoyed in these regions is not inviolable. But it took a national economic crisis along with regionally specific issues, an expertly run campaign, and an eloquent candidate for the Democrats to be victorious in 2008. Building a national majority will require that Democrats balance blue state concerns with red state demands, working class priorities with professional class claims, and economic progressivism with social progressivism, all while navigating the cross-currents of racial and ethnic group divisions. This is no easy task. But, as the saying goes, in great challenge lies great opportunity. For now, though slightly bluer, the country remains a red/blue nation.

## Notes

1. Republicans won control of both the House of Representatives and the Senate in 1994. They lost control of the Senate briefly in 2001 and regained it in 2002. Both houses were lost to the Democrats in 2006.
2. John Harris and Jim VandeHei, "The Obama Revolution," *Politico*, November 4, 2008. Also see Mark Halperin, "Finally, Election Day," *Los Angeles Times*, November 4, 2008. Halperin claims that an Obama win of more than 53 percent of the popular vote over a broad geography would mean a mandate for the Democrat and a potential political realignment.
3. For classic statements of realignment theory, see V. O. Key, "A Theory of Critical Elections," *The Journal of Politics* 17 (1955): 3–18; Walter Dean Burnham, *Critical Elections and the Mainsprings of American Politics* (New York: W. W. Norton,

1970); and James Sundquist, *Dynamics of the Party System: Alignment and Realignment of Political Parties in the United States* (Washington, D.C.: Brookings Institution, 1983). For a critique of the theory, see David Mayhew, *Electoral Realignments: A Critique of an American Genre* (New Haven, Conn.: Yale University Press, 2004).

4. There are numerous examples of such works, but for a few, see: Matthew Lassiter, *The Silent Majority: Suburban Politics in the Sunbelt South* (Princeton, N.J.: Princeton University Press, 2006); Bruce J. Schulman, *The Seventies: The Great Shift in American Culture, Society, and Politics* (New York: Free Press, 2001); Lisa McGirr, *Suburban Warriors: The Origins of the New American Right* (Princeton, N.J.: Princeton University Press, 2001); Sean Wilentz, *The Age of Reagan: A History, 1974–2008* (New York: Harper, 2008); Stephen Skowronek, *The Politics Presidents Make: Leadership from John Adams to George Bush* (Cambridge, Mass.: Harvard University Press, 1993); and Rick Perlstein, *Nixonland: The Rise of a President and the Fracturing of America* (New York: Scribner, 2008).

5. Also suggesting muted support for the Republican regime was the disengagement of voters from the two major parties and the general downward trend in turnout rates that characterized much of the recent era. It is only in the last several elections that voters have begun to reattach themselves to the parties and turn out in greater numbers.

6. See Nicole Mellow, *The State of Disunion: Regional Sources of Modern American Partisanship* (Baltimore: Johns Hopkins University Press, 2008); and Earl Black and Merle Black, *Divided America: The Ferocious Power Struggle in American Politics* (New York: Simon and Schuster, 2007).

7. See Mellow, *The State of Disunion*; Lassiter, *The Silent Majority*; Schulman, *The Seventies*; and McGirr, *Suburban Warriors*.

8. The phrase "emerging Republican majority" was coined by Republican strategist Kevin Phillips in his book, *The Emerging Republican Majority* (New Rochelle, N.Y.: Arlington House, 1969).

9. Phillips, *The Emerging Republican Majority*. For a general history, see Thomas Byrne Edsall and Mary D. Edsall, *Chain Reaction: The Impact of Race, Rights, and Taxes on American Politics* (New York: W. W. Norton, 1992).

10. As quoted in John B. Judis and Ruy Teixeira, *The Emerging Democratic Majority* (New York: Scribner, 2002), 30.

11. Judis and Teixeira, *The Emerging Democratic Majority*.

12. Nicole Mellow, "Voting Behavior: The 2004 Election and the Roots of Republican Success," in *The Elections of 2004*, ed. Michael Nelson (Washington, D.C.: CQ Press, 2005), 77, Figure 7-4.

13. On the persistence of class divisions in party identification, see Jeffrey Stonecash, *Class and Party in American Politics* (Boulder, Colo.: Westview Press, 2000). For a review of some of the reasons for middle class drift, see Edsall and Edsall, *Chain Reaction*; also Lassiter, *The Silent Majority*.

14. "Inside Obama's Sweeping Victory," Pew Research Center Publications, November 5, 2008, http://pewresearch.org/pubs/1023/exit-poll-analysis-2008.

15. Presidential "disapproval" data from 1932 through 2008. Adapted from Gallup Poll data and available at www.presidency.ucsb.edu/data/popularity.php.

16. Calculations based on all major party voters in each of the four regions. The South includes Alabama, Arkansas, Florida, Georgia, Louisiana, Mississippi, North Carolina, South Carolina, Texas, Virginia, Kentucky, Oklahoma, Tennessee, and West Virginia. West includes Iowa, Kansas, Minnesota, Missouri, Nebraska, North Dakota, South Dakota, Arizona, Colorado, Idaho, Montana, Nevada, New Mexico, Utah, and Wyoming. Pacific Coast includes California, Oregon, and Washington. North includes Connecticut, Delaware, Illinois, Indiana, Maine, Maryland, Massachusetts, Michigan, New Hampshire, New Jersey, New York, Ohio, Pennsylvania, Rhode Island, Vermont, and Wisconsin. Alaska and Hawaii, which were

added to the Union after World War II and which regularly vote Republican and Democratic, respectively, are not included in the analysis.

17. See Figure 3-1 in Gerald M. Pomper, "The Presidential Election: The Ills of American Politics After 9/11," in *The Elections of 2004*, Michael Nelson, ed. (Washington, D.C.: CQ Press, 2004), 43.

18. Negative equity data: "Where Homes Are Worth Less than the Mortgage," *New York Times*, November 10, 2008, www.nytimes.com/interactive/2008/11/10/business/20081111_MORTGAGES.html. Unemployment and personal income data: "State by State Polls Compared to Economic Indicators," *Wall Street Journal*, November 1, 2008, http://blogs.wsj.com/economics/2008/11/01/state-by-state-polls-compared-to-economic-indicators/.

19. Everett Carll Ladd Jr., "Liberalism Upside Down: The Inversion of the New Deal Order," *Political Science Quarterly* 91 (1976–1977): 577–600.

20. Andrew Gelman, et al., "Rich State, Poor State, Red State, Blue State: What's the Matter with Connecticut?" *Quarterly Journal of Political Science* 2 (2007): 345–367.

21. "Much-hyped Turnout Record Fails to Materialize, Convenience Voting Fails to Boost Balloting," *American University News*. Press release of American University's Center for the Study of the Electorate, November 6, 2008, www.american.edu/media.

22. Yet of the four broad geographic categories of South, Midwest, Northeast, and West (including the Pacific Coast), only Northeastern whites gave most of their votes to Obama.

23. "Youth Turnout Rate Rises to at Least 52% with 23 Million Voters under 30," *Report of the Center for Information and Research on Civic Learning and Engagement*, Tufts University's Jonathan M. Tisch College of Citizenship and Public Service, www.civicyouth.org.

24. Angus Campbell et al., *The American Voter* (Chicago: University of Chicago Press, 1976, orig. 1960). Note, in particular, their description of Democratic growth after the 1932 election: "When we ask from what levels of society the Democratic Party drew this new strength, we find from our survey data and from the aggregative election figures that the impact of the events of that period appears to have been felt most strongly by the youth, the economically underprivileged, and the minority groups." (p. 153).

25. Organisation for Economic Cooperation and Development data provided in: Dennis Jones and Patrick Kelly, "Mounting Pressures Facing the U.S. Workforce and the Increasing Need for Adult Education and Literacy," *National Commission on Adult Literacy Report*, May 21, 2007.

26. Kirk Johnson, "In Southwest, A Shifting Away from Party Ties," *New York Times*, October 24, 2006.

# 8

# Campaign Finance:
# Fundraising and Spending
# in the 2008 Elections

## Marian Currinder

In September 2008, Democratic presidential nominee Barack Obama raised $153 million, shattering the $66 million single-month record he set one month earlier. By adding 632,000 new donors to his already massive list of contributors, Obama raised more money in one month than most of the 2008 presidential candidates raised in total. His September fund-raising haul amounted to nearly half of what John Kerry raised for his entire 2004 presidential bid. Indeed, by election day, Obama had raised almost $742 million, $46 million more than the $696 million Kerry and President George W. Bush combined raised in 2004.[1]

In a campaign year full of financial ironies, Obama's raising $153 million in the midst of the country's worst financial crisis since the Great Depression may top the list. As Congress and the Bush administration negotiated a taxpayer-funded $700 billion bailout of Wall Street, hundreds of thousands of taxpayers voluntarily forked over millions of dollars to the Democratic nominee's campaign.

Meanwhile, Republican candidates were struggling to raise money. In early October, the National Republican Congressional Committee (NRCC), the fund-raising committee for House Republicans, took out an $8 million loan to spend on competitive races during the last few weeks of the campaign. The list of 2008 campaign finance ironies expanded when the NRCC reported that it procured the loan from Wachovia Bank, which was hit hard by the financial crisis. A few weeks after loaning millions to the NRCC, Wachovia posted a $23.7 billion quarterly loss, the largest ever for a bank.[2]

The fund-raising fortunes of Democratic and Republican candidates contrasted sharply throughout much of the 2008 election. But as the items above suggest, the financial advantage that Democratic candidates enjoyed became even more pronounced as the campaign entered the final stretch. Obama outspent John McCain, the Republican nominee, by margins of 3- and 4-to-1 on advertising in battleground states during the campaign's final weeks and invested heavily in ground-level organization. The Democratic campaign committees in the House and Senate significantly outraised their Republican counterparts, and poured last-minute campaign money into their most competitive races. If there was an upside to the financial crisis, Democrats seemed to have found it.

The story of money in the 2008 elections is full of ironies, surprises, and even a few predictabilities. This chapter examines campaign finance law and campaign spending in the presidential and congressional races in the context of the various anecdotes and idiosyncrasies that made this election one of the most fascinating in recent history.

## Post-2004 Changes in Campaign Finance Law

Campaign spending in the 2008 elections simultaneously accomplished and diminished the goals set forth in decades worth of campaign finance law. Through their rulings and actions, the Supreme Court, the Federal Elections Commission (FEC), candidates, political parties, and organized interests revised the way campaign money was raised and spent in this election.

Campaign finance reform efforts since the 1970s have sought to decrease the influence of wealthy contributors, encourage greater participation by small donors, and improve disclosure. By limiting how much money individuals can contribute, and by establishing a public financing system for presidential candidates, the Federal Elections Campaign Act of 1974 (FECA) attempted to reduce the role of "fat cat" contributors and enhance the role of small donors in federal elections. FECA also aimed to improve disclosure and oversight of the campaign finance system by establishing the FEC. The Bipartisan Campaign Reform Act of 2002 (BCRA), widely known as the McCain-Feingold Act, was intended to further advance these goals by restricting some forms of political advertising and by prohibiting the parties from raising and spending unregulated soft money. Soft money is not subject to FECA rules on the size and source of contributions because it is raised and spent to support party-building activities and issue advocacy. Funds spent in accordance with FECA regulations are known as hard money. Table 8-1 lists the current contribution limits.

After the 2004 election, the U.S. Supreme Court and the FEC issued a number of rulings that modified the law and changed the way money was spent in the 2008 elections. While the Court chipped away at some of BCRA's provisions, the FEC strengthened some of the law's spending and reporting requirements.

The Court's most recent decisions on campaign finance reflect its new composition, with conservative justice Samuel Alito replacing pro-BCRA justice Sandra Day O'Connor in 2006. Prior to the passage of BCRA, groups regulated by the FEC could finance issue ads with soft money as long as the ads did not directly advocate the election or defeat of a candidate for federal office. BCRA placed restrictions on advertising that mentioned candidates by name and required that ads running within sixty days of a general election and thirty days of a primary had to be financed with hard money, and contributors had to be disclosed. In *FEC v. Wisconsin Right to Life* (2007), the Court ruled that ads can only be considered election ads, and thus subject to FEC regulation, if there is no other way to interpret the ad's content. Wisconsin Right to Life (WRTL) had run ads urging viewers to call senators who

**Table 8-1**    Campaign Finance Contribution Limits, 2007–2008

| | To each candidate or candidate committee per election | To national party committee per calendar year | To state, district, and local party committee per calendar year | To any other political committee per calendar year[1] | Special limits |
|---|---|---|---|---|---|
| Individual may give | $2,300* | $28,500* | $10,000 (combined limit) | $5,000 | $108,200* overall biennial limit: $42,700* to all candidates $65,500* to all PACs and parties[2] |
| National party committee may give | $5,000 | No limit | No limit | $5,000 | $39,900 to Senate candidate per campaign[3] |
| State, district, and local party committee may give | $5,000 (combined limit) | No limit | No limit | $5,000 (combined limit) | No limit |
| PAC (multicandidate) may give[4] | $5,000 | $15,000 | $5,000 (combined limit) | $5,000 | No limit |
| PAC (not multicandidate) may give | $2,300* | $28,500* | $10,000 combined | $5,000 | No limit |
| Authorized campaign committee may give | $2,000[5] | No limit | No limit | $5,000 | No limit |

*Source:* Federal Elections Commission.

*These contribution limits are increased for inflation in odd-numbered years.

[1] A contribution earmarked for a candidate through a political committee counts against the original contributor's limit for that candidate. In certain circumstances, the contribution may also count against the contributor's limit to the PAC.

[2] No more than $42,700 of this amount may be contributed to state and local party committees and PACs.

[3] This limit is shared by the national committee and the Senate campaign committee.

[4] A multicandidate committee is a political committee with more than fifty contributors which has been registered for at least six months and, with the exception of state party committees, has made contributions to five or more candidates for federal office.

[5] A federal candidate's authorized committee(s) may contribute no more than $2,000 per election to another federal candidate's authorized committee(s).

were filibustering judicial nominations. Democratic Senator Russ Feingold of Wisconsin, who was up for reelection in 2004, was featured in the ads. The FEC contended that WRTL had violated the law because the ads specifically named a federal candidate. But in the Court's decision, Chief Justice John Roberts wrote, "Discussion of issues cannot be suppressed simply because the issues may also be pertinent in an election. Where the First Amendment is implicated, the tie goes to the speaker, not the censor." The decision meant that organized interests, unions, and corporations could once again air issue ads during elections, as long as they did not directly advocate the election or defeat of a candidate. After sitting out the 2004 election, groups such as these were thrilled to get back in the game.

Following the passage of BCRA, much of the soft money that had previously gone to the parties was redirected to 527 and 501(c) organizations, which are registered and regulated by the Internal Revenue Service rather than the FEC. These groups are allowed to engage in federal election activities as long as they do not expressly advocate the election or defeat of a candidate. 527 groups proved particularly adept at raising unlimited amounts of soft money and became powerful players in the 2004 elections, whereas groups regulated by the FEC remained comparatively silent.

In October 2008, the FEC made its first attempt to determine how explicitly political ads run by interest groups, unions, and corporations can advocate for or against candidates. The commission was asked to review a complaint that the National Right to Life Committee (NRLC) had violated campaign finance rules by specifically naming Democratic presidential nominee Barack Obama in an issue ad. In what is likely to become a pattern with these kinds of reviews, the commission deadlocked. The three Democratic commissioners concluded that the NRLC had violated the rules, and the three Republican commissioners determined that the committee had acted within the law.[3]

The Supreme Court also struck down BCRA's "millionaire's amendment," which allowed candidates who face wealthy, self-financed challengers to collect contributions over the established limit of $2,300 per donor. In *Davis v. FEC* (2008), Justice Samuel Alito, writing for the 5-4 majority, claimed that the Court had "never upheld the constitutionality of a law that imposes different contribution limits for candidates who are competing against each other." By July 2008, self-funding by House candidates hit $59.3 million, surpassing the $59.2 million candidates had spent out of pocket during the entire 2006 election.[4]

The Court also heard a case that did not have federal implications but reinforced the majority's position on strict contribution limits. In *Randall v. Sorrell* (2007), the Court issued a ruling on state-level campaign contribution limits. Vermont's law, which the Supreme Court struck down, restricted individuals from contributing more than $200 to candidates for the state legislature and from contributing more than $400 to gubernatorial candidates. According to the Court, the law made it difficult for challengers to unseat incumbents and for candidates running in primary and general elections to raise adequate money.

The Court's post-2004 campaign finance decisions diminished some of BCRA's attempts to level the playing field between wealthy and less-wealthy candidates. But in the Court's view, some of the law's provisions infringed on citizens' First Amendment rights. While the FEC issued regulations in accordance with the Court's decisions, it also released new regulations that tightened contribution and expenditure requirements.

In response to concerns over the "527 loophole" created by BCRA, the FEC issued rules designed to hold 527 groups more accountable for their federal election activities. According to new FEC regulations, if 527 groups issue appeals to donors indicating that any portion of the solicited funds will be used to support or defeat a candidate, then donors can contribute no more than $5,000 to the group. The idea was to treat 527s that participate in election activities like political action committees (PACs), which can only contribute $5,000 per candidate in each election and can accept no more than $5,000 per calendar year from individuals and other committees. Prior to the FEC's enactment of these rules, individuals could give unlimited contributions to 527s; indeed, more than one-third of the $534 million that 527 groups raised in 2004 came from twenty-five wealthy donors.

The FEC also ruled that 527s making contributions to federal candidates must raise half of their money in contributions of $5,000 or less. The groups are also now required to fund at least half of their operations with hard money—that is, money regulated by the FEC. These new rules, together with the Supreme Court's decision in *FEC v. Wisconsin Right to Life,* mean that 2004 was likely the high mark for 527 spending in federal elections.[5]

In 2007, Congress passed legislation requiring that the names of lobbyists who twice raise more than $15,000 in bundled contributions be disclosed. "Bundlers" collect a large number of individual contributions for a candidate then turn the bundle of contributions over to the campaign. The FEC released draft regulations in September 2007 requiring campaign committees to report the names of their bundlers, but a final vote was delayed by a seven-month standoff between Senate Democrats and President Bush over FEC nominees. In December 2007, only two of the FEC's six commissioners were left after three of President Bush's recess appointments expired. (There was already one vacancy on the commission.) Senate Democrats blocked consideration of any replacements because they objected to one of the president's four nominees. In June 2008, Bush's controversial nominee withdrew his name from consideration, thus clearing the way for the other nominees to be confirmed.[6] After seven months of paralysis, the newly constituted FEC approved the bundling regulations, but the rules did not take effect until after the 2008 election.[7]

Through their recent decisions and rulings, the Supreme Court and the FEC have altered the structure of federal campaign financing. The Court has weakened the law's overarching goal of leveling the campaign finance playing field, arguing that First Amendment rights take precedence. But by continuing to uphold the law's provision that prevents the national party organizations from raising and spending soft money, the Court has indirectly enhanced the role of small donors. As for the FEC, its new regulations governing 527 groups strengthen the law's goal of reducing the influence of fat cat donors. The FEC has also required 527 groups to adhere to stricter reporting and disclosure rules. Additionally, the commission's new bundling reporting requirements advance the law's disclosure goals.

In view of these changes in the law, how did presidential and congressional candidates, the political parties, and organized interests actually raise and spend money in the 2008 elections? Like the Supreme Court and the FEC, these actors helped to reshape the campaign finance landscape in ways that both improved and weakened the law's broad goals.

# The 2008 Presidential Primaries

## 2007: The Race Begins

The protracted and costly battle between Sen. Barack Obama and Sen. Hillary Clinton makes it easy to forget that several other candidates competed for the Democratic presidential nomination. Obama and Clinton established themselves early as formidable fund raisers, making it difficult for the other Democratic contenders to gain financial traction. Collectively, the eight Democratic candidates raised $95.4 million in the first quarter of 2007, $36.1 million of which was raised by Clinton, and $25.8 million of which was raised by Obama. John Edwards raised $14 million, and the remaining five candidates combined took in just over $10 million.

Although Hillary Clinton led the pack in early fund raising, Barack Obama was the big story. Clinton, who entered the 2008 race with the most extensive fund-raising network in Democratic politics, was expected to blow away her rivals. Obama, however, stunned political observers when he raised much more than anyone expected of a recently declared candidate with just two years experience in the U.S. Senate. His first quarter performance vastly undercut Clinton's claim that her ability to raise more money than her opponents would make her nomination inevitable. Clinton had assembled about seventy top fund-raisers from across the country, each of whom pledged to raise as much as $1 million for her campaign. She also formed an extensive network of "Hillraisers," who were expected to collect at least $25,000 each for the campaign.

Despite Clinton's efforts, Obama attracted twice as many donors as she did, more than half of whom gave small amounts. By holding campaign events that cost between $25 and $100, Obama reached out to younger, first-time donors who later could be tapped for more money because they had not yet given the maximum of $2,300. He also recruited a top-notch team of fund-raisers that included some of the biggest names in Democratic politics. These fund-raisers were responsible for reaching out to wealthy donors who could help to quickly build up Obama's campaign treasury. This two-pronged strategy would prove central to his long-term fund-raising success. Obama's refusal to accept contributions from lobbyists and PACs also set him apart from most of his opponents, including Clinton.[8]

Like Clinton, Republican John McCain entered the 2008 race as his party's frontrunner. He had spent the previous two years preparing to run and was expected to far out-raise his Republican opponents in the election cycle's first quarter. But McCain's fund-raising strategy did not work as well as planned. Former Massachusetts governor Mitt Romney led the Republican field with $23.4 million in contributions during the first quarter of 2007. He was followed by former New York City mayor Rudolph Giuliani, who raised $18 million. McCain was third with $14.8 million, but reported only $5.2 million in cash on hand—less than half the amount that Romney and Giuliani had available. After the first quarter finance reports were released, McCain overhauled his finance team and vowed to cut his campaign's profligate spending. The seven other Republican candidates raised much less than the top three contenders. Sen. Sam Brownback of Kansas raised $1.9 million and Rep. Tom Tancredo of Colorado raised $1.3 million; the five other candidates, including former Arkansas governor Mike Huckabee, raised less than $1 million each.[9]

For the first time since the FEC began tracking campaign donations in 1975, Democratic presidential candidates outperformed their Republican opponents in first quarter fund raising. The total raised by the eight Democratic candidates topped the total raised by the ten Republican candidates by more than $30 million. Together, the 2008 presidential candidates raised more than five times the amount candidates raised in the first quarters of 1999 and 2003. These initial figures demonstrated a great deal of early interest in the 2008 race. They also suggested that the battle for each party's nomination was unexpectedly open. The Democratic Party's first viable female candidate faced strong competition from its first viable African American candidate, while John McCain struggled to compete with a telegenic Mormon and "America's Mayor."

Early campaign finance reports also showed that contributors previously aligned with the two most powerful fund-raising networks in recent history—one built by the Clintons, the other by President Bush—were going their own ways rather than once again teaming up. Many of the Clintons' past supporters gave to Obama and other Democratic candidates, and former Bush contributors divided their donations among Romney, Giuliani, and McCain.[10] Indeed, the 2008 presidential campaign's earliest fund-raising reports made clear that the race would be full of twists and turns.

Three months later, by June 2007, the presidential candidates of both parties had already raised $277 million—$5 million more than all the presidential candidates raised in the first year of the 2004 campaign. Obama surged ahead of Clinton, raising $32.8 million during the second quarter of 2007. About one-third of his contributions came over the Internet, and 90 percent of these online donations were less than $100. Clinton raised $21 million, John Edwards brought in $9 million, and Bill Richardson collected $7 million. The four other Democratic candidates raised substantially less during the second quarter. Midway through 2007, Obama had raised more money and had more cash on hand than any of his Democratic and Republican rivals.[11]

Obama also had established a larger donor list than any of his opponents. The 258,000 donors who gave to his campaign during the first six months of 2007 exceeded the combined total of those who gave to the top three Republican contenders—Romney, Giuliani, and McCain—during the same period. Romney continued to outpace his Republican challengers, raising $21 million during the second quarter. Giuliani raised $17 million, and

McCain collected $11 million. The seven other Republican candidates raised much less.[12]

By the end of 2007, Obama and Clinton had raised more than $100 million each. Clinton collected 75 percent of her contributions from individuals who gave $1,000 or more, whereas Obama raised 54 percent of his money from such donors. And while Clinton received only 14 percent of her contributions from donors who gave less than $200 each, Obama collected 32 percent of his money from small donors. This meant that Obama had more donors than Clinton whom he could return to for additional help. John Edwards finished a distant third, with contributions totaling $35 million for the year, and Bill Richardson finished fourth, with $22 million.

Although the Democratic fund-raising momentum clearly stayed with Obama and Clinton throughout 2007, matters were less clear-cut on the Republican side. Giuliani moved into the lead, raising $58.5 million for the year. Romney finished a close second with $53 million, and McCain ended the year with $37 million in contributions. Rep. Ron Paul of Texas, who had gained something of a cult following among self-proclaimed Libertarians, collected a surprising $28 million. Paul's standing in the polls remained consistently low, but his supporters were passionate and raised millions for him over the Internet. Former senator Fred Thompson of Tennessee, who joined the fray midway through 2007, attracted $21.5 million by year's end. Mike Huckabee drew little attention initially but gathered steam later in the year. After raising just over $1 million from January to June, he ended 2007 with $9 million in contributions. Paul was the only Republican candidate to raise most of his donations (61 percent) in amounts of less than $200. Huckabee collected 35 percent in small donations, McCain collected 25 percent, and Romney just 12 percent.

Just before the 2008 primary contests got underway, the FEC authorized seven presidential candidates to receive federal matching funds. To become eligible for matching funds under the law, each of these candidates agreed to spend no more than approximately $50 million for the primaries. Of the seven candidates who chose to rely on the public finance system, only two were considered "top-tier"—McCain and Edwards. McCain, however, later changed his mind and turned down public funding for the primaries. Together, seven candidates received approximately $27 million in matching funds during the 2008 primary season. In 2000, primary candidates received $62.3 million in matching funds, and in 1996 they received $58.5 million.[13] For the four presidential contenders who raised more than $50 million in 2007 (Obama and Clinton had raised twice that amount), public funding was never a consideration. Why participate in a system that caps spending at levels well below what they could raise on their own?

## 2008: The Primary and Caucus Season Begins

On January 3, 2008, Barack Obama won the Iowa caucuses with 38 percent of the vote, proving that an African American candidate could attract white voters. John Edwards finished second with 30 percent, and Hillary Clinton finished a close third, with 29 percent. Obama's unexpected victory proved profitable; he raised $8 million in the first eight days of January. Edwards reported collecting more than $1.6 million in the week following his second-place finish. Meanwhile, the Clinton campaign did damage control by working to convince contributors not to jump ship. Clinton also pursued the financial support of donors who had backed Sen. Joe Biden of Delaware and Sen. Chris Dodd of Connecticut, both of whom dropped out after the Iowa caucuses.[14]

Iowa produced some surprises on the Republican side as well. Huckabee, running on a shoestring budget, was the runaway winner with 34.4 percent of the vote. Romney placed a distant second, winning 25.2 percent, and Thompson edged out McCain for third place, taking 13.4 percent of the vote to McCain's 13 percent. Paul won 9.9 percent of the Iowa vote and Giuliani, the Republican candidate with the biggest campaign war chest, attracted just 3.4 percent. Indeed, Iowa did little to answer the question of who would emerge as the Republican frontrunner. Money—the usual harbinger—offered little in the way of predictive value.

Five days after losing to Obama in Iowa, Clinton pulled out a surprise victory in New Hampshire, winning 39 percent of the vote to Obama's 37 percent. Obama, along with almost every pre-primary poll, had anticipated a second win. Edwards finished a distant third with 17 percent. Clinton's victory in New Hampshire generated $1.1 million in contributions in the next twenty-four hours. Edwards, vowing to stay in the race until the Democratic convention in August, borrowed $9 million by promising to pay it back with federal matching funds. Richardson won just 5 percent and exited the race. With one victory each, Obama and Clinton set their sights on the February 5 "Super Tuesday" contests while continuing to raise money at a breakneck pace.

New Hampshire's Republican primary results bore little resemblance to the outcome in Iowa just five days earlier. McCain won handily, with 37 percent of the vote. Mitt Romney finished second with 32 percent, Huckabee was a distant third with 11 percent, and Giuliani and Paul tied for fourth place with 8 percent each. Following Iowa and New Hampshire, both Huckabee and McCain reported a boost in fund raising. Romney followed up his New Hampshire loss with a major fund-raising push, bringing five hundred of his supporters to Boston for a one-day phone-a-thon. A Romney fund-raiser claimed that the twenty-four-hour event raised more than $4 million.[15]

Heading toward Super Tuesday, Clinton won the Michigan primary (neither Obama nor Edwards was on the ballot) and narrowly defeated Obama in the Nevada caucuses. Obama decisively won the South Carolina primary with 55 percent of the vote. Then, just days before Super Tuesday, Sen. Ted Kennedy of Massachusetts endorsed Obama. Kennedy's strong endorsement helped propel Obama to victory in thirteen of the twenty-two states that held contests on February 5. Clinton won the other nine states, and Edwards dropped out of the race.

One day after Super Tuesday, Clinton revealed that in January she had lent her campaign $5 million. News of the loan surprised many of her donors, who assumed that she was keeping pace with the Obama fund-raising machine. In truth, while his campaign was taking in a remarkable $35 million in January, she raised only $13 million. Forty-six percent of Obama's contributions came from donors who gave $200 or less, compared to 35 percent of Clinton's contributions. Clinton defended the loan and said that it was simply a reflection of how much she believed in her campaign. The fact that she did not publicly disclose the loan until after Super Tuesday, however, suggested that she was aware that it might cast a shadow on her candidacy. News of the loan was followed by revelations that some members of Clinton's campaign staff were working without pay. The anxiety that her donors were experiencing was likely amplified when Obama reported raising $3.5 million the day after Super Tuesday.[16]

McCain followed up his victory in New Hampshire with another in South Carolina. For the first time in more than a year of campaigning, he was situated comfortably at the head of the Republican pack. Huckabee finished second with 30 percent of the vote to McCain's 33 percent. Thompson and Romney received 16 percent and 15 percent, respectively. After McCain won the January 29 Florida primary, his front-runner status was solidified. He attracted more than $12 million in contributions in January—remarkable for a campaign that one month earlier only had about $1 million in cash on hand. Giuliani withdrew from the race after finishing fifth in Florida and endorsed McCain. A week later, on Super Tuesday, McCain captured an impressive array of states and built an insurmountable lead in delegates, prompting Romney to exit the race. Huckabee ended his campaign for the party's nomination in early March, about one month after Romney called it quits.

McCain's Super Tuesday performance brought in a surge in contributions: $11.5 million in February and $15.5 million in March. Seventy-two percent of McCain's March contributions came from donors who gave $1,000 or more. In 2007, when his campaign was nearly broke, McCain had applied for federal matching funds and agreed to adhere to an overall spending limit of $54 million for the entire nomination contest. But once he took the lead and money began to pour in, he asked the FEC for permission to withdraw his application. The FEC permits candidates to exit the program as long as they have not yet received any federal funds or used the promise of federal money as collateral for borrowing money. FEC chair David M. Mason notified McCain that the commission would need to vote on his request, but lacked the quorum to do so because the president and Senate were still in a standoff over commission nominees. McCain decided to proceed as if he had been released from the public finance system, prompting a complaint from the Democratic National Committee (DNC). In August, the FEC voted unanimously to belatedly approve McCain's request.[17] The candidate who had made campaign finance reform one of his signature issues in the Senate was thus spared the embarrassment of having violated campaign finance law. In all, McCain raised a total of $190 million for the nomination campaign.

Meanwhile, the epic battle between Clinton and Obama showed no signs of slowing. The ongoing fight proved profitable for Clinton, who raised $35 million in February, most of it over the Internet. Obama, however, continued to best her, raising almost $57 million. For the first time during the primaries, more than half of both Clinton's and Obama's money came from small donors giving $200 or less. Clinton's March contributions dropped to $21 million; Obama's contributions also dropped, but he still managed to raise $43 million—more than twice what Clinton raised that month. Once again, more than 50 percent of each candidate's contributions came from small donors. The Clinton-Obama battle lasted until June 3, when Obama collected enough delegates to claim the nomination, thus ending one of the longest primary seasons in recent history.

## The General Election

Hillary Clinton's eighteen-month bid to become the Democratic presidential nominee attracted $230 million in contributions. When she left the race in June, however, her campaign was more than $20 million in debt. In a speech to her supporters, Obama hailed his former rival and urged his backers to help retire her debt. Leading by example, he contributed $2,300, the maximum he could give, to her campaign committee.[18] Merging the two candidates' massive fund-raising organizations was a complex undertaking, mainly because of Obama's refusal to accept contributions from lobbyists and PACs. Clinton had twenty-two lobbyists raising money for her campaign, and took in $888,000 in contributions from lobbyists—more than any other presidential candidate in the 2008 election.

After clinching the nomination, Obama announced that his ban on lobbyist and PAC contributions would extend to the DNC. Rejecting any potentially large source of money was risky, but Obama was confident that his army of small donors would make up the difference. He went on to raise more than $51 million in July, almost double what McCain took in that month. By the end of the nomination campaign in August, Obama had raised $428 million and had $77.4 million in cash on hand. During the 2004 primaries, by comparison, President Bush raised $258 million and John Kerry, the Democratic nominee, raised $215 million. Although most of Obama's fund-raising success was from small donors, his campaign relied on at least thirty-five bundlers who raised more than $500,000 each.[19] During the primaries, Obama raised $147.7 million (33 percent of his total) from donors who gave $1,000 or more.

Obama was also confident that he could raise more money for the general election than the $84 million he would be limited to if he accepted public funding. Despite promising otherwise, he thus became the first major-party presidential nominee to reject public funds for the general election campaign. Obama's fund-raisers predicted that he would raise as much as $300 million on his own, mainly by tapping the network of 1.5 million small donors who had contributed to his primary campaign. McCain, who like Obama had agreed to accept public funds, greeted his rival's announcement with a mixture of anger and resignation. Calling Obama's reversal a "big, big deal," McCain pressed the media to cover the story. But public opinion polls showed that the vast majority of Americans saw public financing as a "non-issue."[20] In choosing to accept public funds, McCain—for many years one of the most vocal proponents of campaign finance reform—wound up being seriously disadvantaged by the very system he had long promoted. And even though Democrats had fought for a public financing system in the wake of the Watergate scandal, their candidate chose to extol the free-market virtues of individual campaign donations.[21]

When the national party conventions ended in early September and the general election got underway, McCain had at least one advantage. The Republican National Committee (RNC) had raised more money and had more cash on hand than the DNC. The RNC and the DNC can make unlimited independent expenditures on behalf of their candidates; each national committee can also spend about $19 million in coordination with its party's candidates. Independent expenditures are funds spent on behalf of a candidate but not coordinated with the candidate's campaign. Coordinated expenditures are funds a party spends for services such as polling and media time on behalf of a candidate who has requested it. Because McCain could not make direct use of the $27 million in cash on hand that he had when the general campaign began, he transferred $18 million of it to the RNC and the remaining $9 million to various state party committees.

Presidential candidates, whether they accept public funding or not, can raise money for the national and state party committees which can, in turn, help their campaigns. One way candidates do this is through joint fundraising committees, which are allowed to use the candidates' names to raise money for their parties—money that the parties can then spend to support their campaigns. The majority of contributions to these committees come from donors who give $1,000 or more. According to FEC reports, 75 percent of the contributions to Obama's three joint fund-raising committees were in this range, as were 93 percent of the contributions to McCain's ten committees.[22] Both Obama and McCain relied heavily on major donors, some of whom contributed as much as $70,000, to fill their joint committee coffers. Overall, McCain's joint committees raised $177 million and Obama's raised $184 million.

At the end of August, the RNC had $76.5 million in cash on hand and the DNC had $17.7 million. This meant that McCain and the RNC began the general election with $187.6 million to spend, whereas Obama and the DNC had $95.1 million available.[23] Obama, then, would have to raise about $55 million a month through election day to make up for the $92 million edge that McCain enjoyed at the outset. In addition, the RNC was cashing in on the short-term boost that McCain's selection of Alaska governor Sarah Palin for vice president brought to the ticket. Feeling a new sense of urgency,

Obama's finance team began its final fund-raising push. Suddenly, the candidate who had raised more money than any presidential contender in history was on the financial defensive.

Obama did not stay on the defensive for long, however. He raised an astonishing $153 million in September, shattering the previous one-month fund-raising record of $65 million that he had set in August. The campaign attracted 632,000 new donors in September who gave an average of $86. Almost half of the money Obama raised came in donations of $200 or less. This massive haul put Obama and the DNC on track to outspend McCain and the RNC by a margin of up to 3-to-1 in the final month of the campaign. Together, Obama and the DNC took in $193 million and spent $134 million in September. McCain and the RNC collected $160 million, which included $84.1 million in public funds, and spent $108.6 million. If Democrats had any doubts about Obama's decision to reject public funding, September erased them.[24]

Obama's September fund-raising juggernaut prompted questions about how well the campaign was screening contributions. Most of the questions involved donors who used prepaid credit cards. Because an individual's identity can be masked when using these cards, donors could potentially evade contribution limits. Faced with a huge influx of Internet donations, the campaign chose not to scrutinize contributions as they came in and instead waited until after the money was deposited. This was legal: the FEC does not require front-end screening. Lawyers for both the DNC and the RNC asked the FEC to examine the issue and make recommendations. The issue did not surface until late October, however, and in any event the potentially fraudulent contributions only represented about 1 percent of Obama's funds.[25]

The final few weeks of the campaign featured a barrage of spending. Obama's surfeit of funds was on full display when he purchased thirty minutes for an October 29 primetime infomercial shown on three broadcast television networks (Fox, NBC, and CBS) and on four cable stations (MSNBC, BET, Univision, and TV One). The infomercial likely cost the campaign around $3 million.[26] Despite a last-minute push by McCain and the RNC to blanket battleground states with campaign ads, Obama and the DNC outspent McCain by as much as 4-to-1 on televised ads. The media buy forced McCain to curtail spending on his ground-campaign efforts; he spent half as much as Obama on staffing and opened far fewer field offices. Grassroots staff members were asked to volunteer their time, and the RNC picked up some of the slack for election day get-out-the-vote efforts.[27]

Both candidates were aided by groups that ran ads in key media markets, but these independent efforts were not nearly as extensive as in the 2004 presidential campaign. Spending by 527 groups shrank from $442 million in 2004 to around $200 million in 2008. The FEC had stepped up its monitoring of 527 groups after 2004 and put stricter contribution and expenditure requirements into place. In addition, both McCain and Obama openly discouraged 527 groups from getting involved in the election because they wanted to control the tone and the message of their campaigns. Obama, in particular, worried that overtly negative ads would undermine his message of unity and change.[28] Also, many 527s fell victim to the collapsing economy and were too busy trying to salvage their portfolios to get involved in a meaningful way.

Still, Obama benefited from $50 million in spending by the AFL-CIO, as well as from a massive fund-raising effort undertaken by MoveOn.org. A conservative group, the American Issues Project, ran ads suggesting that Obama had terrorist connections, but its effort tailed off quickly for lack of funds. Overall, Democratic-oriented 527s held a nearly 3-to-1 advantage over Republican-oriented 527s. Although McCain may have benefited from more 527 help, many of these groups were not inclined to back a campaign finance reformer who had actively opposed their role in the electoral process.[29] 501(c) groups were active players in 2008, but their efforts were mostly concentrated on congressional races.

Together, the Republican Party and Republican-oriented groups spent $78 million in independent expenditures to oppose Obama and $6 million to support McCain. The Democratic Party and Democratic-oriented groups spent $14 million opposing McCain and $60 million supporting Obama.[30] One way or another, both parties invested heavily in Obama.

Twenty-two months and $742 million after the 2008 campaign began, Obama won the race for the White House. McCain, who raised $261 million, returned to the U.S. Senate. The 2008 presidential campaign was easily the most expensive in history. The total cost, including spending by the candidates, parties, and outside groups, was an estimated $4.9 billion (see Table 8-2).[31]

## House and Senate Elections

The 2008 congressional elections were also the most expensive in history. Spending by all candidates for Congress reached almost $1.5 billion by October 15, 2008; in 2004, House and Senate candidates spent a total of $715 million. The average cost of winning a seat in 2008 was $1.1 million in the House and $5.6 million in the Senate. The most expensive House race was in New York's 20th District, where candidates spent $9.2 million. Democrat Kirsten Gillibrand won the seat, but was outspent by Republican Sandy Treadwell. The costliest Senate race was in Minnesota, where Republican Norm Coleman and Democrat Al Franken spent more than $35.4 million. (After a recount, Franken won by 225 votes.) The successful House member who spent the least was Democrat Marcia Fudge, who spent just under $50,000 to win Ohio's 11th District seat. And Wyoming's Republican Senator John Barrasso spent only $1.4 million on his reelection. As is typically the case, self-financed candidates did not fare well. Forty-nine congressional candidates spent more than $500,000 of their own money; only twenty-four of them made it onto the general election ballot, and just seven self-financed candidates—six in the House and one in the Senate—won.[32]

Despite record-breaking spending, 306 of the 435 House races were not financially competitive. In 119 congressional districts, challengers did not even

**Table 8-2** 2008 Democratic and Republican Presidential Candidate Receipts and Expenditures

| Candidate | Individual contributions | PAC contributions | Candidate self-financing | Federal funds | Other receipts | Total receipts | Total expenditures |
|---|---|---|---|---|---|---|---|
| *Democrats* | | | | | | | |
| Barack Obama | $656,610,810 | $1,580 | $0 | $0 | $85,040,668 | $741,653,908 | $711,741,924 |
| Joseph Biden | $7,765,311 | $212,745 | $0 | $1,992,225 | $3,208,174 | $9,892,617 | $11,303,869 |
| Hillary Clinton | $195,428,201 | $1,412,071 | $13,175,000 | $0 | $11,630,202 | $221,647,474 | $214,195,821 |
| Christopher Dodd | $8,889,288 | $750,698 | $0 | $1,961,742 | $4,649,783 | $14,112,611 | $15,113,344 |
| John Edwards | $35,117,996 | $0 | –$4,344,469 | $12,882,864 | $4,493,681 | $35,267,208 | $43,721,724 |
| Mike Gravel | $509,929 | $502 | $44,616 | $0 | $6,249 | $561,296 | $556,714 |
| Dennis Kucinich | $4,385,759 | $13,950 | $10,347 | $1,070,521 | $9,501 | $4,419,547 | $5,400,094 |
| Bill Richardson | $21,922,846 | $261,479 | $2,300 | $0 | $65,608 | $22,252,233 | $22,219,621 |
| *Republicans* | | | | | | | |
| John McCain | $200,012,457 | $1,421,629 | $0 | $84,103,800 | $60,011,519 | $261,461,402 | $296,124,438 |
| Samuel Brownback | $3,530,942 | $49,435 | $0 | $0 | $662,069 | $4,242,771 | $4,210,774 |
| James Gilmore | $349,736 | $8,000 | $0 | $0 | $30,409 | $388,395 | $371,940 |
| Rudolph Giuliani | $55,013,474 | $397,259 | $800,000 | $0 | $2,450,758 | $58,665,241 | $58,629,007 |
| Mike Huckabee | $15,991,901 | $54,423 | $0 | $0 | $13,663 | $16,075,487 | $16,043,917 |
| Duncan Hunter | $2,343,063 | $41,273 | $0 | $453,527 | $36,000 | $2,420,336 | $2,809,654 |
| Ron Paul | $34,336,155 | $18,332 | $0 | $0 | $180,402 | $34,534,889 | $30,451,002 |
| Mitt Romney | $59,787,640 | $350,802 | $44,663,736 | $0 | $331,742 | $105,133,920 | $105,117,264 |
| Tom Tancredo | $3,999,589 | $7,525 | $0 | $2,145,126 | $135,844 | $4,144,978 | $6,117,410 |
| Fred Thompson | $23,202,419 | $176,555 | $0 | $0 | $69,507 | $23,448,481 | $23,247,270 |
| Tommy Thompson | $967,322 | $10,174 | $234,760 | $0 | $998 | $1,213,254 | $11,213,254 |

*Source:* Federal Election Commission data released on November 24, 2008.

file campaign finance reports with the FEC, meaning that they neither raised nor spent more than $5,000. An additional 187 challengers filed reports, but did not raise enough to be considered competitive. In 93 percent of House races and 94 percent of Senate races, the candidate who spent the most money won.[33] Table 8-3 shows the huge financial advantage enjoyed by incumbents.

The big story in the 2008 congressional elections was spending by the national parties. The congressional campaign committees for House and Senate Democrats out-raised and outspent their Republican counterparts by large margins. By election day, the Democratic Congressional Campaign Committee (DCCC), the fund-raising committee for House Democrats, had spent more than three times as much as its Republican counterpart, the National Republican Campaign Committee (NRCC), in independent spending. The Democratic Senatorial Campaign Committee (DSCC) had spent twice as much as the National Republican Senatorial Committee (NRSC). By injecting large amounts of money into competitive races, the DCCC and the DSCC were able to protect many of their vulnerable incumbents and support many of their competitive challengers.[34]

Issue advocacy groups also invested heavily in congressional elections. Most of the $350 million these groups raised during the 2008 election was devoted to congressional races, and Democratic-oriented groups such as Move On.org and America Votes held a 3-to-1 financial advantage over Republican-oriented groups, including Freedom's Watch.[35]

## Post-2006 Advantage: Democrats

After the 2006 midterm election, the DCCC and DSCC moved quickly to shore up their campaign accounts. Raising money is much easier for the majority party and, having spent the previous twelve years in the minority, Democrats were eager to cash in. The DCCC's first priority was to protect vulnerable freshmen—the so-called majority makers who propelled House Democrats into the majority in 2006. The committee's Frontline program, which directs money to endangered incumbents, included thirty-one members after the 2006 election. In the first quarter of 2007, these members raised an average of $291,000—a more than $100,000 jump from what the ten or so Frontline members raised in the first quarter of 2005. The DCCC raised $19 million and the NRCC collected $15.8 million during the same quarter. On the Senate side, the DSCC took in $13.7 million to the NRSC's $7 million. Despite these discrepancies at the congressional level, the RNC maintained a comfortable fund-raising edge over the DNC. By April 2007, the RNC held an $8 million cash advantage. Most of the money that these two committees raised, however, was devoted to the presidential race.[36]

The early fund-raising figures set the financial tone for the remainder of the 2008 election. The DCCC and the DSCC continued to bask in the glow of the 2006 elections and dominated second and third quarter fund raising. By late 2007, only 22 percent of the 229 House Democrats seeking reelection faced challengers who had filed campaign finance reports with the FEC.

**Table 8-3** Incumbent Advantage in the 2008 Election

|  | | | | *Senate* | | | |
|---|---|---|---|---|---|---|---|
|  | Democrats | | | | Republicans | | |
| Type of candidate | Number of candidates | Total raised | Average raised | Number of candidates | Total raised | Average raised |
| Incumbent | 16 | $146,993,389 | $9,187,087 | 25 | $214,189,613 | $8,567,585 |
| Challenger | 58 | $82,887,794 | $1,429,100 | 31 | $16,986,791 | $547,961 |
| Open seat | 9 | $34,345,149 | $3,816,128 | 15 | $24,842,670 | $1,656,178 |
| Grand total | 83 | $264,226,332 | $3,183,450 | 71 | $256,019,074 | $3,605,902 |

|  | | | | *House* | | | |
|---|---|---|---|---|---|---|---|
|  | Democrats | | | | Republicans | | |
| Type of candidate | Number of candidates | Total raised | Average raised | Number of candidates | Total raised | Average raised |
| Incumbent | 237 | $306,969,806 | $1,295,231 | 198 | $232,904,004 | $1,176,283 |
| Challenger | 308 | $101,003,269 | $327,933 | 278 | $90,103,860 | $324,115 |
| Open seat | 126 | $70,684,429 | $560,988 | 145 | $77,852,033 | $536,911 |
| Grand total | 671 | $478,657,504 | $713,349 | 621 | $400,859,897 | $645,507 |

*Source:* Center for Responsive Politics. Based on data released by the Federal Election Commission on November 6, 2008. Figures include all candidates who have filed reports.

Meanwhile, 38 percent of the 191 House Republicans running for reelection faced such challengers. Democratic incumbents facing challengers had raised an average of $693,951, whereas Republican incumbents had raised an average of $468,083. The twenty-five most vulnerable Democratic incumbents had raised an average of $942,450. Their twenty-nine Republican counterparts had collected an average of $684,700.[37]

By the end of 2007, the DCCC had comfortably moved from a defensive to an offensive position. Committee chair Chris Van Hollen of Maryland determined that vulnerable House Democrats were financially well positioned to win reelection and shifted his focus to winning open seats in Republican districts. Twelve of the thirty-one "Frontline Democrats" lacked serious competition, and nine finished the year with more than $1 million in cash on hand. The DCCC's "Red to Blue" program moved front and center and began directing money to promising Democratic candidates in about two dozen open seat races.[38] Senate Democrats continued to outraise their Republican counterparts as well.

The NRCC ended 2007 with $5.4 million in cash on hand—much less than the DCCC's $35 million. The NRCC had raised about $50 million in 2007, but had to devote substantial funds to paying down debts the committee racked up in 2006. NRCC chair Tom Cole of Oklahoma called on his colleagues to give to the committee and many heeded his call. Members can make unlimited transfers from their personal campaign accounts to the congressional campaign committees and can also give $5,000 from their leadership PACs. Leadership PACs are fund-raising committees connected to members of

Congress that are typically used to support both personal and party goals. Both parties in the House now require their members to pay dues to the campaign committees. The amount of money a member is expected to contribute typically corresponds with his or her seniority and rank. Between 2002 and 2006, the DCCC doubled its reliance on member contributions and the NRCC tripled the share of contributions it received from Republican members. Party leaders typically set the tone: by August 2008, House Speaker Nancy Pelosi of California, House Majority Leader Steny Hoyer of Maryland, and House Minority Leader John Boehner of Ohio each had given more than $1 million to their party campaign committees. Members who do not ante up risk being passed over for plum committee assignments and leadership posts.[39]

The NRCC also joined forces with the NRSC to establish a joint fundraising account that matched donations from Republican House members and senators. Many members of Congress also formed joint fund-raising committees with each other in 2008 for the purpose of sharing donors, sharing venues, or building a reputation as a strong fund-raiser. Most congressional joint fundraising committees combined a well-known lawmaker with a lesser-known member to help the lesser-known member raise money. Republican members of Congress also joined forces with a state or federal party committee to raise money for both themselves and the party.

Congressional Republicans raised a respectable amount of campaign money in 2007, but Democratic fund raising was in overdrive. In addition to receiving help from the party committees, candidates also relied on PACs and individual contributions. Both parties' incumbents received about half of their contributions from PACs. In addition, challengers raised about 25 percent of their money from small contributors, compared to just 10 percent for incumbents. And both incumbents and challengers collected about 30 percent of their funds from large donors who gave $1,000 or more.[40]

## 2008: The News Gets Worse for Republicans

House Republicans bleakly rang in the New Year by calling in the FBI to investigate irregularities in the NRCC's finances. The investigation centered on Christopher Ward, a former employee of the NRCC who subsequently worked as a contractor for the committee. Ward also served as treasurer for dozens of Republican campaign committees. The NRCC had not conducted an independent audit since the 2002 election; prior to 2002, when Rep. Tom Reynolds of New York took over as chair of the committee, audits had been conducted annually. Federal authorities determined that Ward had diverted about $1 million from the NRCC to his personal accounts. This amounted to roughly 20 percent of the committee's $5 million in cash on hand. Several Republican lawmakers said that Ward had also stolen money from their personal campaign committees.[41] The scandal did little to brighten Republican prospects in 2008.

After Republicans lost three special elections in previously Republican districts in the spring of 2008, Democrats proclaimed that no district was safe for Republicans. The NRCC spent $1.8 million on ads that tried to tie the Democratic special election candidates to Obama, but the strategy proved unsuccessful. On the heels of these losses, Republican leaders advised their candidates to craft individual, rather than party-based, campaign strategies. Candidates were also advised not to count on the NRCC for financial assistance. "Candidates will have to demonstrate that they're worth the investment," Cole said. "We will have to be pretty brutal."[42]

When the DCCC and DSCC announced that they would continue to take money from lobbyists and PACs, despite Obama's ban on such contributions to his own campaign, congressional Republicans saw an opportunity to paint their opponents as hypocrites. Most Democratic congressional candidates joined their party's campaign committees in rejecting Obama's ban on contributions from lobbyists and PACs. Members of Congress tend to raise a much higher proportion of their campaign money from PACs than do presidential candidates, and most were reluctant to cut off those funds. Unfortunately for Republicans, the hypocrite label did not stick and Democrats continued to raise money at record pace.

Heading into the final months of the 2008 election, congressional Democrats had three times more cash on hand than the Republicans. At the beginning of June, the DCCC had $47.2 million in the bank and the DSCC had $38.5 million. The NRCC had just $6.7 in cash on hand and the NRSC had only $21.6 million. June also brought news that the Republicans' preferred candidate to run against Sen. John Kerry of Massachusetts did not have enough signatures to get on the ballot and that an independent candidate in Oregon, who would have taken votes away from the Democratic candidate challenging the vulnerable Republican Senator Gordon Smith, had dropped out of the race.[43] As of election day, the Democratic congressional campaign committees had raised a combined total of $255 million, compared to $182 million for the Republican committees.

## Party Independent Spending

The dominant story line in the final leg of the 2008 election was whether congressional Democrats would be able to translate their huge financial advantage into major gains in the House and Senate. Both parties had to make tough decisions about which races to invest in and which to ignore. By the end of October, the DSCC had made $53.2 million in independent expenditures, compared to the NRSC's $27.4 million. The DSCC invested heavily in eleven states being defended by Republican incumbents. Two weeks before election day, the DSCC spent more than $3 million opposing North Carolina Senator Elizabeth Dole, three times more than the NRSC spent opposing her challenger, Kay Hagan. Dole lost the election. Both committees invested just over $1 million in the Oregon Senate race, and Gordon Smith, the Republican incumbent, lost as well. The DSCC spent $1.5 million in an unsuccessful attempt to unseat Senate Minority Leader Mitch McConnell in Kentucky and another $2.8 million attacking Georgia Senator Saxby Chambliss.[44] Although Chambliss eventually won, he was forced into a runoff with Jim Martin in December. High levels of last-minute spending helped Senate Democrats pick up at least six seats in the 2008 election.[45]

On the House side, the DCCC spent $52.3 million in independent expenditures through October, compared to $11.4 million for the NRCC. Indeed, the DCCC made more independent expenditures than any other committee during the 2008 election. Democrats invested $500,000 or more in forty-one House races; their spending in twenty-seven of these races topped $1 million. Of these races, only ten involved Democratic incumbents. Playing offense allowed the Democrats to invest heavily in challengers and open seat candidates. The NRCC invested $500,000 in nine races, including those of six Republican incumbents. Both committees spent about $250,000 in thirteen additional races, with the Democrats spending more on challengers and open seat candidates. With just two weeks left in the 2008 campaign, the Democrats poured money into at least sixteen of the closest House races, spending upwards of $500,000 in half of them. The NRCC put last-minute money into twelve races, but spent much less overall.[46] Independent spending by the DCCC helped House Democrats pick up at least twenty seats.[47]

## Issue Advocacy Spending

In a May 25, 2008 Fox News Sunday appearance, DCCC chair Chris Van Hollen challenged NRCC chair Tom Cole to join him in calling for an end to soft-money political ads. Cole called the request a "political stunt" and accused Van Hollen of being insincere. The exchange was sparked by news that a conservative 501(c)(4) organization named Freedom's Watch was expected to pour millions of dollars into House and Senate races. Van Hollen claimed that the NRCC, which was struggling to raise money, had essentially contracted out its operation to Freedom's Watch.[48] The group had originally announced that it would spend around $200 million opposing Democratic candidates in congressional races. In the end, Freedom's Watch was hit hard by the financial crisis and significantly scaled back its operation. By mid-October, the group had spent $30 million on congressional races—a fraction of what it had intended to spend.

Most of the $350 million in issue advocacy spending during the 2008 election benefited Democratic candidates in congressional races. Although spending by 527 groups was down from 2004, 501(c) groups picked up the slack. 501(c) groups can do everything 527 groups do, as long as "partisan campaign activity" does not become their primary function. They are also exempt from some of the reporting requirements that 527 groups must comply with. The increased activity of 501(c) groups in 2008 provided an attractive, less regulated outlet for soft-money spending on issue advocacy. 527 groups spent $185 million by mid-October, and 501(c) groups were expected to spend somewhere around $200 million by election day. Spending by these groups was concentrated in a few dozen competitive House and Senate races. For example, Republican-oriented groups spent about $11 million on Colorado's close Senate race, while their Democratic counterparts spent about $4 million. Republican Senator Gordon Smith of Oregon received about $6 million in help from three Republican-oriented groups—more than the NRSC spent on his race. In addition to investing in television and radio advertising, these groups spent heavily on "ground war" activities like canvassing, e-mailing, and phone-banking. In fact, two of the top Democratic-oriented groups, America Votes and Change to Win, focused almost entirely on the ground war, as did one of the top Republican groups, the College Republican National Committee.[49]

Many 501(c) groups maintain that their activities are not intended to influence elections, but rather are a continuation of their grassroots activities concerning policy issues. In 2008, however, a number of these groups invested in advocacy campaigns that might reasonably be considered electioneering. America's Agenda: Healthcare for Kids, for example, spent more than $13 million on television ads thanking twenty-six members of Congress in close races who had supported their efforts. All of the ads were paid for by a contribution from PHARMA, the pharmaceutical industry's trade group, which advocates expanded health insurance for children. At issue is whether the ad campaign's primary purpose was to influence races or keep pressure on Congress to expand children's health insurance. The Sierra Club, Planned Parenthood, and the National Rifle Association are among the organizations that claim 501(c) status for political purposes.[50]

Disproportionately heavy spending on behalf of Democratic candidates and causes, combined with difficult political circumstances, proved too much for congressional Republicans in 2008. Some survived tough races, but many lacked the resources to put up a strong fight.

## Conclusion

The story of money in the 2008 elections was one of change and continuity. The presidential race illuminated both the strengths and weaknesses of the nation's campaign finance system. The race was also full of ironic twists and turns. On the Democratic side, the candidate who raised the most money won his party's nomination, but only after a long, drawn-out fight. On the Republican side, money provided little in the way of predictive value. Notably, John McCain won his party's nomination despite teetering on the edge of bankruptcy several times during the primary campaign.

Obama's campaign attracted an astounding four million donors, thereby dispelling the notion that big-money contributors determine a candidate's fundraising fate. Using technologies like e-mail and text messaging, Obama successfully convinced millions of people that small contributions can make a huge difference. By encouraging greater participation, he advanced one of campaign reform law's most important goals, but by rejecting public financing for his own campaign, he also rejected the goal of keeping campaign costs and expenditures down. Since the election, many critics have argued that Obama's decision to bypass public funding was a step backward for campaign finance reform. But others see Obama's fund-raising prowess, and particularly his reliance on small donors, as a step toward leveling the campaign-funding playing field.[51]

A proponent of the presidential public finance system, McCain agreed to accept public funds in the general election and wound up tremendously handicapped by the very system he has long supported. Because McCain accepted public funds, the FEC is required to conduct an extensive post-election audit of his campaign coffers; adding insult to injury, the audit will likely cost McCain millions of dollars in accounting and legal fees. Meanwhile, the FEC is unlikely to audit the questionable donations that Obama received through the Internet because he declined public financing.[52] McCain's reputation as a reformer may have also lost him support from 527 and 501(c) groups unwilling to spend money on his behalf because of his antipathy toward them. Being a reformer, it seems, has its costs.

With all the talk of change the 2008 election brought, many aspects of campaign finance remained constant. Although the increased role of small donors in the presidential campaign signaled greater participation in the elections process, congressional candidates continued to rely heavily on PAC money and large contributions from individual donors. This was particularly true of incumbents, who raised only 10 percent of their money from small donors. And as in past congressional elections, the candidates who spent the most won the most. Tighter regulation of 527 groups led to the increased participation of 501(c) groups, proving that money, like water, will always find an outlet. As in previous elections, the elections of 2008 brought about both major change and more of the same.

## Notes

1. Lindsey Renick Mayer, "Obama's $150 Million," www.opensecrets.org/news/2008/10/obamas-150-million.html; and Federal Elections Commission, http://fec.gov.
2. David M. Drucker, "Sources: NRCC Secures $8 Million Loan for Final Election Push," *Roll Call*, October 8, 2008; and Zachary A. Goldfarb, "Wachovia Reports Historic Loss," *Washington Post*, October 23, 2008, D1.
3. "Citing 9/11 Ad, DCCC Calls for Cash against Feeney," *CongressDailyPM*, October 24, 2008.
4. Mather Murray, "Money Can't Buy Them Love," *Washington Post*, July 31, 2008.
5. Thank you to Sue S. Lagon for providing me with information on recent Supreme Court and FEC rulings.
6. Matthew Mosk, "Vacancies on FEC Filled as 5 Win Senate Approval," *Washington Post*, June 25, 2008, A6.
7. "FEC Bundling Rule Won't Come in Time for Elections," *CongressDailyPM*, September 9, 2008.
8. Anne E. Kornblut and Matthew Mosk, "Obama's Campaign Takes in $25 million: He Nearly Matches Clinton, with Twice as Many Donors," *Washington Post*, April 5, 2007, A1; Dan Balz, "Fundraising Totals Challenge Early Campaign Assumptions," *Washington Post*, April 17, 2007, A1; Jeffrey H. Birnbaum

and Matthew Mosk, "Clinton Fundraising Goes Full Force," *Washington Post,* February 7, 2007, A8; and Matthew Mosk and John Solomon, "Obama Taps Two Worlds to Fill 2008 War Chest," *Washington Post,* April 15, 2007, A1.

9. Campaign Finance Institute, "Big $1,000+ Donations Supply 79% of Presidential Candidates' Early Money," April 16, 2007, http://cfinst.org.

10. Dan Balz, "Fundraising Totals Challenge Early Campaign Assumptions," April 17, 2007, www.washingtonpost.com/wp-dyn/content/article/2007/04/16/AR2007041601705.html.

11. Campaign Finance Institute, "The Presidential Campaigns Are Setting Records," July 16, 2007, http://cfinst.org; John Solomon, "Obama Takes Lead in Money Raised; Pressure on Clinton Is Expected to Grow," *Washington Post,* July 2, 2007, A1; and Jose Antonio Vargas, "A Foundation Built on Small Blocks: Growing Internet Use Helps Obama to a Wide Base and a Money Lead," *Washington Post,* July 16, 2007, A10.

12. Ibid.

13. FEC, "FEC Approves Matching Funds for 2008 Presidential Candidates," December 20, 2007, http://fec.gov/press/press2007/20071207cert.shtml.

14. Matthew Mosk, "Clinton Tops Obama in Year-End Fundraising: Both Candidates Benefit From Early Victories," *Washington Post,* January 10, 2008, A14; and Anne E. Kornblut and Shailagh Murray, "N.Y. Senator Defies Polls, Edges Obama," *Washington Post,* January 9, 2008, A1.

15. Ibid.

16. Shailagh Murray and Matthew Mosk, "Clinton Lent Her Campaign $5 Million: Delegate Race with Obama Is Nearly Even," *Washington Post,* February 7, 2008, A1.

17. Matthew Mosk and Glenn Kessler, "FEC Warns McCain on Campaign Spending," *Washington Post,* February 22, 2008, A1; and Jim Kuhnhenn, "FEC Frees McCain from Spending Limit for Primaries," August 21, 2008, WTOPnews.com.

18. Anne E. Kornblut and Matthew Mosk, "Obama, Clinton Join Together in Show of Unity: Former Rivals Stress Goal of Bringing Democrats Together," *Washington Post,* June 27, 2008, A4.

19. Kevin Bogardus and Jordan Fabian, "Dem. Unity Tough on K St," *The Hill,* June 6, 2008, 1; Matthew Mosk, "Obama Raised More than $51 Million Last Month; and Democratic Candidate's Monthly Total Is Nearly Double that of His GOP Rival," *Washington Post,* August 17, 2008, A8.

20. Shailagh Murray and Perry Bacon Jr., "Obama to Reject Public Funds for Election," *Washington Post,* June 20, 2008, A1; and Jeffrey M. Jones, "Campaign Financing Appears to Be Non-Issue for Voters," October 30, 2008, www.gallup.com.

21. Linton Weeks, "Did Obama Kill Public Campaign Finance?" October 22, 2008, www.npr.org.

22. Campaign Finance Institute, "After Holding Financial Advantage in Primaries, Obama Likely to Achieve Only Parity with McCain in General," September 25, 2008, http://cfinst.org.

23. McCain's $84.1 million in public funds plus the RNC's $76.5 million; Obama's $77.4 million in cash on hand plus the DNC's $17.7 million.

24. Campaign Finance Institute, "Obama's October Surprise: A 60–40 Democratic Financial Advantage?" October 21, 2008, http://cfinst.org; and Michael Luo, "Obama Raises More than $150 Million in September," *New York Times,* October 20, 2008.

25. Matthew Mosk, "Campaign Finance Gets New Scrutiny," *Washington Post,* September 26, 2008, A1; and Matthew Mosk, "Obama Accepting Untraceable Donations," *Washington Post,* October 29, 2008, A2.

26. Jim Rutenberg and Brian Stelter, "Obama, Purse Swelling, Plans Half-Hour TV Ad," *New York Times,* October 9, 2008.

27. Michael Luo, "Obama Raises More than $150 Million in September"; and Matthew Mosk, "In Final Stretch, McCain to Pour Money into TV Ads," *Washington Post,* October 31, 2008, A3.
28. Jonathan Weisman and Michael D. Shear, "Obama, McCain Aim to Curb 527s," *Washington Post,* May 14, 2008, A6.
29. Bill Swindell, "527s Stuck in Port as Other Organizations Jump into Fray," *National Journal,* October 23, 2008; Matthew Mosk, "Economic Downturn Sidelines Donors to '527' Groups," *Washington Post,* October 19, 2008, A9; and Campaign Finance Institute, "501 (c) Groups Emerge as Big Players Alongside 527s," October 31, 2008, http://cfinst.org.
30. Center for Responsive Politics, www.opensecrets.org/pres08/indexp.php.
31. Center for Responsive Politics, "Money Wins Presidency and 9 of 10 Congressional Races in Priciest U.S. Election Ever," November 5, 2008, www.opensecrets.org.
32. Ibid. Final candidate spending reports were not reported to the FEC until December 4, 2008.
33. Center for Responsive Politics, "Money Wins Presidency and 9 of 10 Congressional Races in Priciest U.S. Election Ever"; and Campaign Finance Institute, "A First Look at Money in the House and Senate Elections," November 6, 2008, http://cfinst.org.
34. Campaign Finance Institute, "A First Look at Money in the House and Senate Elections."
35. Campaign Finance Institute, "501 (c) Groups Emerge as Big Players alongside 527s."
36. Chris Cillizza, "Democrats Grab Money Advantage in 2007's First Quarter," *Washington Post,* April 20, 2007, A6; and Lauren W. Whittington, "Frontliners Get Quick Cash Start: Frosh Post Solid Totals," *Roll Call,* April 16, 2008.
37. Campaign Finance Institute, "CFI Analysis of FEC House Candidate Reports through Sept. 30," October 30, 2007, http://cfinst.org.
38. David Drucker, "DCCC Targets 40 GOP Seats," *Roll Call,* December 20, 2007.
39. Emily Cadei, "Incumbents Feed the Party Coffers," October 6, 2008, *CQ Weekly,* 2642.
40. Campaign Finance Institute, "House Democrats Hold an Early Financial Advantage in Critical 2008 Match-ups," February 19, 2009, http://cfinst.org.
41. Paul Singer, "No NRCC Audits in Five Years," *Roll Call,* February 25, 2008; and Paul Kane and Dan Eggen, "GOP Campaign Arm Missing Cash: FBI Investigating Treasurer over Lack of Auditing," *Washington Post,* March 7, 2008, A4.
42. David M. Drucker, "NRCC's Tough Road: Weak Incumbents May Be Left Behind," *Roll Call,* June 17, 2008.
43. Shira Toeplitz, "Democratic Committees Maintain Cash Advantage," *Roll Call,* June 23, 2008.
44. Campaign Finance Institute, "CFI Announces New Tool for Tracking the Parties' Independent Spending Shifts during the Campaign's Closing Week," October 28, 2008, http://cfinst.org.
45. Two seats (Georgia and Alaska) were still undecided as of this writing.
46. Campaign Finance Institute, "CFI Announces New Tool for Tracking the Parties' Independent Spending Shifts during the Campaign's Closing Week."
47. Five seats were still undecided.
48. Jackie Kucinich, "NRCC Chairman Cole Fires back at 'Hypocritical' Challenge," *The Hill,* June 3, 2008; and Lauren W. Whittington, "DCCC Goes for Broke: New Site Hits Freedom's Watch," *Roll Call,* July 31, 208.
49. Campaign Finance Institute, "501 (c) Groups Emerge as Big Players Alongside 527s."
50. Ibid. and Bill Swindell, "527s Stuck in Port as Other Organizations Jump into Fray."
51. Linton Weeks, "Did Obama Kill Public Campaign Finance?"
52. Kenneth P. Vogel, "Obama Likely to Escape Campaign Audit," *Politico,* November 11, 2008.

# 9

# The Meaning of the 2008 Election

David R. Mayhew

The "meaning" of any election is a socially constructed product. We are still trying to figure out the meaning of the election of 1800, which has generated some interesting books lately.[1] What does it really mean that Jefferson beat Adams? On the practical side, the assessments of elections right after they occur by journalists, academics, politicians, and others are a feature of the electoral cycle itself. What is it that just happened? We need to know. Many voices weigh in. Quick comparisons are made, quick judgments are rendered, and those judgments often enter into the ensuing political life of the country.

Without much question, the paramount meaning or significance of the 2008 election is that an African American candidate was elected president of the United States. That makes it an extraordinary event. It is historic. It may reshape racial relations in the United States. But I have little to say about the matter here, since the significance is plain to all. Also, I have little to say about the election's demographics, which are pretty well vetted in this volume, as well as in the media. Nor do I say anything about whether the nomination of Sarah Palin for vice president cost the Republicans. Possibly it did, but nobody really knows.

What does that leave? I offer here certain quick comparisons, frames, judgments, and perspectives of other sorts about the presidential and congressional elections of 2008. My bents are toward history and simple statistics.

## An Open-Seat Presidential Election

Counting 2008, the United States has now had fifty-six presidential elections, beginning with the first held in 1788. What can be said about this long experience that might help frame the one in 2008? I would like to steer past any speculation about "realignments" or "critical elections." I do not believe that these ideas lead anywhere useful.[2] A good basic ordering question for the two-century-plus history of U.S. elections seems to be: When an election took place, did the party then holding the presidency run an incumbent candidate? In two of those fifty-six elections, 1788 and 1824, that question doesn't seem to make much sense, but in the other fifty-four instances it does.[3] Then, a follow-up question for each of these fifty-four instances is: For an in-office party, did running an incumbent presidential candidate, as opposed to navigating an open-seat election, affect its chances of keeping the presidency?

As can be seen in the top half of Table 9-1, running an incumbent candidate seems to help a party. In roughly two-thirds of the relevant instances—twenty-one cases out of thirty-one—incumbent presidential candidates have won reelection. Most recently, Bill Clinton in 1996 and George W. Bush in 2004 did so. No surprise. There are several reasons for this incumbency advantage.[4] Once in office, presidents acquire skills, enjoy prerogatives, and can deploy resources. Most presidents have conducted previous winning campaigns—an education of sorts. Also, like prize fighters who keep winning fights, presidents are in general alpha politicians by nature, whereas most losers in the presidential realm rank in comparison as betas.[5] Voters, for their part, may be risk averse—why take a chance on a novice in the White House? Or voters may be stuck in their previous voting behavior that favored a particular politician.[6]

Of greater relevance to the election of 2008 is the bottom half of Table 9-1—the twenty-three open-seat presidential elections. Until 2008, in-parties navigating open-seat elections kept the White House only 50 percent of the time. They had eleven wins and eleven losses. The election of 2008 has added another case to the loss column, rendering an up-to-date record of eleven wins and twelve losses. On balance in American history, in-office *parties* trying to keep the White House have enjoyed no electoral advantage whatever when they have failed to run in-office *candidates*.

A side question might be: Does it help an in-party to run an incumbent vice president for the presidency? The 2008 election was the only one since 1952 featuring neither an incumbent president nor an incumbent vice president. The historical evidence bearing on this question is vastly too slim to allow much purchase, but I doubt it. The logic seems weak. Serving very publicly as second banana for four years under an all-powerful president doesn't seem to add up to much of a credential. And the retiring presidents haven't always been helpful. In 1968, President Lyndon Johnson made Hubert Humphrey look weak. In 2000, was Bill Clinton a plus for Al Gore? (Gore didn't think so.) For the record, there have been three move-up successes—John Adams in 1796, Martin Van Buren in 1836, and George H. W. Bush in 1988. There have been three move-up failures—Nixon in 1960, Humphrey in 1968, and Gore in 2000. There is also the odd case of Thomas Jefferson in 1800, who won as an incumbent vice president challenging an incumbent president of the other party.

I am arguing here that the full historical universe of open-seat presidential elections provides a kind of yardstick. How does the contest of 2008 register on that yardstick? To draw some comparisons, let me shift from the binary won-loss record to a consideration of popular vote shares. That means dropping the three earliest elections in U.S. history from the open-seat data set of twenty-three, since the early contests of 1796, 1808, and 1816 do not have usable popular vote data.[7] That leaves twenty open-seat contests. For each of them, a question or two can be addressed regarding the major-party share of the national popular vote.

One question is: Lacking an incumbent candidate, how well did the in-party do? See Table 9-2, which ranks the twenty results from worst to best. The median performance is 49.6 percent of the major-party vote—very close

**Table 9-1**   Has the Party Holding the Presidency Kept It?

| Elections with an incumbent candidate running | |
|---|---|
| Yes, kept the presidency (N = 21) | No, lost the presidency (N = 10) |
| 1792–Washington | 1800–J. Adams lost to Jefferson |
| 1804–Jefferson | 1828–J. Q. Adams lost to Jackson |
| 1812–Madison | 1840–Van Buren lost to W. H. Harrison |
| 1820–Monroe | 1888–Cleveland lost to B. Harrison |
| 1832–Jackson | 1892–B. Harrison lost to Cleveland |
| 1864–Lincoln | 1912–Taft lost to Wilson |
| 1872–Grant | 1932–Hoover lost to F. D. Roosevelt |
| 1900–McKinley | 1976–Ford lost to Carter |
| 1904–T. Roosevelt | 1980–Carter lost to Reagan |
| 1916–Wilson | 1992–G. H. W. Bush lost to Clinton |
| 1924–Coolidge | |
| 1936–F. D. Roosevelt | |
| 1940–F. D. Roosevelt | |
| 1944–F. D. Roosevelt | |
| 1948–Truman | |
| 1956–Eisenhower | |
| 1964–L. B. Johnson | |
| 1972–Nixon | |
| 1984–Reagan | |
| 1996–Clinton | |
| 2004–G. W. Bush | |

| Elections without an incumbent running (with winners named) | |
|---|---|
| Yes, kept the presidency (N = 11) | No, lost the presidency (N = 12) |
| 1796–J. Adams | 1844–Polk |
| 1808–Madison | 1848–Taylor |
| 1816–Monroe | 1852–Pierce |
| 1836–Van Buren | 1860–Lincoln |
| 1856–Buchanan | 1884–Cleveland |
| 1868–Grant | 1896–McKinley |
| 1876–Hayes | 1920–Harding |
| 1880–Garfield | 1952–Eisenhower |
| 1908–Taft | 1960–Kennedy |
| 1928–Hoover | 1968–Nixon |
| 1988–G. H. W. Bush | 2000–G. W. Bush |
| | 2008–Obama |

*Note:* Omitted from the calculations are 1788, when the presidency was new, and 1824, when all the serious contenders for the office were of the same hegemonic party.

to 50–50 that the binary win-loss pattern would suggest. Tied at that median figure are the in-party Republicans who lost to Grover Cleveland in 1884 and the in-party Democrats who lost to Nixon in 1968. (Note that this 1968 value, involving just the major-party vote, ignores the third-party vote that year for George Wallace.) Worst-performing, at the top of Table 9-2, were the in-party Democrats in Warren Harding's landslide Republican victory of 1920. Best-performing were the in-party Republicans in 1928, when Herbert Hoover benefited from a booming economy and the Democrats' nomination of a Roman Catholic candidate, Al Smith. In the top half of the table one gets a whiff of

Table 9-2    Percentages of the Major-Party Popular Vote Won by the Incumbent Parties' Candidates in Open-Seat Presidential Elections

| Year | Incumbent party | Winning candidate | Incumbent party percentage |
|------|-----------------|-------------------|---------------------------|
| 1920 | Democrat | Harding (Republican) | 36.1 |
| 1860 | Democrat | Lincoln (Republican) | 42.5[1] |
| 1952 | Democrat | Eisenhower (Republican) | 44.7 |
| 1852 | Whig | Pierce (Democrat) | 46.4 |
| 2008 | Republican | Obama (Democrat) | 46.6 |
| 1848 | Democrat | Taylor (Whig) | 47.3 |
| 1896 | Democrat | McKinley (Republican) | 47.3 |
| 1876 | Republican | Hayes (Republican) | 48.5 |
| 1844 | Whig | Polk (Democrat) | 49.3 |
| 1884 | Republican | Cleveland (Democrat) | 49.6 |
| 1968 | Democrat | Nixon (Republican) | 49.6 |
| 1960 | Republican | Kennedy (Democrat) | 49.9[2] |
| 1880 | Republican | Garfield (Republican) | 50.1 |
| 2000 | Democrat | G. W. Bush (Republican) | 50.3 |
| 1836 | Democrat | Van Buren (Democrat) | 50.9[3] |
| 1868 | Republican | Grant (Republican) | 52.7 |
| 1988 | Republican | G. H. W. Bush (Republican) | 53.9 |
| 1908 | Republican | Taft (Republican) | 54.5 |
| 1856 | Democrat | Buchanan (Democrat) | 57.8 |
| 1928 | Republican | Hoover (Republican) | 58.8 |

[1] This is the Stephen Douglas share of the Abraham Lincoln plus Douglas vote.

[2] This is a vexed result. The figure rises to more than 50.0 if the Alabama popular vote is counted in a plausible, albeit unconventional, way.

[3] The Whig vote adds together the vote for three regional candidates.

various kinds of disaster—the grim aftermath of World War I downing the Democrats in 1920, the breakup of the Union depressing the Democrats in 1860, the Korean War harming the Democrats in 1952, the backwash of the Mexican War possibly damaging the Democrats in 1848, and the great, long-lasting depression of 1893 continuing to damage the Democrats in 1896.

How about Barack Obama's victory in 2008? See the underlined row in Table 9-2. From the perspective of this table, the performance of the in-party Republicans in 2008 was not great. At 46.6 percent, they did three points worse than the historical median.[8]

Another application of the open-seat yardstick is possible. See Table 9-3, which reorganizes the data of Table 9-2 to show something different. Here, the winning presidential candidates are ranked according to their popular vote percentages, regardless of whether they ran as nominees of the in-party. In-party or out-party, how did the winners perform in open-seat contests? At the top of the table, note that the big open-seat winners were Harding in 1920 and Hoover in 1928. At the bottom of the table appear George W. Bush in 2000 and Rutherford B. Hayes in 1876—both lofted to office by the Electoral College despite losing the national popular vote. In general in the table, note that open-seat elections tend to be close. Fifteen of the twenty winners have won with less than 55 percent of the major-party popular vote. Where is Obama? Close to the middle of the pack at 53.4 percent. According to this

**Table 9-3**  Winning Candidate's Percentage of Major-Party Vote in Open-Seat Presidential Elections, 1936–2008

| Year | Winning candidate | Party | Vote percentage |
|------|-------------------|-------|-----------------|
| 1920 | Warren Harding | Republican | 63.9 |
| 1928 | Herbert Hoover | Republican | 58.8 |
| 1856 | James Buchanan | Democrat | 57.8 |
| 1860 | Abraham Lincoln | Republican | 57.5[1] |
| 1952 | Dwight Eisenhower | Republican | 55.3 |
| 1908 | William Howard Taft | Republican | 54.5 |
| 1988 | George H. W. Bush | Republican | 53.9 |
| 1852 | Franklin Pierce | Democrat | 53.6 |
| 2008 | Barack Obama | Democrat | 53.4 |
| 1868 | Ulysses Grant | Republican | 52.7 |
| 1848 | Zachary Taylor | Whig | 52.5 |
| 1896 | William McKinley | Republican | 52.5 |
| 1836 | Martin Van Buren | Democrat | 50.9[2] |
| 1844 | James Polk | Democrat | 50.7 |
| 1884 | Grover Cleveland | Democrat | 50.4 |
| 1968 | Richard Nixon | Republican | 50.4 |
| 1880 | James Garfield | Republican | 50.1 |
| 1960 | John F. Kennedy | Democrat | 50.1[3] |
| 2000 | George W. Bush | Republican | 49.7 |
| 1876 | Rutherford Hayes | Republican | 48.5 |

[1] This is the Abraham Lincoln share of the Lincoln plus Stephen Douglas vote.
[2] The Whig vote adds together the vote for three regional candidates.
[3] This is a vexed result. The figure falls to less than 50.0 if the Alabama popular vote is counted in a plausible, albeit unconventional, way.

standard, he scored slightly higher than William McKinley in 1896, yet slightly lower than George H. W. Bush in 1988.

The 2008 election brought one of the worst showings for an in-party facing an open-seat presidential election in U.S. history. It was the fifth worst showing in the twenty instances. The voters' news for the GOP was bad. Compared with all performances in open-seat circumstances, however—that is, innocent of all considerations of which party held the White House ex ante—the Obama percentage of 53.4 percent was solid yet close to average. He did not win by a landslide margin of ten points or better, as Dwight D. Eisenhower did in 1952 and Harding did in 1920.

At this point, perhaps another comparison is useful. This one assembles popular-vote as well as electoral-vote data for certain recent presidential winners regardless of any considerations having to do with which party was holding the White House at the time or which candidates if any were incumbents. Just the relevant uncooked facts. Table 9-4 lists not all the recent presidential winners but rather those whose victory margins were roughly comparable to Obama's. Omitted are the two close George W. Bush elections and Ronald Reagan's 1984 landslide. Like Reagan in 1980 and George H. W. Bush in 1988, but unlike Bill Clinton in either of his elections, Obama won a majority of the popular vote. Obama's popular-vote edge looks something like Clinton's in 1992.

Table 9-4    Victory Showings, in Recent Presidential Elections, in the Vicinity of Obama's

| Year | Winner | Winner's percentage of total popular vote minus runner-up's percentage | Winner's percentage of total popular vote | Electoral votes won |
|------|--------|------|------|------|
| 1980 | Reagan | 9.7 | 50.7 | 489 |
| 1988 | G. H. W. Bush | 7.8 | 53.4 | 426 |
| 1992 | Clinton | 5.6 | 43.0 | 370 |
| 1996 | Clinton | 8.5 | 49.2 | 379 |
| 2008 | Obama | 6.8 | 52.7 | 365 |

# Homeostasis

So much for open-seat elections. Here is another perspective. In certain ancient philosophies, the world keeps repeating itself. Things go round and round. By contrast, the idea of progress is modern. In a decently functioning two-party system, the ancient view seems to be right, at least in one respect. Party control of a government goes back and forth. For one thing, if both parties aim for the median voter in a plausible way, updating their ideologies and issue menus as need be, a system should equilibrate. For another, the opposition party is always available to point out mistakes and profit from them.

If all this is true, then each of the parties in a two-party system, over a long period of time, should fare about equally in elections. Has that been true in the case of U.S. presidential elections? The answer is yes. Consider the record from 1828 to 2008—a total of forty-six elections, omitting the pre–Andrew Jackson era. The Democrats have won the White House in twenty-one of these elections, the Republicans (in combination with, before them, the Whigs) in twenty-five. Three of those Republican victories (1876, 1888, and 2000) were Electoral College wins in which the popular vote went the other way.[9] With that correction, the Democrats' record is twenty-four and twenty-two. In those forty-six elections, the median Democratic share of the major-party popular vote has been 50.4 percent.[10] (Their mean share has been 49.5 percent.) In the post–World War II era, the Democrats have won the presidency seven times and the Republicans nine times, with each of the two parties winning the popular vote eight times.[11]

Also, if the equilibration idea is valid, party control of the presidency should bounce back and forth. Generally speaking, it does. The statistician Daniel J. Gans has noted, for example, that in the sequence of presidential elections from 1856 to 1980, the distribution of "runs" by party (Jimmy Carter, for example, was a run of one for the Democrats; Reagan and George H. W. Bush were a run of three for the Republicans) did not differ significantly from what you would expect to get in a distribution of runs of heads and tails through coin flips.[12] Since World War II the party controlling the White House has kept it in eight elections, but lost it in eight. This pattern renders fanciful any idea that the American political system, at least in recent times, has been fostering any long-lasting party "eras" in the sphere of presidential politics. Things have tended to bounce back and forth. Republican strategist Karl Rove could build for the short term, which is a major accomplishment, but probably no one can build for the long term. Not at the presidential level.

Here is the commonsense point. The election of 2008 was, among other things, an equilibrating election. Parties in power tend to slip. Parties out of power tend to rise. On the former point, one authoritative estimate has it that, controlling for all else, the party occupying the White House loses half a percentage point of the popular vote for every four years in office.[13] In the present case, all else equal, that would mean a slash of the Republican share of the vote in 2000, 49.7 percent, to 48.7 percent in 2008, which is just two points off John McCain's showing of 46.6 percent.

There are reasons for such equilibration. One line of theorizing is that, over time, parties out of power succeed in assembling "coalitions of minorities" of various types that for whatever reason grow discontented with the in-crowd. Governments tend to disappoint.[14] Another possibility is that, generally speaking, we are too optimistic in life. Stylized psychology seems to say so. Optimism is good for individual survival. Perhaps incoming parties, and the electorates that support them, systematically overestimate what is accomplishable in office and then are disappointed. Yet another possibility is ontological. From the standpoint of a chief executive—an elected one or not—what is the world really like out there? Anyone who has ever run an organization has probably reflected that unfavorable items turn up more often in the in-basket than favorable ones. That kind of pattern can take a political toll.

Finally, in a very convincing interpretation, one recent line of scholarship points to ideological equilibration.[15] Once in office, the argument goes, a party tends to enact policies suited to its own ideological side of the median voter—Democrats to the left, Republican to the right. This goes down well for awhile, since it may be a corrective to the previous party's off-center performance in the opposite direction. But then such behavior gets on voters' nerves, and they correct by switching back to the other party. The history of officeholding and policymaking, that is, tends to be dialectical.

This is a simple, basic idea that has good empirical grounding in the American experience of recent decades. Certainly the idea resonates if it is applied to the eight-year George W. Bush administration and its surrounding politics. In both domestic and foreign policy, the Bush White House operated on the right-hand side of the line. Its rightward bent was emphatic, from the tax cuts of 2001 through the Iraq War through, for example, energy policy, environmental policy, cultural policy, and the White House's attempt to partially privatize Social Security in 2005. By this reckoning Obama's victory was a theoretically well-grounded ideological correction. Many elections have had that quality.

## Events, Contingency, Luck

Here is yet another perspective. In offering it, I wade deeper into waters of overdetermination, but so be it. As political scientists, we like to traffic in measurable regularities and, generally speaking, that is what we do. The two perspectives on the meaning of the 2008 election discussed above are instances of that propensity. So is the kind of econometric analysis that uses regularly measurable economic data to explain the outcome of elections. Data on inflation, unemployment, and changes in per capita income can be marshaled and deployed with elegance and profit. The confidence intervals may be wide, and the explained variance may fall considerably short of completeness, but the enterprise tends to work. In the 2008 election, for example, Ray Fair's prediction model worked well.[16]

Yet we tend to overlook unique, or at least odd or sparsely occurring, kinds of events as causes of electoral patterns or results. Such happenings are not so tractable. They don't fit into equations well. Historians dwell on them, but social scientists tend not to. The kinds of events I have in mind might be a shock to everybody, such as volcanic eruptions, or they might be spurred by governments, the instruments of governments, or other actors. But generally speaking, they come as a surprise. A paradigmatic instance is the blowing up of the Madrid trains three days before the Spanish election of 2004. Spain's conservative government had been heading toward a victory or at worst a photo finish, but the bombing of the trains discombobulated Spanish politics, although not in any simple or deterministic way. Instead, the governing party seems to have reacted to the event foolishly, or been perceived to do so, and the opposition Socialists, apparently as a consequence, walked away with the election. Had no trains blown up, there would have been no opportunity for the government to react foolishly. A result like this cannot be explained by claiming that it was predetermined by conventional indicators, or by the match-up of well-embedded left-right voter preferences to the ideological offerings of the politicians.

How about the American experience? In this country's history, there seems to be an ample helping. Here are some instances, both events and plausible non-events—the latter of which are, although especially dicey propositions, intriguing and empirically rooted parts of the record. In 1864, absent the surprising victories by Union armies in Atlanta and the Shenandoah Valley in September and October, the Democrat George McClellan, rather than Abraham Lincoln, seems to have been headed for victory in the November election—Lincoln certainly thought so.[17] During World War II, a non-event seems to have undermined the incumbent Democrats in the 1942 midterm, while an event seems to have helped them in the 1944 presidential election. Unfortunately for FDR, the successful Allied landing in North Africa didn't quite meet the November 1942 election deadline, but D-Day in June 1944 was more propitiously timed. President Roosevelt was not pressuring the military, but he was apparently aware of the political implications both times: "Just as the 1942 mid-terms had influenced the Torch [North Africa] decision, so the looming 1944 presidential elections affected the Trident [D-Day] ones."[18]

Two more non-events. In 1968 President Lyndon B. Johnson angled to announce Vietnam peace talks just before the presidential election, which might have helped the Democratic candidate Humphrey. Yet the Republican candidate Nixon did not fancy a peace move just then, and apparently his agents dickered with the South Vietnamese government to help ward one off. No peace move occurred.[19] In 1980 President Carter would have loved to wire a settlement of the Iranian hostage crisis just before the election, but the Iranian government wasn't amenable. Politicians know the electoral potential of events and of their opposite: non-events that are all too visible or tangible.

Events and non-events such as these lie in the noneconomic realm. Of more relevance to 2008 is the economic realm. American history is, among other things, a saga of economic panics, crashes, banking crises, and the like. These events are not easily measured or plugged into equations. They can affect the conventional economic indicators, and often do, but not always in the short term, and their widespread immediate effects can include fear among voters about mortgages, credit, bank accounts, and job loss. In the econometrics tradition, these fears are not conventional indicator material. Also, panics or crashes can by themselves be scary spectacles—like Pearl Harbor or 9/11 in a different vein—even if they do not generate widespread economic hardships in the short run.

Voters can react to scary economic spectacles. Yet there is an odd aspect to American history. Never before 2008 did a major panic or crash occur during the run-up to an election—either a presidential election or a midterm. The list of panics or crashes looks something like the following: 1819, 1837, 1857, 1873, 1907 (a currency crisis), 1929, 1937, and 1987 (a Wall Street crash).[20] Certainly, some of these events had electoral effects—but at a temporal distance. Until 2008, no panic coincided with an election.

Now we have an instance.[21] Wall Street and a good deal more crashed in September 2008. With what consequence? "Crushed by the crash" is probably as good a judgment as any about what happened to John McCain during the 2008 election. True, the economic indicators for the year were not great anyway, and the various homeostatic factors discussed above were operating to his disadvantage. Yet the polls showed that the race was roughly even in early September (McCain was even slightly ahead for awhile), and it takes a brave prognosticator to predict an election outcome when close competitors face two more months of happenings, which may include gaffes, scandals, revelations, media bombshells, al-Qaida videotapes, driving-under-the-influence leaks, and the rest.[22]

The crash in September 2008 seems to have sent south not only McCain's numbers, but also those of Republican candidates for the House and Senate. "In the postmortem analyses of the presidential contest," one pre-election analysis of the election went, "the financial meltdown will likely mark the tipping point."[23] A post-election assessment agreed: "As the economy sank, the fortunes of Obama—as the Democratic candidate after eight years of Republican rule—inevitably rose. McCain could have performed flawlessly and still succumbed to economic reality."[24] Meanwhile, additional House districts tipped toward the Democrats, and what had seemed like five endangered Republican Senate seats expanded into eight.

As with the Madrid trains in 2004, the causal path at work here was apparently complex and contingent rather than simple and deterministic. National security, McCain's strong point, gave way to economics as a popular concern. A premium got placed on economic management as opposed to cultural expression. The Republicans looked somewhat foolish when McCain rushed back to Washington, D.C., in hopes of brokering a settlement, only to meet House Republicans scattering like stirred-up chickens as the $700 billion bailout loomed. As much as anything, a primal fire-the-management verdict seems to have set in among voters—even if McCain wasn't exactly the management.

Paging Machiavelli and the tides of *fortuna*. In political terms, the eight-year administration of George W. Bush followed an arc of, among other things, luck. Absent the supreme gift of the butterfly ballot in Palm Beach County, Florida, in 2000, leaving aside everything else that happened in Florida that year, Bush wouldn't have reached the White House.[25] Absent the grim events of 9/11, Republicans might have fared worse in the elections of 2002 and 2004, which were dominated by national security concerns. In 2006 Iraq collapsed into apparently irretrievable (although on today's evidence, it wasn't) sectarian violence in exactly October of that year, just before the midterm. For the Republicans, the 2006 midterm was devastating. Then in September 2008 came the Wall Street crash. The gods have their ways.

## The Electoral College

No one can tell exactly what elections would be like if American presidents were selected directly by nationwide popular vote. The issues and mobilization strategies might change somewhat. Also, tactical maneuvers under the current system—the parties' battleground state appeals and the rest—can swerve the popular vote share in particular states by tenths of a percentage point or more. For this reason, there is no reason to rate the precise state-specific results that we see now as being somehow an exact gold-standard truth.

Still, it is interesting to witness how presidential elections have played out within the existing Electoral College system. Table 9-5 uses a technique to probe into deviations, so to speak, and into possible party bias, in the sixteen presidential elections since World War II, including 2008.[26] The first column of percentages gives each Democratic presidential candidate's share of the major-party national popular vote. The second column gives the Democratic candidate's popular vote share in the median Electoral College state, counting the District of Columbia as a state.[27] That is the state that turns out to be pivotal once all the fifty-one are weighted according to their Electoral College votes and laid end to end according to their Democratic presidential vote share. The pivotal state is the one that contains the median elector. In 2004, for example, it was Ohio with 48.9 percent for John Kerry. In 2000, it was Florida with 49.995 percent for Al Gore. The last column in Table 9-5 gives, for each election, the difference between the values supplied in the two preceding columns.

**Table 9-5**   Democratic Share of Major-Party Presidential Vote

| Year | Winner | Percentage share of nationwide popular vote | Percentage share of median Electoral College unit | Difference |
|------|--------|------|------|------|
| 1948 | Truman | 52.3 | 50.5 | +1.8 |
| 1952 | Eisenhower | 44.5 | 44.2 | +0.3 |
| 1956 | Eisenhower | 42.2 | 42.6 | −0.4 |
| 1960 | Kennedy | 50.1 | 50.4 | −0.3 |
| 1964 | Johnson | 61.3 | 62.4 | −1.1 |
| 1968 | Nixon | 49.6 | 48.7 | +0.9 |
| 1972 | Nixon | 38.2 | 38.7 | −0.5 |
| 1976 | Carter | 51.1 | 50.9 | +0.2 |
| 1980 | Reagan | 44.7 | 45.7 | −1.0 |
| 1984 | Reagan | 40.8 | 40.5 | +0.3 |
| 1988 | Bush 41 | 46.1 | 46.0 | +0.1 |
| 1992 | Clinton | 53.5 | 52.8 | +0.7 |
| 1996 | Clinton | 54.7 | 55.2 | −0.5 |
| 2000 | Bush 43 | 50.3 | 49.995 | +0.3 |
| 2004 | Bush 43 | 48.8 | 48.9 | −0.1 |
| 2008 | Obama | 53.4 | 54.0 | −0.6 |
| Mean |  | 48.85 | 48.84 | +0.006 |

During these sixteen elections, ignoring the pluses and minuses, the mean absolute divergence between the nationwide popular vote share, taken straight, and its expression in the median Electoral College unit has been 0.575 percent—a bit more than half a percentage point. A split result came to pass in 2000, when Gore won the national popular vote but lost the election. But the deviations, so to speak, have been very small. They have ranged as high as 1.0 percent in 1980 and 1.8 percent in 1948—although the high absolute values for those two years may be related to the presence of third-party candidates.[28]

That is the deviations data. As for partisan bias, it has on average hugged zero. See the reading in the lower right-hand corner of Table 9-5. In eight of the sixteen elections, the Electoral College deviations have slightly favored the Democrats; in the other eight they have slightly favored the Republicans. In the two most recent elections, 2004 and 2008, favor has gone slightly to the Democrats. Here is one way of presenting the intuition. Consider the following counterfactual: if, say, 3.5 percent of the popular vote were arbitrarily shaved off Obama's major-party percentage in every state, he would fall slightly behind McCain in the national popular vote. But he would still win at least an Electoral College tie by taking Iowa with 54.7 percent and then secure a sure-fire victory in the House of Representatives in which the Democrats dominate most state delegations.[29] George W. Bush's victory in 2000 tracked a similar, although in that case Republican advantage, featuring Florida.

By this standard, the lack of a systematic partisan bias in the Electoral College during the last sixteen elections comes close to being uncanny. It probably explains why there is so little interest in getting rid of the Electoral

College. In general, neither party has been consistently disfavored. Neither party can expect to be disfavored next time. After 2000, there was a brief ripple of reform sentiment among Democrats. But it went away and seems unlikely to return.

## Race

Nothing caused more comment during the 2008 election than race. Would there be a "Bradley effect" in which the African American candidate fared much worse than the polls had predicted? In other ways, would Barack Obama be significantly damaged by being an African American? The answer to these questions seems to be no, or not much. For the Democrats, using 2004 as a baseline, the white vote did indeed subside in parts of the South and in Appalachia.[30] Yet across the country as a whole it did not, and Obama carried three southern states compared to none for Gore and Kerry. Exit polls showed Obama running about two percentage points better than Kerry among white voters, about five points better among blacks (who had already been voting 90 percent Democratic anyway), and about eleven points better among Hispanics.

What can be said about these demographic patterns of voting? On the one hand, the white vote for the Democratic presidential candidate certainly did not implode. That is a major result. For the very long term it is even an astonishing result, given the Democrats' long history, lasting into the Woodrow Wilson presidency in the 1910s, as the party of white supremacy.

With some hesitation, I offer a possibly illuminating comparison in Figure 9-1. It juxtaposes Obama's victory in 2008 with that of Kennedy, the only Roman Catholic elected to the presidency, in 1960. How does religion then compare with race now? The comparison has difficulties. Roman Catholics considerably outnumber African Americans. And the black vote, as noted, has registered very high for Democrats in recent times and could scarcely have risen much higher in 2008.

Even so, Figure 9-1 offers a comparison by featuring an "index of religious voting" for 1960 and an "index of race voting" for 2008.[31] The percentage of Catholics, as opposed to Protestants, who voted for Kennedy in 1960, is compared to the percentage of blacks, as opposed to whites, who voted for Obama in 2008.[32] In 1960, for example, 78 percent of Catholics voted for Kennedy, but only 38 percent of Protestants voted for him, yielding an index value of 40. In Figure 9-1, the 1960 and 2008 elections are juxtaposed vertically, with the immediately preceding and (in 1960's case) succeeding elections branching to the left and right. As can be seen, the candidates' religious identities in 1960 seem to have brought an enormous (although temporary) jolt to the parties' coalitional structure.[33] Millions of Catholics voted Democratic who likely otherwise wouldn't have. Millions of Protestants voted Republican who likely otherwise wouldn't have. In 2008, race seems to have brought a much smaller jolt. The index value for race did

**Figure 9-1**   Indexes of Race and Religious Voting

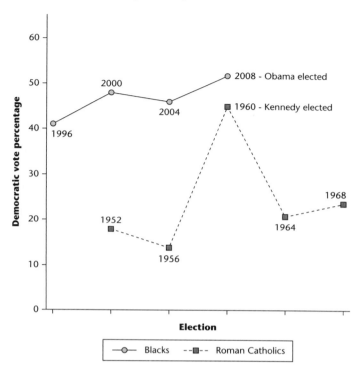

Sources: Religious voting index from Nelson W. Polsby and Aaron Wildavsky, *Presidential Elections: Strategies and Structures of American Politics,* 10th ed. (New York: Chatham House, 2000), 317–319. Race voting index from "Dissecting the Changing Electorate," *New York Times,* November 9, 2008, WK5.

Notes: The solid line indicates the percentage of blacks voting for the Democratic presidential candidate, minus the percentage of whites voting that way. The dashed line indicates the percentage of Roman Catholics voting for the Democratic presidential candidate minus the percentage of Protestants voting that way.

reach a peak in 2008,[34] but, generally speaking, the white vote stayed about the same for the Democrats. In all likelihood, if the white vote had caved for the Democrats in 2008 to the degree that the Protestant vote did for them in 1960, John McCain would be president.

Yet there is more to the story. The differential gains for the Democrats, by race, between 2004 and 2008, are noteworthy.[35] Obviously, African-, Hispanic-, and Asian-Americans are supplying a new edge to the Democratic Party coalition. This trend is not new. It is, among other things, a gradually appearing product of the Voting Rights Act of 1965 and the Hart-Celler Immigration Act of 1965.

Nor is this the first time in U.S. history that a major expansion of the electorate by race, religion, or ethnicity has elevated one of the parties. The coming into politics of the Scotch-Irish aided the Jeffersonian and Jacksonian Democrats during the early nineteenth century. In the 1850s and 1860s, Irish

Catholic immigration augmented the Democrats, and accretions of German Protestants and newly enfranchised African Americans augmented the Republicans. From the 1890s through the 1930s, Italian, Jewish, and Slavic immigrants augmented the Democrats (who also benefited politically as their southern state parties disfranchised African Americans). In recent times, the coming into politics of African-, Hispanic-, and Asian-Americans seems to be replicating, for the Democrats, the eastern and southern European script of a century ago. Trends like these can be powerful aids to a party. Yet note that in the end, at least in this country's two-party system, such trends have not countermanded the forces of luck and homeostasis. Opposition parties, even if demographically challenged, have a way of bouncing back and catching up.

## How Big Was Obama's Victory is 2008?

Well, it certainly was solid. A 53.4 percent showing is impressive, not least because Obama won a majority of the popular vote. He is only the fifth Democrat since the Civil War to do that, the others being Samuel Tilden in 1876, Franklin D. Roosevelt (four times), Lyndon B. Johnson in 1964, and Jimmy Carter (very narrowly) in 1976. Also, the 2008 election brought the Democrats a party-wide victory. Their share of the national popular vote for the House of Representatives exceeded 54 percent in the 2006 midterm. In 2008, it rose above 55 percent. Rare is the record of sequential gains in House and Senate seats that the Democrats enjoyed in 2006 and 2008.

Yet there are caveats. Voter turnout did not balloon in 2008 as many had projected.[36] The Democrats' victory was peculiarly, perhaps uniquely, a Washington, D.C., victory. The party's performance tailed off in elections for governor and state legislature.[37] Exhibiting rare discrimination, voters seem to have taken dead aim at just the Bush White House and congressional Republicans. Also, in the face of a difficult political context, the Republican showing at the presidential level in 2008, 46.6 percent, arguably wasn't all that bad. The party came out of the election damaged but alive. It is out there; it will come back.[38] Even the 2008 turnout pattern offers grounds for Republican optimism. One reason that turnout didn't soar as much as it might have is because many unenthusiastic Republicans stayed home. They probably won't stay at home forever.[39]

Luck also played a role in 2008. In purely partisan terms, perhaps the best long-term news for the Democrats is that the Wall Street crash of 2008 occurred on the Republican watch. A disaster like that can delegitimize a party for quite awhile. Witness the Democrats under Grover Cleveland confronted by the depression of 1893, the Hoover Republicans confronting the depression of 1929, or the Carter Democrats confronting the double-digit inflation and other economic troubles of the late 1970s.[40] In all three cases, it wasn't just a governing party that was discredited. Also left in the dust was each governing party's doctrine of political economy.[41] Association with disaster is not a winning hand.

Yet there is a caution. In these previous cases, the governing party was not only afflicted by economic disaster but had an extended chance—years—to wrestle with it. Generally speaking, those parties flailed around. In the present case, the Wall Street crash of 2008 afflicted the Bush administration too late to allow that administration much of a chance to wrestle with it. It's the Obama administration that will have to do so.

# Notes

Thanks to Joseph Sempolinski for his help on this work.

1. See Bernard A. Weisberger, *America Afire: Jefferson, Adams, and the Revolutionary Election of 1800* (New York: William Morrow, 2000); Bruce Ackerman, *The Failure of the Founding Fathers: Jefferson, Marshall, and the Rise of Presidential Democracy* (Cambridge, Mass.: Belknap Press, 2007); and Edward J. Larson, *A Magnificent Catastrophe: The Tumultuous Election of 1800* (New York: Free Press, 2008).

2. For an extended statement on this question, see David R. Mayhew, *Electoral Realignments: A Critique of an American Genre* (New Haven, Conn.: Yale University Press, 2002).

3. For a full presentation of this analysis, see David R. Mayhew, "Incumbency Advantage in U.S. Presidential Elections: The Historical Record," *Political Science Quarterly* 123, no. 2 (Summer 2008): 201–228. In 1788, there was no incumbent party. In 1824, during a brief one-party era, the incumbent party collapsed into competing factions of various ideological shades.

4. The statistical advantage accruing to incumbent candidates in presidential elections is discussed in Herbert F. Weisberg, "Partisanship and Incumbency in Presidential Elections," *Political Behavior* 24 (December 2002): 339–360; Ray C. Fair, *Predicting Presidential Elections and Other Things* (Stanford, Calif.: Stanford University Press, 2002), 46–51; and David Samuels, "Presidentialism and Accountability for the Economy in Comparative Perspective," *American Political Science Review* 98 (August 2004): 425–436, at 428–429.

5. See John Zaller, "Politicians as Prize Fighters: Electoral Selection and Incumbency Advantage," in *Politicians and Party Politics,* ed. John G. Geer (Baltimore: Johns Hopkins University Press, 1998).

6. See Sendhil Mullainathan and Ebonya Washington, "Sticking with Your Vote: Cognitive Dissonance and Voting," paper presented at the American Politics Seminar, Yale University, September 5, 2007. Another possibility that lurks here is strategic behavior. Do the out-parties put up weak presidential candidates because they see that they can't win? Do incumbents of the in-party decide not to run again when the electoral omens are bad? These possibilities are discussed in Mayhew, "Incumbency Advantage," pp. 219–225. It seems likely that strategic behavior makes a minor contribution, at best, to the pattern here in Table 9-1.

7. In all those three, by the way, the in-party kept the White House. Absent those three contests, the in-party's historical win-loss record since the 1820s falls to a lackluster eight and twelve.

8. The reading for 2008 is based on early unofficial returns.

9. On the other side, however, there is the vexed instance of 1960. It is not clear which candidate won a national popular-vote edge in the Kennedy-Nixon contest of that year. Conventional wisdom has it that Kennedy did, but the facts are complex. At issue is the count of the popular vote in Alabama. See Neal R. Peirce, *The People's President* (New York: Simon and Schuster, 1968), 102–107; Brian

J. Gaines, "Popular Myths about Popular Vote-Electoral College Splits," *PS: Political Science and Politics* 34 (March 2001): 71–75; George C. Edwards III, *Why the Electoral College Is Bad for America* (New Haven, Conn.: Yale University Press, 2004), 48–51; and V. O. Key Jr., "Interpreting the Election Returns," in *The Presidential Election and Transition 1960–61*, ed. Paul T. David (Washington, D.C.: Brookings Institution, 1961), 150.

10. The Whig vote for 1836 adds together the vote for three regional candidates. The Stephen Douglas vote is the Democratic vote for 1860. Since this calculation involves the major parties, the William Howard Taft vote is the Republican value for 1912.

11. That is, the record is eight and eight if the clouded 1960 result is counted as a Democratic popular-vote win.

12. Daniel J. Gans, "Persistence of Party Success in American Presidential Elections," *Journal of Interdisciplinary History* 16 (Winter 1986): 228–230. Gans also finds (230–233) that in the absence of repeat major-party candidates (such as George W. Bush in 2004 and Adlai Stevenson in 1956), the previous presidential election holds virtually no predictive value for the current election—either in predicting the victorious party or the parties' shares of the popular vote.

13. See Larry M. Bartels and John Zaller, "Presidential Vote Models: A Recount," *PS: Political Science and Politics* 34 (March 2001): 17.

14. Anthony Downs, *An Economic Theory of Democracy* (New York: Harper and Row, 1957).

15. Robert S. Erikson, Michael B. MacKuen, and James A. Stimson, *The Macro Polity* (New York: Cambridge University Press, 2002).

16. http://fairmodel.econ.yale.edu/vote2008/index2.htm. On the other hand, well-executed election forecasts can be embarrassing, as most of them were in 2000.

17. See the analysis in James M. McPherson, *Tried by War: Abraham Lincoln as Commander in Chief* (New York: Penguin, 2008), chap. 10.

18. Andrew Roberts, *Masters and Commanders: How Roosevelt, Churchill, Marshall and Alanbrooke Won the War in the West* (London: Allen Lane, 2008), 370. On this aspect of the 1942 midterm, see also H. W. Brands, *Traitor to His Class: The Privileged Life and Radical Presidency of Franklin Delano Roosevelt* (New York: Doubleday, 2008), 685–686, 690–691.

19. See Larry Berman, *Nixon, Kissinger, and Betrayal in Vietnam* (New York: Free Press, 2001), 29–36.

20. A brief discussion appears in John Steele Gordon, "A Short Banking History of the United States," *Wall Street Journal*, October 10, 2008, A17.

21. It has been argued that Republican presidents during recent decades, as opposed to Democratic ones, have excelled in rigging the economy in their party's favor as a new presidential election rolls around. The experience of 2008 looks like, among other things, a world-class disconfirmation of that idea.

22. On this subject, see the time-line analysis of the last few months of the presidential election of 2000 in Richard Johnston, Michael G. Hagen, and Kathleen Hall Jamieson, *The 2000 Presidential Election and the Foundations of Party Politics* (New York: Cambridge University Press, 2004).

23. Jennifer E. Duffy, "Senate GOP Downsizing Again," *National Journal*, November 1, 2008, 18. Other pre-election assessments of the effects of the crash include Jay Cost, "On the State of the Race," September 30, 2008, www.realclearpolitics,com/horseraceblog/2008/09/on_the_state_of_the_race_1.html; and Adam Nagourney and Megan Thee, "Poll Finds Obama Gaining Support and McCain Weakened in Bailout Crisis," *New York Times*, October 2, 2008.

24. "The Great Debates," *Newsweek*, November 17, 2008, 106.

25. On the butterfly ballot, see Henry Brady et al., "Law and Data: The Butterfly Ballot Episode," *PS: Political Science and Politics* 34 (March 2001): 59–69.

26. For purposes of calculation here, I have assigned all of Nebraska's five electoral votes in 2008 to McCain. That is despite the success of the Democrats in winning one of those votes by prevailing in the Omaha congressional district.

27. The District of Columbia enters the calculations in 1964.

28. The Henry Wallace and Strom Thurmond candidacies in 1948; the John Anderson candidacy in 1980.

29. As I have calculated the immediate post-election returns, the median Electoral College unit for 2008 is, as it happens, a blend of Colorado and Iowa since those two Obama states meet at the 269-269 juncture once the 51 units are arrayed in the order of their Obama percentages. In Table 9-5, the value in the Electoral College column for 2008 is an average of Colorado's 53.4 percent and Iowa's 54.7 percent. I have pegged Colorado at 53.4 percent and also the Obama nationwide share at 53.4 percent. But those figures are fragile as I write, so there is a certain lack of closure.

30. See "For Most of the Country, a Blue Shift," *New York Times,* November 6, 2008, P1.

31. The model for these calculations is an "index of class voting" employed by Robert R. Alford in *Party and Society* (Chicago: Rand McNally, 1963).

32. These are percentages of the total popular vote. Races other than whites and blacks are ignored in the calculations for 1960, as are religions other than Catholics and Protestants in 1960.

33. See the analysis in Philip E. Converse et al., "Stability and Change in 1960: A Reinstating Election," *American Political Science Review* 55, no. 2 (June 1961): 269–280.

34. Actually, the race index reading for 1984, when whites flocked to Reagan in his reelection landslide but blacks didn't budge, surpassed that of 2008. The value for 1984 is 54.

35. This is leaving aside any differential changes by race in voter turnout, which at any rate do not seem to have been overwhelming.

36. Early assessments include: "Report: '08 Turnout Same As or Only Slightly Higher than '04," *CNN Political Ticker,* November 7, 2008; and Chris Cillizza, "5 Myths about an Election of Mythic Proportions," *Washington Post,* November 16, 2008.

37. Charles Cook, "Obama's Short Coattails: Democrats' Downballot Gains Weren't as Great as Some Had Hoped: It May Take a While to Figure Out Why," NationalJournal.com, November 7, 2008; and Alan Greenblatt, "Slow and Steady Wins in State Races; Democrats Take Over One More Governorship and Modestly Expand Their Power in State Legislatures," *Congressional Quarterly Weekly,* November 10, 2008, 3019–3021.

38. It is not unknown for a major party to collapse and vanish. The Whigs did so in the 1850s. But that fate is most unlikely for a major American party today. One reason is that the states around 1900, through detailed regulation of the parties' organizations and nominating processes, turned the Democrats and Republicans into something like public utilities. By law, the barriers to entry are low: Ambitious politicians and popular ideas can infuse rather easily into one or the other of the major parties. By contrast, the legal barriers to entry are rather high for third parties bidding to enter the system. On the move to heavy regulation of the American parties, see Leon D. Epstein, *Political Parties in the American Mold* (Madison: University of Wisconsin Press, 1986), chap. 6.

39. This could be a reversion. Earlier in U.S. history, it is estimated, inter-electoral change in party fortunes depended more on differential party mobilization and turnout, as compared to inter-election change via voter conversion. The latter pattern is said to have become more prominent in the latter half of the twentieth century. See W. Phillips Shively, "From Differential Abstention to Conversion: A

Change in Electoral Change, 1864–1988," *American Journal of Political Science* 36, no. 2 (May 1992): 309–330.

40. On the Carter case, see Robert J. Samuelson, *The Great Inflation and Its Aftermath: The Past and Future of American Affluence* (New York: Random House, 2008).

41. Although the record is less clear, another possible case is the fate of the Democrats in the late 1830s. The panic of 1837 and its painful aftermath seemed to help loft the Whigs to power in the 1840 election and also cast doubt on the doctrine of political economy espoused by the governing Democrats under Andrew Jackson and Martin Van Buren in the 1830s. See Michael F. Holt, "The Election of 1840, Voter Mobilization, and the Emergence of the Second American Party System: A Reappraisal of Jacksonian Voting Behavior," 16–58 in *A Master's Due: Essays in Honor of David Herbert Donald*, eds. William J. Cooper Jr., Michael F. Holt, and John McCardell (Baton Rouge: Louisiana State University Press, 1985).